Environmental Quality and Food Supply

Environmental Quality and Food Supply

EDITED BY

Philip L. White, Sc.D.
Secretary, Council on Foods and Nutrition
Director, Department of Foods and Nutrition
American Medical Association

AND

Diane Robbins, R.D.
Nutritionist, Department of Foods and Nutrition
American Medical Association

FUTURA
PUBLISHING COMPANY
1974

Copyright © 1974
Futura Publishing Company, Inc.

Published by
Futura Publishing Company, Inc.
295 Main Street
Mount Kisco, New York 10549

L.C.: 73-89336
ISBN: 0-87993-037-3

Printed in U.S.A. by
NOBLE OFFSET PRINTERS, INC.
New York, N.Y. 10003

Acknowledgements

Special recognition and gratitude are expressed to the Symposium planning committee: Mike H. Baker, Melvin R. Bandle, Frank Barton, James L. Breeling, C.O. Chichester, Ph.D.; William J. Darby, M.D.,Ph.D.; Asher Finkel, M.D.; Jack Finkley, M.D.; Albert C. Kolbye Jr., M.D.; Granville Larimore, M.D.; Bernard Liska, Ph.D.; Donald J. Moore; Emil M. Mrak, Ph.D.; and Shiela Sorocool, M.D.

We extend our thanks to C.O. Chichester, Ph.D. and Emil M. Mrak, Ph.D. for their presentation of the case as summarized in the Introduction.

Our appreciation is expressed to Nancy Selvey, R.D. and Mary Ellis, R.D. of the AMA Department of Foods and Nutrition for their editorial assistance.

Philip L. White Sc.D.
Diane Robbins, R.D.

Acknowledgments

Contributors

R. Stephen Berry, Ph.D.
Professor of Chemistry
University of Chicago
Chicago, Illinois

Helen L. Cannon
Branch of Exploration Research
U.S. Department of the Interior
Geological Survey
Denver, Colorado

Alan Carlin
Director, Implementation Research Division
Office of Research and Monitoring
Environmental Protection Agency
Washington, D.C.

Duane Chapman, Ph.D.
Professor of Resource Economics
Cornell University
Ithaca, New York

C. O. Chichester, Ph.D.
Professor of Food and Resource Chemistry
College of Agriculture
University of Rhode Island
Kingston, Rhode Island

J. M. Coon, Ph.D.
Professor and Chairman
Department of Pharmacology
Jefferson Medical College
Philadelphia, Pennsylvania

William J. Darby, M.D., Ph.D.
President
The Nutrition Foundation
New York, New York

Samuel S. Epstein, M.D.
Swetland Professor of Environmental Health
School of Medicine, and Human Ecology
Department of Pharmacology
Case Western Reserve University
Cleveland, Ohio

Eugene E. Erickson, Ph.D.
Technical Director
North Star Research Institute
Minneapolis, Minnesota

Charles R. Goldman, Ph.D.
Professor of Limnology
Division of Environmental Studies
University of California
Davis, California

Paul R. Graham
Commercial Development Manager
Monsanto Company
St. Louis, Missouri

Herman F. Kraybill, Ph.D.
Scientific Coordinator
Environmental Carcinogenesus
National Institutes of Health
Bethesda, Maryland

T. W. Kwon, Ph.D.
Head, Food Resources Laboratory
Korea Institute of Science and Technology
Cheong Ryang
Seoul, Korea

Oscar A. Lorenz, Ph.D.
Professor of Vegetable Crops
College of Agriculture and Environmental Sciences
University of California
Davis, California

Walter A. Mercer
Director, Wester Research Laboratory
National Canners Association
Berkeley, California

Emil M. Mrak, Ph.D.
Chancellor Emeritus
University of California
Davis, California

Frederick Sargent, II, M.D.
Provost
Western Washington State College
Bellingham, Washington

Carlos Schlesinger, Ph.D.
INTEC
Arenido Santa Maria
Santigo, Chile

Stanley Segall, Ph.D.
Department of Biological Sciences
Drexel Institute of Technology
Philadelphia, Pennsylvania

Samuel I. Shibko, Ph.D.
Division of Toxicology
FDA
Washington, D.C.

E. Paul Taiganides, Ph.D.
Agricultural Engineering Department
Ohio State University
Columbus, Ohio

Fred H. Tschirley, Ph.D.
Pesticides Coordinator, Science and Education
U.S. Department of Agriculture
Washington, D.C.

B. L. Weir, M.S.
Research Associate
Department of Vegetable Crops
University of California
Davis, California

John H. Weisburger, Ph.D.
Vice President for Research
American Health Foundation
New York, N.Y.

Table of Contents

Contributors vii

Introduction xvii

Chapter 1 1
Fitness of the Ecosystem
Ecosystem, environmental quality, natural ecosystem, human ecosystem, urbanization, the farm as a
monoculture, exploitation of the ecosystem, supra-
ethical criterion.
Frederick Sargent II

Chapter 2 7
Power Structure and Environment
Pollutants, magnitude and nature of pollution,
problems of developing countries, environmental sani-
tation problems, transfer of technology.
Carlos Schlesinger

Chapter 3 17
Ecology and Human Health Engineering
Water development, ecologic change, demographic
changes, topsoil exhaustion, use of thermal energy
produced by atomic reactors, recycling plant food
wastes, solid waste management.
Charles Goldman

Chapter 4 25
By-Product Recovery as a Resource
Environmental quality of South Korea; resources;
farm residues, animal wastes, cellulose, rice bran,
coconut water, tapioca waste; sewage as a nutrient
resource, industrial development.
T. W. Kwon

Chapter 5 39
Benefits of Pollution Control
Health related damages, identifying pollution control benefits, agricultural production aids, cost-function for production aids, intensive and extensive agriculture.

Alan P. Carlin

Chapter 6 49
Costs of Pollution and Recycling
Wastes as resources, resource recovery, conversion of solid waste to fuel, food processing wastes, rumen contents of beef cattle, composting, dehydrating.

E. E. Erickson

Chapter 7 61
Agricultural Wastes
Ecological disruption, industrialization, animal waste management, natural versus unnatural by-products, the earth's biosphere, coprology.

E. Paul Taiganides

Chapter 8 67
The Economic Consequences of Regulation or Prohibition of Agricultural Chemicals in American Agriculture
Consequences of chemical regulation, land-chemical substitution, economic consequences of nitrogen fertilizer restriction, farm residue increase, soil erosion.

Duane Chapman

Chapter 9 79
Pesticides in Relation to Environmental Quality
Toxicity and transportability, DDT, benefits and risks of pesticides, dietary intake of pesticides, host resistance, biological control, chemical growth modifiers, pest management.

Fred H. Tschirley

Chapter 10 87
Fertilizers
Phosphorus contamination, nitrogen utilization, nitrate contamination, denitrification, water pollution.

Oscar A. Lorenz

Chapter 11 93
Nitrate Accumulation in Vegetables
Effects of nitrates and nitrites on animals, establishment of nitrate standards of food for humans, environmental conditions relating to nitrate accumulation, nitrate content of vegetables, sources of nitrogen, effects of temperature, rate of nitrogen fertilization.

Oscar A. Lorenz and B. L. Weir

Chapter 12 105
The Food System and Environmental Quality
Magnitude of the problems of food processing and waste reduction, in-plant modifications and changes, treatment of waste waters, in-plant survey data, dry peeling fruits and vegetables, blanching wastes, feasibility of research accomplishments, industrial responsibility.

Walter A. Mercer

Chapter 13 115
Energy Use and Energy Waste
    A. Energy Accounting
        Diseconomies, economy curves, energy dissipation, regional climate change.
    B. Principles of Thermodynamic Thrift
        Energy husbandry, thermodynamic potential, the automobile manufacturing system, energy costs of production, reduction of national energy budget.

R. Stephen Berry

Chapter 14 131
The Philosophy of Acceptable Risk and the Prac-
ticality of Maximum Safety
   World food risks, technology assessment and risk
benefit, societal criteria of acceptable safety, rational
judgement, irrationality of scientist-turned-politician,
Scientific McCarthyism, needs beyond scientific perspective, scientists and politicians, essentiality of mutual understanding, examination of the decision making process.

William J. Darby

Chapter 15 143
Natural Toxicants of Geologic Origin
   Selenium, arsenic, cadmium, lead, amphibolite,
nickel, fluorine.

Helen L. Cannon

Chapter 16 165
Naturally Occurring Toxicants in Foods
   Natural components of foods, toxicity versus hazard, safety numbers for chemical components, safety
through technology, abnormal or unusual circumstances, delayed effects, nutrition education.

J. M. Coon

Chapter 17 173
Unintentional Additives in Foods
   Synthetic chemicals, determination of health significance, assessment of chemical hazards, metabolic
pathways of chemicals, safety appraisal, levels of hazard occurrence.

Herman F. Kraybill

Chapter 18 185
Phthalates: A Story in the Making
   Entry of phthalate esters into the environment and
human body, physical properties, Flory-Higgins Interaction Parameter, permanance, plasticizer volatility,

plasticizer synthesis technology, polymer-plasticizer process, plasticizer uses and markets, biodegradation of phthalates, natural occurrence of phthalate moiety.

Paul R. Graham

Chapter 19 207
Toxicology of Phthalic Acid Esters
Exposure to phthalic acid esters, available toxicity data, subacute and chronic toxicity studies, regulated uses of phthalates, migration of phthalates from packaging material.

Samuel I. Shibko

Chapter 20 227
The Etiology and Prevention of Cancer
Etiology factors, types of cancer, carcinogenic risks to man, mutagenesis, environmental factors and cardiovasular disease, and prevention.

John H. Weisburger

Chapter 21 241
Definition of Risk; Priority for Safety
Federal decision making process, regulatory process, technological innovations, new chemical products, data base, efficacy, identity of food additives, toxicity evaluation, and chemical carcinogenesis.

Samuel S. Epstein

Introduction

This book evolved from the Symposium on Environmental Quality and Food Supply sponsored by the Council on Foods and Nutrition and the Council on Environmental, Occupational and Public Health of the American Medical Association. Distinguished authorities in areas of food and resource chemistry, by-product recovery, pollution control, food production and processing, agriculture, soil science, consumerism, legislation, environmental engineering, pesticides, health science, and toxicology discussed their special concerns about the quality of the environment in relation to maintaining a safe and nutritionally adequate food supply.

The participants accepted the challenge to approach the two-fold problem of (1) the adverse effects of certain environmental factors on the quality of our food and (2) the adverse effects of our food production and processing systems upon the environment.

A present day madness exists within our society pertaining to the environment and the safety, adequacy, and quality of our food supply. There is concern about the continuous rise in costs of food and the implementation of advanced technology. Unfortunately, we were late in recognizing the seriousness of these problems. We now find ourselves in a potentially hazardous situation as a result of public neglect and the failure of our lawmakers to make early, constructive efforts to curtail these vexing problems.

Many of the problems we now face can be attributed to the industrialization of modern civilization. When people moved from farms to the cities in great numbers, our society became dependent on a food supply which required delivery to an urban environment. Farm production has reached the point where one worker who produced food for five people may now produce food for forty people. We have concentrated our production into centralized locations. Accompanying this increased concentration of production, there is an increased concentration of wastes. Unless these wastes are reutilized, the concentration of pollutants also increases. We process approximately 70% of the food supply in the United States, thus adding to the problem of processing and packaging wastes.

Concern and uncertainty of the environment and our food supply touches the farmer, the food processor, the naturalist, the politicians and government, and the consumer. The farmer is restricted by regulations pertaining to the disposal of agricultural wastes such as stubble, orchard prunings, or brush which results from the clearing of lands. Such restrictions are proper, but costly, and often result in increased costs of foods. Nitrate contamination creates a serious problem for the farmer in relation to animal production. The majority of cattle in the United States are raised in feedlots before going to the packing company. The tremendous quantity of wastes deposited by the cattle result in a large annual accumulation of nitrogen, phosphorus, and potassium. The wastes from these animals can contaminate ground water, surface waters, rivers, and lakes. Bacterial contamination from feedlots and resulting public health hazards is another aspect of concern in the area of nitrogen contamination.

The farmer is experiencing a frequency of new regulations with respect to the use of pesticides. Many pesticides are being banned and he must seek alternatives to pesticide use. Several alternatives are currently being considered. The breeding of crops that are resistant to disease, particularly to those transmitted by insects may be one possibility. Research in areas for the development of insect sterility to control insect vectors and the utilization of attractants and hormones for pest control is also being conducted toward efforts to alleviate the pest control problem.

Developing protocols for the testing of safety and deciding upon a method to use in implementation are problems now confronting the food processor. A galaxy of regulations especially in regard to the safety of food products and the disposal of wastes has created a great deal of concern and confusion to the food processor. The disposal of empty pesticide containers, in particular, presents a serious problem. Some state laws, such as California, require the fencing in of empty containers. At the same time, their highway administrators have made it mandatory that containers be entirely sealed or closed when transported along highways to disposal sites. The alternative of destroying these containers by pyrolosis creates a controversy over whether there is an added contribution to air pollution. This causes naturalists to be concerned with the possibility of residues escaping from the containers and harming wildlife and our water supply. As a result, the containers continue to stack up and consumer costs continue to rise.

Similar problems are being experienced with respect to cannery wastes. In the past, cannery waste was hauled to open country, spread over the land surface, where it was permitted to dry, and then plowed under. New arrangements must now be made due to residential complaints concerning odors and flies. Many land application sites have been closed which makes it difficult to dispose of the large volume of cannery wastes.

The increase in consumer interest for high quality food has resulted in a distrust of many food processors. Consumers fear (sometimes unreasonably) that foods are not nutritious, that they are contaminated, and that they are inadequately labeled. The news media often concentrates on highlighting the dramatic or unusual incidents and the exceptions, which cause the consumer to become even more skeptical.

In approaching these problems, we must examine the food production and processing systems as well as food safety and health effects. This will facilitate our ability to actively engage in efforts which will solve environmental and food supply problems. Public risks to life and health as well as public benefit must be major considerations in the decision making processes. Thorough evaluation must be made of the available alternatives in relation to all the risks and benefits involved in possible courses of action. We must strive most of all to be objective in our decision-making process as we implement the total systems approach. But, before doing this, the actual problems must be identified.

It is felt that solutions to these environmental and food supply problems are totally feasible if our priorities are redefined. The social aspects of the rapid changes and problems confronting us must be weighed carefully. This will require the cooperation of all types of institutions, industry, government, and the public in order to appropriately expend efforts to improve the quality of our food supply. Thus, the context of this book is to provide an enlightenment and understanding of the interaction of the environment and food supply in hopes of improving the quality of our national habitat.

Fitness of the Ecosystem

FREDERICK SARGENT, II, M.D.

Emphasis on the ecosystem - as a concept of the total environment - broadens the context in which to consider food production.[1,2]

A natural ecosystem is comprised of a biotic community and its abiotic environment. Solar energy drives this system. Nutrients flow from the environment into the organisms of the biotic community and, via food chains, through these organisms, finally recycle back to the environment.

During the past 2.6 billion years, the environment has gradually changed. Organisms played no small part. For example, the green plant is responsible for the oxygen contained in the atmosphere. At the same time, as the organisms changed, they adapted to the gradually altering environmental circumstances and conditions. Organisms became fit for environment, and our environment became fit for organisms as a consequence of this evolutionary process.

This is fitness of the ecosystem, a fundamental ecological concept. It allows one to define "environmental quality." Under this concept, a quality environment is one that provides a set of conditions and circumstances necessary for organisms to expand their potentials to the fullest development and the most harmonious expression.

While the environment may be fit, it is not necessarily optimum for all organismic functions. A fit environment provides the qualities essential for survival of organisms. Because the environment is generally inoptimum for one or more functions, each organism exploits the environment to the best of its advantage. This exploitation adds qualities that make the environment more habitable.

For about 500,000 years, man has gradually been transforming the natural ecosystem into the human ecosystem. This transformation began with the discovery of fire. It has passed through several seral stages, which we identify as anthroposeres: gathering, hunting and fishing, herding, agriculture, and industry. The existing anthroposere is urbanization.

With urbanization, there is a migration of people to the city. Such trends are now world-wide, and in many of the developed nations the majority of the population resides in urban areas. In the United States, for example, it is estimated that about 70% of the population is urbanized.

The city may be conceptualized as a configuration of structures, spaces, and institutions designed to accommodate large numbers of people into a small area, and provide its residents with a habitable environment. Although the city gives the appearance of an independent existence, the survival of its inhabitants depends on a continuing input of a variety of foods, fibers, and raw materials. These flows depend, in turn, on complex linkages with far-flung renewable and nonrenewable resources provided by the food-producing system.

The productive unit of the food-producing system is a man-made ecosystem, the farm. The farm is generally a monoculture, an intensive technological enterprise devoted to growing a single species of domesticated plant or animal. The farm is maintained as an immature ecosystem, for that is the most productive. The harvest is taken from the land and processed through an intricate agricultural industry. Because, essentially, none of the harvest is returned to the land, large quantities of nutrients are extracted from the soil. These are returned annually as fertilizers. To assure maximal productivity, the domesticates are selectively bred to resist pests, drought, and other severe weather conditions. To reduce the competition from weeds, insects, fungi, and molds, the domesticates are protected by a variety of biocides. Many of the domesticates have been so intensively bred for specific purposes that they are solely dependent on man for their continued existence. This farm is an intensively managed technological enterprise. Only a small fraction of the labor force (about 5% in the United States) is engaged in farming.

Man moves to transform the land into a domesticated landscape of plants and animals serving his purposes. He already uses 41% of the total land surface for croplands, rangelands, and managed forests.[3] In the future, it is probable that he will use 50% in these ways and rely more on further intensification of management, rather than expansion of use to marginal lands to increase productivity.[3] As he exploits more and more of the land, he threatens wild gene pools which are essential to invigorate his already rather narrow food base.

The city and the farm exemplify phases in the transformation of the natural ecosystem into the human ecosystem. This transformation is proceeding inexorably. It appears that man has decided that he can manage all the resources of the biosphere. It is no longer the resources that limit decisions; it is the decisions that make the resources. Along this course, the climactic anthroposere will be the total transformation of the natural ecosystem. At the present stage in his evolution, man has locked himself into a course that may well bring him to the climax visualized before he has acquired the skills, knowledge, and wisdom for managing such an ecosystem. He cannot, with any certainty, foretell the consequences of the transformation in which he is engaged. Furthermore, he cannot yet design alternative processes for his ecosystem which will assure him of survival. In spite of these deficiencies, man must make some tough decisions in the decades ahead, decisions which are value judgments, decisions which will affect his cultural traditions.

Man's evolution has been anagenetic. It has exhibited increased independence from the external environment accompanied with more precise and sensitive sense organs and concentration of the nervous system with consequent knowledge, feelings, awareness and emergence of the mind. For man, cultural evolution has become more important than biological evolution; and it is cultural evolution that drives the transformation of the ecosystem.

The transformation or exploitation of the ecosystem is proceeding on a global scale. Exploitation on this scale entails responsible action, efficient mechanisms of transformation of information, and particular preparation of the recipients to receive that information. A central issue is to decide what ethical beliefs will guide this transformation. These beliefs must be assessed for their effectiveness as guides for evolution according to some "supra-ethical criterion" related to the facts emerging from the study of human biology and human evolution. I suggest that the supra-ethical criterion must have an environmental focus. It must be the concept of the fitness of the ecosystem.

Adopting such a supra-ethical criterion will be difficult, for man is by nature morally ambivalent. As Toynbee[4] states it "man's moral performance is inevitably handicapped by the built-in self-centeredness which is another name for life itself, and which is consequently implanted in each species of Man as it is in each specimen of every other species of living creatures." Man is uniquely adaptive and superior to other forms of life. Man can occupy the entire habitable globe. Any attempt to regulate this occupancy will be viewed as threatening to his self identity and will be resisted. Only if man can come to understand ecological principles and incorporate them into his cultural behavior might there be an open-ended future.

For these reasons, I would assign highest priority to developing comprehensive knowledge of just how ecosystems function. Man must comprehend the operations of not only the natural ecosystems, but also of the man-made ones, particularly the food-producing system and the urban system. Pioneer work on such investigations has already been initiated under the International Biological Program. These studies will be continued under the Project on Analysis of World Ecosystems of the Scientific Committee on Problems of the Environment of the International Council of Scientific Union and the Man and Biosphere Program of UNESCO.

References
1. Sargent, F II: Nature and Scope of Human Ecology, Sargent, F II (ed.) in *Human Ecology*, Amsterdam, North Holland Publishing Co., in press, 1973.
2. Sargent, F II: Fitness of Ecosystem, Sargent, F II (ed.) in *Human Ecology*, Amsterdam, North Holland Publishing Co., in press, 1973.

3. Work Group on Ecological Effects, Matthews, WH; Smith, FE; and Goldberg, (eds.), in *Man's Impact on Terrestrial and Oceanic Ecosystems.* Cambridge, The MIT Press, 1971, pp 4-5.
4. Toynbee, A: *Experiences,* New York, Oxford University Press, 1969, p 287.

Power Structure and Environment

CARLOS SCHLESINGER, Ph.D.

Human activities inevitably and increasingly introduce material and energy into the environment. When that material or energy endangers or is liable to endanger man's health, his well-being, or his resources directly or indirectly, it is called a pollutant. This definition suggests that desirable activities can produce undesirable side effects; and this is true even of achievements that have benefited mankind in preventive medicine, agriculture, and industrial development.

In addition to prevailing natural conditions, three factors in particular determine the magnitude and nature of the pollution problem, whether at the local or global level:

The size of the human population;

The rate of production and consumption; and

The level and use of technology.

While the total stress resulting from these factors is increasing, the capacity of the environment to deal with their side effects is finite.

Pollution of one sort or another occurs throughout human society, and the effects of any given pollutant are frequently the same wherever they are felt. It is true that the present situation results principally from immoderate application of technology in industrialized countries. The developing countries, however, are already affected by this situation. With increasing industrialization and urbanization, the developing countries are encountering the same problems and dealing with more and more of the same pollutants as developed countries. At the same time, it is also true that the stage of development affects both the perception of pollution as a problem and the resources and priority assigned to dealing with it.

There is one very important difference between pollution problems and environmental problems as a whole of industrialized and developing countries. In the former, the present problems result largely from increasing affluence. In the latter, they are inherent factors in a continued state of poverty such as health hazards due to inadequate sanitary facilities.

With regard to pollution prevention and control, the developing countries are in a potentially favorable situation, answers to their present problems can be provided by development itself. At the same time, they can draw on the experience of the more industrialized countries. Then, as their own countries expand, they should be able to avoid the mistakes and malpractices that characterize industrial development hitherto and led to the present pollution crisis.

The current concern with the human environment has arisen at a time when the energies and efforts of the developing countries are being increasingly devoted to the goal of development. To a large extent, this current concentration on environmental issues has emerged out of the problems experienced by the industrially advanced countries. These problems are largely the outcome of a high level of economic development. The creation of large productive capacities in industry and agriculture, the growth of complex systems of transportation and communication, the evolution of massive urban conglomerations, all have been accompanied, in one way or another, by damage to or disruption of the human environment. They have attained such major proportions that in many communities they already constitute serious hazards to human health and well-being. In some ways, the dangers extend beyond national boundaries and threaten the world as a whole.

The developing countries are not unconcerned with these problems. They have an obvious and vital stake in them to the extent of their impact on the global environment and on their economic relations with industrialized countries. They also have an interest in the problems to the extent that the problems tend to accompany the process of development and are already beginning to emerge with increasing severity in their own societies. The developing countries would clearly wish to avoid the mistakes and distortions that have characterized the patterns of development of industrialized societies.

However, the major environmental problems of developing countries are essentially of a different kind. They are predominantly problems that reflect the poverty and lack of development of their societies. In both towns and countryside not merely the quality of life, but life itself is endangered by poor water, housing, sanitation, and nutrition, by sickness and disease, and by natural disasters.

These are problems no less than those of industrial pollution. They clamor for attention in the context of concern with human environment. They are problems which affect the greater mass of mankind. It is evident that the kind of environmental problems that are of importance in developing countries can be overcome by the process of development itself.

It might be assumed that measures adopted by developed and developing countries to deal with these problems involved in preserving the balance of the environment will have direct or indirect effects on the structure and trends of world trade. It seems unlikely that measures of this kind can affect all international trade transactions, or even that they can bring about radical changes in the structure of the operations.

However, Latin American countries in the world market have certain considerations which can probably be taken as a useful basis. In the first place, it should be noted that the current value of exports from the 20 Latin American states amounted to $12,190 million in 1968, and $13,360 million in 1969.[1] Although these figures are the highest values ever recorded for Latin America's sales, the annual growth rate has lagged behind that of world exports, and even behind that of exports from all developing countries.

As a result, Latin America's share in world exports has fallen steadily from 11.1% in 1950, to only 6% to 7% in 1960, and 4.8% in 1969.[1] Among the various factors which have determined this steady downward trend is the excessive concentration of trade on a few primary products, which have had no share in the rise in sales of the more dynamic sector of trade, that is, manufactures. Added to these are the well-known problems of the instability of the world market for primary products and the chronic deterioration of the terms of trade, which have generally meant that the purchasing power of exports is growing at a slower annual rate than their volume. Except in one or two cases, the efforts of the Latin American countries to alter the composition of their exports have not shown any striking results, notwithstanding the fact that in many of them the share of manufactured products in total exports have shown significant increases.

For Latin America as a whole, the share of manufactures in total exports continues to be small although rising slowly: from 2.5% in 1955 to 3% in 1960, and 7.5% in 1968.[1] In view of these facts, it would be interesting for the Latin American countries to consider the circumstances in which the industrialized countries are gradually putting measures into practice to reduce environmental pollution in their principal manufacturing centers, and how this could alter their production costs and import policies.

In both cases, international economic relations could suffer gradual pressures, which might affect the balance of payment of the Latin American countries and ultimately their trade prospects. In the light of problems of this kind, some effects of the environmental sanitation measures adopted in developing countries are identified.

SOME FAVORABLE EFFECTS

It has been estimated that adjustments in the United States economy to take care of environmental sanitation problems could push up production costs about 10%. If such adjustments do not lead to additional quality requirements for Latin American products, this might result in a possible expansion of the margin of competition for Latin American industries. The environmental sanitation measures adopted elsewhere could mean that raw material processing and export industries might be relocated in Latin American countries, which would raise the total value of its exports.

This transfer might be a temptation to industries in developed countries, which spend large amounts of time and money on controlling pollution. Added to this factor, in some cases, is the desire to turn to account the advantages of subcontracting, possibly to reduce labor costs. Such industries would be established in parts of Latin America where nature could take care of eliminating the pollution or wastes resulting from manufacturing activities, and stave off for long periods of time the injurious effects of pollution on mankind.

The question is, however, whether nature is really eliminating pollution in less densely populated developing areas. It is well-known that pollution of the high seas is practically worldwide. How long will it be before air pollution is discovered to be a universal problem, and at world meetings all countries will be charged with the responsibility of protecting this common asset, the seas and the air?

One example of the aim to relocate pollution-causing industries in countries which are better equipped by nature to absorb such contamination is Japan's tentative suggestion that Chile should export granulated iron to that country instead of iron ore. This would raise the total value of Chilean exports of this metal. Another factor that might favor Latin American trade would be the greater demand from industrialized countries for natural raw materials to replace synthetic products. The manufacture of synthetic products causes more pollution and often involves recycling difficulties with serious waste disposal problems.

SOME ADVERSE EFFECTS

Increases in prices of Latin American imports are usually from countries where environmental sanitation measures result in increases in production costs that are not sufficiently compensated for by government subsidies. Such measures could, thus, have an adverse effect on Latin America's terms of trade. A second adverse effect might be a ban on certain imports from Latin American countries which fail to meet the standards established as part of the environmental sanitation program in importing countries. What happened in the case of Argentine meat, which was excluded from the markets of industrialized countries on health grounds, could also happen in the case of other products which Latin America is currently exporting.

The establishment by the United States of a maximum sulfur content of 1% in the fuels used in urban centers is a threat to Venezuelan fuels, whose sulfur content is 2.5%.[2]

Another disadvantage could be increased customs protection in countries whose production costs have increased to comply with environmental sanitation standards. Customs duties would probably be increased for products whose manufacturing processes contaminate the environment or for more complex products which utilize the former as inputs and whose prices would rise accordingly.

It is estimated that production costs would rise approximately 5% to 10%, according to the industrial process. This proportion should be high enough to affect world demand. In a more detailed study of the subject, it would be useful to examine the present exports of products whose manufacturing processes pollute the environment in Latin American countries, and exports of articles which are used as inputs of those products. Latin America exports large quantities of some of these commodities: pulp and paper, petroleum, and petrochemical products. Processed foodstuffs, which are in danger of being excluded on quality grounds, may also be excluded because of increased customs protection when production costs of importing countries are pushed up in order to comply with environmental sanitation requirements.

It should be remembered that many of the processes that pollute the environment are precisely those that are needed to expand the region's industrial exports, given the existing technology in Latin America. Moreover, if Latin America takes advantage of one of the possible favorable effects of the sanitation measures that might be enforced by developed countries, (the relocation in Latin America of industries which cause pollution), there would be a greater danger of developed countries stepping up their customs protection against the products of those industries.

Exports from countries that have adopted no pollution control regulations and must compete on the markets of countries which not only have adopted them, but make full use of this fact in advertising their products, would find themselves in a psychological disadvantage vis-a-vis the consumer. The psychological disadvantage might give rise to opposing campaigns, such as that launched by the United States against cheap labor in Japan.

EFFECTS ON TRANSFER OF TECHNOLOGY

If criteria that take account of environmental problems are introduced into international economic relations, economic problems may arise in the transfer and assimilation of new technology. It must be remembered that at the present time, the transference of technology is an induced process through which developing countries receive from the more advanced countries their prevailing techniques.

Economic problems such as production, costs, and size of markets are transferred together with the technology and set cetain limits on the economic decisions connected with their adaptation to enterprise in developing countries. Operating in relatively small markets, Latin American industry has yielded a very poor rate of return on investments and has frequently required protection policies in its incipient stages. Hence, the tendency has been to reduce any additional cost which might even further diminish the economic efficiency of the new sectors.

In the spearhead sectors of industry, the transference of technology should be considered sector by sector, so as to determine where the adaptation of foreign techniques is economically viable, and where they should be used in their actual form.

In agriculture, for example, there seems to be ample scope for developing countries to prevent the environmental deterioration - erosion and soil depletion among others - already observed in other parts of the world. The same observation could be applicable to fishing, where certain advance techniques can be selected in order to prevent a reduction in the stock of fish.

The main problem seems to lie in the industrial sector, where the transfer of techniques is an interdependent process, since it is obviously difficult to keep abreast of technical programs in a sector without participating in most of the innovations that are subsequently added. Because this involves an expensive chain investment process, Latin American countries could find it difficult to establish an economic policy for selecting techniques that would substantially modify the structure of a given sector.

From all this, it may be deduced that the relationship existing between the worldwide substitution of techniques and the purchase and transfer of techniques have certain repercussions on the balance of the environment, which developing countries will find it difficult to escape as they become more industrialized. The economic cost of off-setting or eliminating such effects, added to the production costs of a developing economy, may seriously hamper the developing countries industrial developing efforts. If developing countries intend to implement an industrial development policy, with the necessary provisions to counteract the adverse effects of industrialization on the environment, they will certainly need the financial machinery to absorb the cost involved.

Another major concern of developing countries vis-a-vis international cooperation is financial aid. As noted, the Latin American countries may, through international trade relations, find themselves faced with unfavorable situations which may involve financial losses. Moreover, the protection of the natural resources and living levels, particularly when this means joining in an international effort to avert worldwide dangers, may introduce additional financial burdens in their already tight developing budgets. Therefore, it is justifiable to consider the need to obtain financing over and above that which is already envisaged for development. Such economic assistance would make it possible to deal with environmental problems without detriment to other pressing needs.

This subject has been discussed in general terms by the international agencies which channel financial assistance. Because they understand this need, there is hope that the proper solution will be found.

References

1. El Medio Humano en America Latina, Comission Economia para America Latina, (UN) E/CN. 12/398, 1971.
2. Pitts, JN and Metcalf, RL: *Advances in Environmental Sciences and Technology*, New York, Wiley- Interscience, 1969, vol 1 pp 25-39.

Ecology and Human Health Engineering

CHARLES R. GOLDMAN, Ph.D.

In the last decade there has been a rapid development of widespread public concern over progressive environmental deterioration. Predictions of fuel shortages that have been treated in the past as purely rhetorical questions, are now a reality. Our awareness of the seriousness of global pollution is heightened daily by the tremendous outpourings from the news media concerning gasoline, electricity, food shortages, smog alerts, contaminated water supplies, nuclear plant leakages, oil spills, the demise of wild animal populations—in short, environmental problems abound and public awareness as a whole may even be near the saturation point. Scientists have used highly sophisticated instruments and theoretical models both to detect and even predict the rate of environmental degradation. Now that the extent of environmental destruction is being realized, the efforts of science and technology should increasingly be directed toward developing the means of dealing with these global problems.

Three aspects of engineering in relation to ecology and human health will be considered here: (1) the relationship of large-scale development of water resources to the ecological change such developments produce, (2) the utilization of thermal and organic wastes in food production, and (3) the general problem of achieving a higher degree of resource recovery in the next few decades.

WATER RESOURCE DEVELOPMENT

Colossal schemes of water transfer and hydroelectric impoundment have characterized this century. They have involved ambitious water transport projects designed to transfer large quantities of water over considerable distances. The course of water development throughout the world in the twentieth century has been almost entirely without regard to environmental effects of these projects. For at least half a century the majority of these have been accepted on the basis of progress with very little concern for environmental impact. The frontier attitude that the wilderness was there to tame has prevailed. Only in the last two decades that has there been a significant counter movement against water development.[1]

In many cases the environmental impact resulting from this proliferation of large-scale water projects has been severe. In some parts of the world the construction of large dams, flood control works, and complex water distribution systems have had devastating effects on the environment. We now have a history of some of the mistakes of some of these grandiose water schemes. These mistakes are sufficiently evident to caution and direct the modern water developer toward making more ecologically sound decisions than his predecessors. As an example, schistosomiasis, a tropical disease caused by parasitic blood flukes, became a much more serious problem after the construction of the Aswan Dam on the Nile River. We have seen major invasions of water weeds in many of the impoundments created by the African dams, and have had serious problems in relocation of human populations that were displaced by African water projects. We have had losses of soil fertility resulting from the entrapment of sediments behind dams. Again the most famous example is the recession of the Delta of the Nile resulting from the Aswan Dam. This recession of the Nile Delta shoreline caused by the reduction of sediment load has exposed estuarine areas of the Delta to the saline waters of the Mediterranean, thereby drastically changing the ecological milieu of the Delta.[2] The California State Water Project has resulted in adverse effects on the environment including the reduction of fresh water through the Sacramento-San Joaquin Delta to 1/7 of its previous average.[3,4] This imposes the threat of irreparable harm through downstream pollution and upstream invasion of salt water.

Other subtle yet serious effects of these ambitious water

projects are the demographic changes. Water projects stimulate population growth in these areas by providing irrigated land and water supplies. Some demographic changes are beginning to appear in relation to the California Water Project. One of the best known opponents of the California water plan, Congressman Jerome Waldie, has said that what Southern California needs now is air, not water; that to supply additional water at this time is to promote population growth and further tax the nearly exhausted air supply!

In some cases, water plans can provide the leverage to modernize food production in an entire country. In a recent mission to Honduras an examination was made of the dam site of the El Cajon Project, a $100 million hydroelectric scheme damming three rivers above San Pedro Sula for the purpose of providing power for Guatemala, Honduras, and possibly Nicaragua.[5] A variety of ways that the dam might be very detrimental to the area were expected to be discovered. After examining the site, however, it was found that such a dam could provide the impetus for change in resource utilization which is drastically needed in this area. The forests that are used for grazing are extensively and frequently fired to discourage the growth of herbs, new growth of trees, and ticks. With the loss of nitrogen fixing plants growth is slow and fertility of the soil has steadily decreased. For several centuries the farmers have practiced a bush-fallow or slash-and-burn agriculture. The watershed is burned annually to clear the brush for planting corn, rice, or beans. The slopes are planted almost to the vertical on a thin soil mantle overlying limestone. Through erosion on these steep burned slopes, the limited topsoil is being rapidly lost. This slash-and-burn agricultural rotation that is characteristic of most of Central America has already led to serious and irreparable loss of the thin soil mantle. If loss of this non-renewable resource continues in Honduras the agricultural base will be exhausted within a relatively short time.

Hopefully, if the El Cajon project is financed by the World Bank, it will provide the financial leverage and political drive to begin a serious soil conservation program in Honduras. It is badly needed and without it, the population will not have a sufficient food supply in the very near future. The importance of involvement in basic ecological problems cannot be over-emphasized.

USE OF THERMAL ENERGY
PRODUCED BY ATOMIC REACTORS

The per capita energy consumption is expected to quadruple by the end of the century.[6] The controversy over the potential hazards of atomic reactors still rages but, in view of the current and projected critical power demands of the country, the establishment of great numbers of atomic reactors is predicted. If these atomic reactors are developed to provide the electrical energy for which our civilization appears to have an ever-increasing and insatiable appetite, there will be surplus heat which can be utilized in food production. If nuclear plants are located along coastal waters, there will be an appreciable warming of these waters, with the real possibility of utilizing this heat for thermal enhancement as opposed to thermal pollution. The analogy can be made to the fate of sewage produced from a sewage treatment plant: if correctly used for fertilizer it is of value, but if allowed to enter a waterway it becomes a pollutant.

There is an alternative—near San Diego the Santee Water District reclaims a million gallons of water per day for recreational use and irrigation which otherwise would flow directly to the sea. Water reclamation is already extremely important in South Africa and has promise for the arid parts of many countries.

Aquaculture, which has been of vital importance to many countries, is increasingly important throughout the world and provides a potential utilization of this heat in protein production. There very clearly is a need to supplement current research and production by efforts in this area. Production within the shrimp industry is certainly far below potential. Shortages in the supply of lobsters are common. Certainly the oyster industry, threatened or destroyed by pollution, is foundering on a world-wide scale. Freshwater crayfish are as important to the Scandinavians as turkeys are to Americans and promise to be an increasingly important product of aquaculture.

The possibility of utilizing some of our thermal and chemical wastes in promoting aquaculture is being investigated, particularly in northern climates. The Swedes, Danes, and Norwegians are interested in increasing the production of marine fish through warming water. There is shrimp culture activity in Florida and work in the field is now underway in British Columbia. As food production, particularly protein, becomes an increasingly important world-wide problem, such research and development should be strongly encouraged.

ECONOMICALLY FEASIBLE RESOURCE RECOVERY

The food industry has been basically ignored in the quest for pollution control of solid wastes, but hopefully this will not continue. The petrochemical industry because of the publicized hazards of pesticide usage has borne some of the brunt of the environmental movement. It is an absolute certainty that the environmental crisis, the global pollution we are experiencing, will continue and become much worse before we see any real improvement. However, in view of impending shortages of natural resources, resource recovery, particularly of irreplaceable metals, must soon become a reality.

Man's conversion of natural resources to wastes at accelerating rates will force us to direct our mining efforts to our vast accumulation of solid wastes. Aquaculture, too, may prove to be a promising means of utilizing these wastes.

Even if pesticides are excluded from our consideration of pollution, the food industry produces additional pollutants that find their way into the nation's waterways. Many of these have a high biochemical oxygen demand (BOD) and once treated in settling ponds, wastes are discharged into our waterways with very little attention to the nitrogen and phosphorous they still contain. Thus, great quantities of fertilizers are delivered to the world's water courses promoting excessive growth of algae and higher aquatic plants. Secondary treatment in sewage plants, in effect, converts an organic nutrient to an inorganic form therby making it more readily available for algal growth.

An unusually imaginative Swedish industrialist, Dr. Rubin Rausing, inventor of the TetraPak, or pyramid-shaped milk carton so prevalent in Europe, at one time decided that he would attempt to produce a sterile milk. He organized his barn, animals, and veterinarians and almost succeeded in the task. As he progressed he discovered that he had a solid waste problem. Dr. Rausing then developed a unique processing technique for cow manure. Within a few years, he discovered that the cow manure he was processing into a particularly high grade fertilizer was worth more than the milk he was producing—a very unusual situation in food production economy! But it does indicate that certain food industry by-products or wastes may be converted to another product that will increase the profit margin and at the same time decrease an ever-expanding solid waste problem.

The introduction of the California crayfish into northern Europe to replace the northern European crayfish *Astacus,* which is being steadily killed off by a fungus infection, may also be useful in recycling the waste products from food plants. The crayfish, delicious to eat, is also an effective scavenger along the littoral zone of lakes. Crayfish might well be put to service by the food industry in utilization of some of the by-products now entering our waterways as pollutants. By combining the processes of waste disposal and food production, organic wastes could be converted from sources of pollution to sources of sustenance for the world's burgeoning population.

In considering Ecology and Human Health Engineering, engineers and biologist must work together in attacking the staggering problem of global pollution. The problems of waste disposal are so closely related to the necessity for resource recovery, that we must plan and work together toward a common goal.

Solid waste management must eventually include economically feasible resource recovery. Most of the machinery is available, but there is a need to link up effectively the components of a complete system. A variety of waste disposal experiments are in progress, but adequate government funding of research and development in this field is severely lacking. What now is considered to be an interesting experiment or a good public relations activity by the container industry, will soon become a real necessity.

References

1. Goldman, CR; McEvoy, James; and Richerson, Peter (eds.): Environmental Quality and Water Development, A Report for the National Water Commission, Washington, D.C., San Francisco, WH Freeman & Co, 1973.
2. Hedgpeth, J: Protection of Environmental Quality in Estuaries, In Goldman, CR; Richerson, P; and McEvoy, J (eds.), *Environmental Quality and Water Development*. San Francisco, WH Freeman, 1973, p 233-249.
3. Ludwick, A and Teclaff, E: A History of Water Development and Environmental Quality, In Goldman, CR; Richerson, P; McEvoy, J (eds.), *Environmental Quality and Water Development,* San Francisco, WH Freeman, 1973, p 26-77.
4. Seckler, D (Ed.): California Water: A Study in Resource Management, U C Press, 1971, 348 pp.
5. Goldman, CR: El Cajon Project Feasibility Study, vol 5, *Ecology*, 1972, 63 p.
6. Holden, C: Energy: Shortages Loom, but Conservation Lags, *Science* **180**:1155-1156, 1973.

By-Product Recovery as a Resource

T.W. KWON, Ph.D.

By-products and wastes leading to environmental disruption originate in collective human activities, such as urbanization, cultivation, and industrialization. Typical examples are metabolic wastes of mankind and animals, nonedible portions of agricultural and fishery products and various underutilized products from industrial activities and modern living.

Through increasing population, urbanization, and industrialization such products are concentrated locally to an extent exceeding nature's capacity to take care of them and therefore they create a world-wide pollution problem. If such products can be utilized for human benefit they will no longer be by-products or wastes and will instead become new resources to augment the diminishing supply of existing material resources.

A concentration of wastes in a specific place may cause serious pollution, but, from a positive viewpoint, this waste is also a concentration of new resources awaiting utilization. In principle, more severe pollution should make the utilization of waste economically feasible. Hence, we must find ways to make use of this principle.

EXAMPLE OF CHANGING ENVIRONMENTAL QUALITY IN A DEVELOPING REGION: SOUTH KOREA

South Korea, over which the Republic of Korea now exercises jurisdiction, is about 100,000 square kilometers in area and represents 43% of the Korean peninsula. Agrarian land is some 20% of the total land area, and the population of 32 million depends mainly on cereal grains.

Until 1961 the Korean economy suffered from all the symptoms of underdevelopment. Launching of the first five-year Economic Development Plan in 1962, however, pushed the Korean economy toward industrialization, whereas, agriculture had previously been dominant. The per capita GNP (gross national product) grew from $90 in 1961 to $198 in 1969. During the same period the mining and manufacturing share in GNP increased from 14.9% to 26.1% while that of agriculture and fisheries decreased from 43.8% to 28.1%.[1]

Because of this industrialization Korea is no longer a clean country. The high levels of air and water pollution around major cities demonstrate the lack of safeguards. Pollution in the Han River has reached the point where the intake of the Seoul water supply system must be relocated upstream. Air pollution in Seoul has reached levels which have been shown to be damaging to human health. Industrial development in Ulsan and other places has already resulted in considerable damage to trees, crops, and fisheries.

The pollutants may be in gaseous, liquid, or solid form. The gaseous and liquid pollutants originate mainly from industrialization and partly from urbanization. Solid waste may be derived from urban refuse, industrial operations, and agricultural activities. It is interesting to note that in both developed and developing countries more solid waste came from agricultural sources than all other sources combined.[2]

BY-PRODUCTS AS FOOD SOURCES

In the present discussion, we consider as potential food sources those biodegradable by-products and wastes that are in solid form. Agricultural and fishery by-products, cannery wastes, and municipal sewage may be included in this category. Agricultural by-products and municipal sewage in particular are the important wastes in developing countries whose food processing and the fishery industries are in a rather early developmental stage.

Farm Residue and Animal Waste

They represent only a small portion of the photosynthetic products produced by the cultivation of crops which are harvested as food while much larger portions remain as by-products. Farm animals also produce a considerable amount of waste. In Korea farm residues such as cereal husks and straw constitute the largest quantity of solid waste which amounts to about 20 million tons a year on a dry basis.[3] About one-third of this total is in the form of manure. In the United States farm residues are reported to be more than 600 million tons of which one third is manure.[4]

The need to convert agricultural waste to usable products is becoming more and more imperative. The discarded materials are bringing about a fast-growing pollution problem. Even when these discarded materials are burned many of the combustion products are serious pollutants. At the same time the food supply from conventional sources is far from being sufficient in the face of rapidly increasing demands for greater quantity and better quality. Thus, the need clearly exists for developing new foods from nonconventional sources such as agricultural wastes. Agricultural wastes can be utilized directly as a feed ingredient and indirectly as an energy source in food production by microorganisms. With limited arable land and under given climatic conditions such as those in Korea, fermentation may offer the best opportunity to produce additional foods.

Although precise data are not available, it is estimated that about 50% of the rice husks and cereal straws in Korea are utilized as fuel in villages.[3] With rapid economic development use of waste as fuel may be terminated gradually. Use of such waste in industry may thus be a desirable means for its disposal, contributing as it will to improvement of farm income and maximum utilization of domestic resources.

Korea imports respectively over 70,000 tons of fish and soybean meal and about 100,000 tons of molasses for the foodstuff and fermentation industries. It is roughly estimated that about 3 million tons of cereal straws and rice husks (equivalent to 20% of the total) and about 200 thousand tons of poultry manure could be collected economically. With the recovery of these resources Korea could stimulate development of the fermentation industry and save a considerable amount in foreign exchange.

Cellulose

Among the constituents of waste, cellulose ranks high in application to fermentation processes (Table I). Research in the U.S. is in progress on the use of bagasse and urban solid wastes for industrial purposes.[6,7] In this research the waste materials are utilized as a new source for single-cell protein production and the wastes are eliminated at the same time. In addition, the challenge in using animal waste as a raw material for producing feed is to convert the waste to a more digestible and nutritious form by fermentation.[4] Similar research projects are taking place at the Korea Institute of Science and Technology.

Table I.—Chemical Composition of Several Farm Residues[5]

	Water(%)	Protein(%)	Fat(%)	Cellulose(%)	Ash(%)
Rice husk	8.0	3.0	0.8	40.7	19.1
Rice straw	7.5	3.9	1.4	33.5	14.5
Barley straw	10.0	3.7	1.6	37.7	6.0

Rice bran

Rice bran constitutes about 9% of rough rice. The bran contains more fats, protein, and vitamins than milled rice (Table II). Although such nutrients are sorely needed this valuable by-product has not been efficiently utilized in Korea and other rice-eating countries. The bran produced in Asia and the Far East amounts to about 8 million tons. Edible oil available from this source would be valued at $300 million.[9] Against this potential the actual production is about 10% due to the economic and technical problems attendant on development of this industry. Korea produces about 300 thousand tons of rice bran annually but only 13% of the total bran is utilized for oil production.

The majority of rice mills are of small capacity and outmoded (which affects bran quality), and they are widely scattered over rural areas (which complicates collection of a sizable quantity of the bran). Both—quality and quantity—are prerequisites for profitable extraction of oil. Research is needed on

Table II.—Chemical Composition of Rice Bran and Milled Rice[8]

	Rice Bran(A)	Milled Rice(B)	A/B
Carbohydrate(%)	46.6	91.5	0.5
Protein(%)	14.6	7.6	1.9
Lipid(%)	13.4	0.3	44.7
Thiamin(ug/g)	27.9	0.8	34.8
Niacin(ug/g)	408.6	18.1	22.6
Pyridoxin(ug/g)	32.1	4.5	7.1
Pantothenic acid(ug/g)	71.3	6.4	11.1
Riboflavin(ug/g)	2.68	0.26	10.3

the various aspects of the rice bran oil industries starting with the rice milling operation to produce bran of a higher oil and protein content than at present and to make it more feasible to extract oil and utilize the defatted bran as feedstuff for livestock. Modernization of rice mills on a large scale will allow collection and extraction of rice bran to be carried out more effectively and economically. It would be even more ideal if in modernization of rice mills the solvent extractive milling (X-M) process could be adopted.[10] This new rice milling technology offers more rice, oil and defatted bran, and of better quality than those obtained from conventional milling. The clean, high-protein rice bran can now be utilized as an ingredient in processed foods. Thus, if it is effectively used, rice bran will provide extra food to Asiatic countries without the necessity of employing additional land for cultivation of crops. Unfortunately, the solution to this urgent problem involves high capital investment, mostly in terms of foreign exchange.

Coconut water

The coconut industry is an important one in many developing countries in Asia. The estimated annual coconut production during 1960 to 1965 reached a level of 2.7 million tons and accounts for about 80% of world production.[11] About 60% was exported to developed countries, earning over $230 million annually during the same period. The fact, however, that this region has the lowest per capita consumption of protein and that copra cake and meal are a cheap source of good quality protein should give priority to the exportation of the oil instead of the copra. Assuming an approximate 10.4% protein content for desiccated coconut, the possible annual production of the protein is estimated to be at least 260 thousand tons.

Coconut water, a clear liquid found in the center of fresh nuts, is considered a waste in the region where copra is manufactured. Coconut water contains all the nutrients required for growth of a microorganism, and, thus, can be utilized as a fermentation substrate (Table III). However, its sugar content is only about 2%, not sufficient for vinegar production.

In the Philippines more than 75 billion nuts were used for copra manufacture during 1970. Over 1.5 billion liters of coconut water could be obtained from this assuming the average water content of each nut to be 0.2 liters. If one-fifth of this were used for vinegar manufacture, there would be about 210 million liters of vinegar available to supply the needs of about 6 million Philippine families. [13] In Ceylon, trials have been made to investigate the feasibility of utilizing coconut water to obtain a potable spirit. [12]

Table III.—Proximate Constituents of Coconut Water [12]

Total solid	4.71%
Total sugar	2.08
Other organic solid	2.01
Ash	0.62

Tapioca waste

In Thailand the tapioca starch manufacturing industry contributes significantly to water pollution. The ideal solution would be by-product recovery from the discharge of such factories in a way which would off-set the cost of waste treatment or result in a profit to the industry. The extraction of organic nutrients from the tapioca effluents through microbial cultivation deserves consideration as a possible solution. [14]

The tapioca root is very rich in carbohydrates, mainly starch, and is, therefore, used as a raw material for the production of starch. Wastes produced by a starch factory can be divided into two types: solid pulp and solid wastes. The pulp is pressed to remove excess water, sun-dried and sold as tapioca meal to be used for animal feed. One ton of dried pulp is produced from about 100 tons of fresh roots. The pulp has a high carbohydrate content but is low in fat and protein (Table IV).

Table IV.—Chemical Composition of Tapioca Pulp [14]

Moisture	12.7%
Ash	9.1
Fibre	8.1
Fat	1.0
Protein	2.5
Carbohydrate	65.9

The liquid wastes are composed of root wash water and separate waste water. The root wash water mainly consists of cork cells, sand, and clay particles. After alum coagulation the treated root wash water is recycled. Extraction of the dissolved solids is suggested by substantial quantities of organic nutrients in the separator waste water. Microbial cultivation is also suggested since alum coagulation of the separator waste water was found to be ineffective.

Yeast has attracted perhaps the greatest interest among microorganisms considered as a potential protein source. Its ability to grow well in the range of 25° to 40°C at low acidity, with a minimum growth factor requirement, makes it most suitable. The approximate composition of the settled waste water is shown in Table V. When the waste was used in laboratory experiments without added nutrients, it was clearly shown that a reduction of 60% or better in the 5-day BOD (biochemical

Table V.—Proximate Composition of Settled Waste Water [14]

Total solid	0.99%
Total sugar	0.60
Organic matter	0.75
Ash	0.16
pH	6.2

oxygen demand) could be attained. The production of yeast solids would then amount to about 40% of the total solids present in the waste water. A similar process may be applicable to waste recovery from sweet potato starch manufacturing in Korea.

Other wastes

There are several other agricultural wastes available, such as sweet potato pulp, corn cobs, and soybean hulls. However, the quantity of such items collectable economically is too small to justify commercial recovery operations in Korea. [15]

Malaysia produces about 4 million tons of hevea latex annually. The nonrubber materials contained in the latex amounted to about 100 thousand tons of material which at present is normally discarded as waste in nearby streams. This procedure aggravates stream pollution and represents a direct loss to the land of valuable plant nutrients. A method for employing the waste as a fertilizer is already used to some extent. A possible use for the waste is conversion into livestock feeds through the cultivation of algae. [16]

ANALYSIS OF POTENTIAL USE
OF SEWAGE AS A SOURCE

Seoul's population (about 6 million) produces around 230,000 tons of sewage per day [17], and is the main pollutant of the Han River. Today's conventional waste-water treatment processes strip organic nutrients from the water for ultimate disposal as gas and sludge solid. Future food and water shortages, however, will necessitate the development of a process for extracting and conserving the nutrients to produce food or feed under controlled conditions and provide treated water for reuse. Today the most economical method of water reclamation is suggested to be high-rate oxidation pond systems where treatment is effected by algal-bacterial symbiosis.

Sewage usually contains essentially balanced nutrients for algae. The organic substances, however, that are present in sewage must be broken down by bacteria to provide essential elements in a form available to the algae. One process that has been very successful is diagrammed in Figure 1. In the process, bacteria oxidize organic wastes to create nutrients available for algae, while the algae use solar energy and carbon dioxide from the air to incorporate these nutrients into their cells. Oxygen is coincidentally produced and is available to the bacteria for the oxidation of additional waste. The net result of this cycle is that organic matter in the waste is converted into algal cells for livestock feed while water is reclaimed in the process.

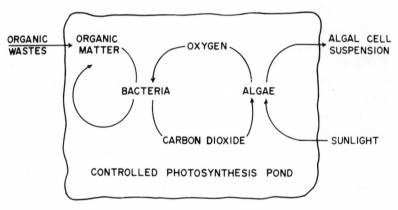

Figure 1.—Cycle of controlled photosynthesis in organic wastes. [19]

Research on a pilot-plant scale on this process in Thailand, Israel, Malaysia [18], and the United States [19] has apparently been successful. The benefit to an urban center of using the waste-water treatment algae production system include water pollution control in the urban environment, provision of animal feed without the use of already limited land and water resources and resource conservation through reclamation and reuse.

BY-PRODUCT RECOVERY VS. DEVELOPMENT OF INDUSTRY AND AGRICULTURE IN DEVELOPING COUNTRIES

Some of the problems facing developing countries in terms of ensuring an adequate food supply are:

• The heavy water requirements for conventional crop production.

• Protection of water resources from pollution.

• Efficient utilization of land and conservation of resources to produce more food and feedstuffs.

Conserving raw materials through reuse has been applied to solid water in the past. This has been particularly true during periods of national strife when raw materials are in short supply. Production of yeast from the sulfite waste-liquor of a paper mill is a well-known example of successful waste recovery with benefits in terms of environmental protection and added profit for the industry. The fermentation system through which single-cell protein and reusable water are obtained from solid and liquid waste through microbial action is perhaps the most promising approach in providing a feasible solution to these problems.

At present the Soviet Union is the only country producing alcohol and yeast from cellulosic agricultural waste on a commercial scale. In the Soviet Union this reduction industry has increased 86%, while other industries as a whole increased 69% during 1959 to 1965.[20] While such industry is technically possible [20-21], the question lies with its economic feasibility. The economics of the operation depend highly on geographical location, availability of resources, and the degree to which these types of by-product utilization industries are necessary to supply domestic demands.

In terms of economics, developed countries have the advantage since such wastes are concentrated by mechanized farm operation on a large scale. It is less attractive in developing areas because the operations are on a small scale and use manual labor. In fact, cellulose is the most abundant form of organic matter and accounts for one-third of the total plant material on earth. Protein, other food ingredients and major chemicals can be produced by fermentation processes with cellulose as a source. Oil supplies are being used up rapidly whereas, in contrast, plants are converted at a very slow rate to fossil form by geological processes. [22] Fermentation may thus supply more food while at the same time restore the chemical side of the carbon cycle (Figure 2).

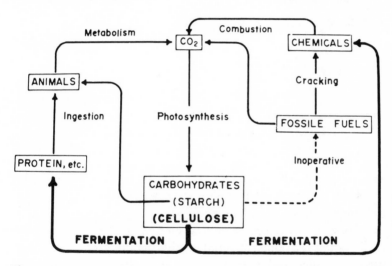

Figure 2.—Fermentation may restore chemical side of cycle and give more foods.

Wastes that are low in nutrients can be concentrated effectively and rather cheaply by the addition of other wastes which are high in solids. A semi-dry mash is obtained which is then pressed—a relatively inexpensive procedure—and used as animal feed or in some cases as fertilizer.

The dream of developing countries is to accomplish rapid industrial and agricultural development without environmental pollution. In already developed countries pollution control requirements place heavy financial burdens on some industries [23],

and may result in price increases of salable commodities up to
10% (Table VI). According to a recent analysis pollution has
increased tenfold while population has grown only 43% since
World War II. Pollution per capita has therefore increased sevenfold. [24]

Table VI.—Despite Cost Increases in the US from Pollution Control [23]

Food and live animals	1 to 5%
Beverages and tobacco	1 to 5
Crude materials	1 to 10
Mineral fuels and petroleum products	5 to 10
Oils, fats and waxes	5 to 10
Chemicals	5 to 10
Manufactured goods	5 to 10
Machinery and transport equipment	5 to 10

Are all these part of the natural course of development?
There must be better or alternate ways for advances in development which prevent or reduce pollution.

Of course experiences of the developed countries should be
carefully analyzed and reflected in the planning of developing
countries. Advice and joint research from developed countries
and the United Nations could provide developing nations with
guidance for minimizing the pollution produced while attaining
industrial development.

The examples discussed so far only indicate the potential in
developing countries. The potential is there and the techniques
are feasible. How to also achieve economic feasibility is the
question that arises. The economics, however, may not be a
world-wide problem. What may not be economical in one area
may be economical in other areas. Further detailed studies in
laboratories or on a pilot-plant basis are needed to define a
working system before full-scale commercial operations are initiated. To clean up the polluted part of the world while keeping

the unpolluted part clean is the common obligation of mankind for the coming generation.

References

1. Industry in Korea, The Korea Development Bank, Seoul, 1970.
2. Rhee, CJ: Present Status of Solid Waste Treatment, *New Technology* (Korea) 4:2, 1972.
3. Kwon, TW: Industrial Use of Agricultural By-Products, *New Technology* (Korea) 2:16, 1970.
4. From Agricultural Wastes to Feed or Fuel, *C&EN* 14, 1972.
5. Morrison, FB: *Feeds and Feeding*, Clinton, Iowa, the Morrison Pub. Co., 1959.
6. Han, YW and Srinvasan, VR: Isolation and Characterization of a Cellulose-Utilizing Bacterium, *Appl. Microbiol,* 16:1140, 1969.
7. Srinivasan VR, and Han, YW: Utilization of Bagasse, *Cellulases and Its Application,* 1969, (Adv Chem Ser 95:447-60)
8. Matz, SA: *Cereals as Food and Feed*, Westport, Conn., AVI, 1959.
9. Research Problems in the Development of Rice Bran Oil Industry in the ECAFE Region, AIDC/IR/R.5, Economic Commission for Asia and the Far East, 1967.
10. Nowlin, JF: X-M Process for Solvent Extractive Milling of Rice, ID/WG 89:3, United Nations Development Organization, 1971.
11. Co-operation in Industrial Research for the Development of the Coconut Industry in the ECAFE Region, AIDC/IR/R.8, Economic Commission for Asia and the Far East, 1967.
12. Jayatissa, PM; Jeya Raj, EE; Triimanna, ASL; and Senamayake, UM: Utilization of Waste to Obtain Potable Spirit, Paper presented to the Work study on Waste recovery by microganisms, University of Malaya-UNESCO/ICRO, 1972.
13. Diokno-Palo, N: Vinegar Production from Sugared Coconut Water, University of Malaya-UNESCO/ICRO, 1972.
14. Sundhagul, M: Feasibility Study of Tapioca Waste Recovery, Paper presented to the Work study on waste recovery by organisms, University of Malaya-UNESCO/ICRO, 1972.
15. Lee, YH and Yang IW: Fermented Foods from Agricultural By-Products, *New Technology* (Korea) 2:34, 1970.
16. John, CK: Utilization of Waste Material in Hevea Latex, Paper presented at Work study on waste recovery by microrganisms, University of Malaya-UNESCO/ICRO, 1972.
17. Chung, TW: Culture and Production of Microalgae from Municipal Waste Water, *New Technology* (Korea) 2:15, 1971.
18. McGarry, CG: The Technology of Mass Algae Culture from Wastes; and Maheswaran, A: Sewage Processing, Papers presented at the Work study on waste recovery by microrganisms, University of Malaya-UNESCO/ICRO, 1972.

19. Oswald, WJ and Golueke, CG: Large-Scale Production of Algae, Ma-
    teles, R and Tannenbaum, SR (eds.): in *Single-Cell Protein*, Cam-
    bridge, Mass, MIT press, 1968, p 271.
20. Kozalor, AI: Changes in the Overall Production of the Hydrolysis
    Industry, *Gidrolizi Lesokhim*, Prom. 18:25, 1965.
21. Kehr, WQ: Microbial Degradation of Urban and Agricultural Wastes,
    San Clemente, CL (eds.): *Environmental Quality; Now or Never*,
    Continuing Education Service, Michigan State University, East Lans-
    ing, 1972, p 184.
22. Scientists Forecast Changes Due by 2000, *C&EN*, 1970, p 68.
23. Pollution Control; A World Trade Problem, *C&EN*, 1971, p 16.
24. Closing Circle on Environmental Economics, *C&EN*, 1972, p22.

Benefits of Pollution Control

ALAN P. CARLIN

The purpose of this paper is to describe the principal types of benefits and how information on them could be used to help determine the economically optimum level of control. However, it should be understood that as an economist I define benefits in terms of their value to man while those people primarily oriented towards an ecological point of view might have a different value system.

The interaction of health aspects between environmental quality and food supply, requires a brief review of what the major pollutants (or residuals) resulting from modern agriculture are (see Table I). These pollutants lead to a variety of damages to plants, animals, man himself, and property of value to him. Those pollutants that sometimes result in health damages to man are starred in Table I. Table II indicates some of the major categories of pollution control benefits and the principal means for measuring them. Although not intended to be all inclusive, this table features most of the more important categories of pollution control benefits.*

MAJOR CATEGORIES OF POLLUTION CONTROL BENEFITS

These benefits range from physical damages through recreational and aesthetic, to what has been called option demand by those in the economics profession. Physical benefits refer to

---

*Perhaps the major category not listed is that of environmental risk, i.e., the risk that pollution will result in an environmental catastrophe of some sort. Depending on the nature of the possible catastrophe, this risk could be classified as a sub-type under any of the above types.

Table I—Major Residuals From Agriculture

Air Pollution
Particulate matter* from
  Processing operations
    Cotton ginning
    Alfalfa dehydrators
  Wind erosion of unprotected soil
Oxidants* from burning of
  Plant residuals, including forest residuals
  Processing wastes

Water Pollution
Stream sediment from additional water erosion of unprotected soil
Plant nutrients from fertilizer runoffs causing:
  Eutrophication
  Nitrate in well water*
Inorganic salts and minerals from irrigation
Biochemical oxygen demand (BOD) from
  Animal wastes
  Processing wastes

Solid Wastes
Residues from farm, ranch, and forestry operations
Processing wastes

Infestions Agents and Allergens*
Animal disease agents
Plant disease organisms
Allergens and poisonous weeds
Insect vectors

Pesticides*
Insecticides
Fungicides
Nematocides

---

*Indicates possible adverse impact on human health.

Source: Based on Cecil H. Wadleigh, *Wastes in Relation to Agriculture and Forestry,*
U.S. = Department of Agriculture Miscellaneous Publication No. 1065, Washington,
D.C., March 1968, Appendix II.

Table II—Major Pollution Control Benefits and their Measurement

Principal Types of Benefits	Principal Means for Measurement
Physical	Valuation of pollution effects
Recreational	Estimates of added use and its value with less pollution
Aesthetic	Expressed willingness-to-pay; variations in property values with pollution levels
Option demand	Expressed Willingness-to-pay

savings achieved by avoiding the direct adverse effects of pollution on man's health, on the animals, plants, and property that he values, and on production costs external to the pollution source. The cracking of automobile tires and other rubber products as a result of high concentrations of photochemical oxidants is an example of an adverse physical effect that has been demonstrated.

Recreational benefits are the added benefits that man would receive from extra recreational opportunities available to him if pollution did not exist. An example is the opportunity to swim in a formerly polluted water body. Current information suggests that the principal water pollution control benefits may be in the recreational area. In other words, the principal value of a clean river may be that it would create additional recreational opportunities compared to those available if it were polluted.

Aesthetic benefits refer both to the added visual or other sensory benefits to man when he is not exposed to pollution as well as to a more nebulous, but nevertheless, important satisfaction that many people receive from simply knowing that water is "clean" even if they do not see it. The removal of floating noxious solids from a water body would be likely to result in this type of benefit to those who viewed it.

Option demand benefits arise as a result of retaining the option of doing or seeing something, even if the individuals involved have no present plans to exercise it. Perhaps the best-known example of this, although it does not involve pollution control, is a decision made several years ago to preserve the Grand Canyon without building hydroelectric dams in it. Many of the people who supported that decision had no intention of going to or visiting the inner canyon in which the dams would have been located, but they still had a desire to retain the option of doing so. This option demand benefit is also to be found in the area of pollution control. Feelings expressed for the preservation of rare wildlife species from the dangers of pollution, for example, suggest that many people feel such benefits exist.

PRINCIPAL MEANS FOR
QUANTIFYING BENEFITS

Table II also lists the principal means that presently exist to quantify these benefits of pollution control. In order to quantify physical benefits, the most direct route is to attempt to determine what the physical effects are, and then attempt to place a value on them. Since the physical effects of pollutants on man and things of value to man usually vary according to the pollution levels causing the damages, it is useful to attempt to define a physical damage function relating the two such as is illustrated in Figure 1. If economic values are then placed on the damages, an economic damage function such as is shown in Figure 2 results.

In the case of recreational benefits, the easiest approach appears to be through estimating the added use that would result in the presence of less pollution.

Aesthetic benefits can be quantified by using two alternative approaches. One is to attempt to find areas where a substantial change in pollution level has occurred, and then attempt to correlate these changes with changes in local property values. To use this approach successfully, it is necessary to determine what part of the change in property values is attributable to the aesthetic portion of the benefits of pollution control, an often

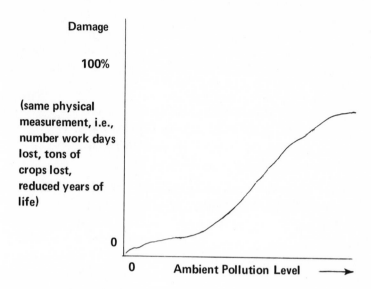

Figure 1. —Physical Damage Function

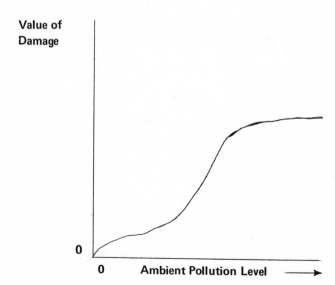

Figure 2. —Economic Damage Function

difficult task. Another approach for quantifying aesthetic benefits is by sampling a representative cross-section of the population and asking them what they would be willing to pay for
improved aesthetic benefits. This latter approach also appears to
be the most feasible route in the case of option demand.

APPLICATION TO DETERMINING
THE ECONOMICALLY OPTIMUM
LEVEL OF POLLUTION CONTROL
FOR AGRICULTURE

Assuming that we know what major environmental damages
result from agriculture and have estimates as to the benefits of
pollution control, we must next decide how to apply this
information to the problem of determining the economically
optimum level of pollution. This assumes that the necessary
effort and research required to ascertain the benefits has been
expended so that empirical rather than just theoretical measures
are available. It should also be mentioned that in reality there
are many other more practical considerations taken into account in determining pollution control levels than the economic
benefits and costs, most importantly the many specific provisions of the legislation written by Congress.

The following analysis of agricultural production aids, such as
fertilizer or pesticides, could be carried out given sufficient
effort and bold enough assumptions to solve many data inade-
quacies.

For any given level of production aid use, one could attempt
to calculate the resulting general or ambient pollution levels
that might cause damages. This usually requires some knowledge of how pollutants travel from one spot to another, so as
to determine how the release of pollutants in agricultural fields
will affect their concentrations in areas where they will affect
man or things of value to man. Then, using an economic damage
function for that pollutant, one could relate production aid use
to the resulting economic damages from physical causes. If
similar relationships were constructed for recreational, aesthetic, and option demand damages, a composite function could be
constructed relating damages to production aid use. If these

economic damages were then added to the net additional direct or market cost of using the production aid (as shown in idealized form in the lowest of the three curves in Figure 3), it would be possible to derive the net additional cost of using the aid including non-market or external costs (as shown, again in idealized form, in the middle curve).

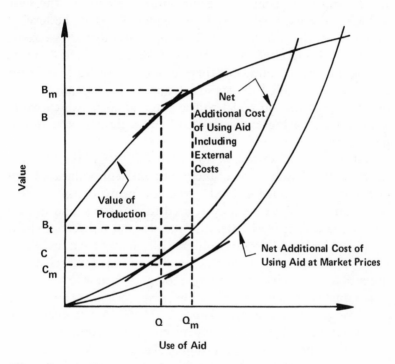

Figure 3. —Optimum Use of Environmentally Damaging Agricultural Production Aid

The upper curve shows the total benefits in terms of increased agricultural production to be derived from using the agricultural production aid. It begins at the left showing the value of production without use of the production aid, production increases with relatively moderate amounts of the production aid, and then the effects as the marginal return starts falling off.

In a perfectly competitive market in which the external costs are not taken into account, the use of the production aid will be

at the level labeled Q_m, m referring to market, this is the level
at which the benefits (value of production) are maximized
relative to the cost of using the agricultural production aid for
this idealized case.*

Taking the external costs (largely environmental damages)
into account, the optimum use of the production aid will be
smaller since the benefits are maximized relative to the costs
including the external costs (the middle curve) at the level Q.
Level Q is the optimum, taking into account the external
damages. This level of use of the aid could be achieved either by
setting an upper bound on the amount of use (level Q in this
case), which is called the standards approach, or imposing a tax
on the use of the aid equal to the external costs, which would
automatically achieve the desired results through the market
mechanism.

A major complication in any such analysis is the fact that
many of the damages are a function of ambient pollution levels,
rather than of emission levels; whereas, many of the costs of
pollution control are directly related to emissions, and not the
resulting ambient levels. Because the relation between ambient
levels and emission levels is only partially understood, usually in
terms of complex mathematical models of unproven reliability,
the problem is, indeed much more complex than it first appears.

In conclusion, a great deal of knowledge is lacking concerning
the cost of environmental damages. The EPA has decided to
carry out one of the first organized efforts toward a multi-
pollutant approach to this problem. However, we are able to
spend only about $750,000 a year on the problem of develop-
ing benefit estimates and the closely related one of developing
compatible cost of control estimates. So far, we have arrived at
very few answers, but are concentrating our resources on attempting to develop national "point estimates", rather than
damage functions. These "point estimates" attempt to measure
the benefits to the nation if pollution were reduced to the level
specified in EPA ambient standards. Further development

---

*Technically, it is the level of use of the aid at which the value of production minus
the net additional cost of using the aid at market prices is at a maximum; it is also
the point at which the tangents to these idealized curves at those points are parallel.

would be necessary if functional relationships which relate benefits/damages to various levels of pollution control are to be developed similar to that shown in Figure 2. Regional estimates might be even more useful than national estimates in determining optimum pollution control levels.

Finally, it is necessary to raise (although not answer) a more general question as to whether some U.S. agricultural policies encourage the intensive use of agricultural production aids, with their resulting environmental damages. More precisely, the question is whether such policies result in excessive use (from the point of view of economic efficiency as discussed earlier) of production aids, especially when the environmental damages or external effects are taken into account. If they do, some reduction in damages can be obtained by modifying these policies.

Uncited References

Anderson, J Jr and Crocker, D: The Economics of Air Pollution: Literature Assessment, *Project Clean Air: Task Force Assessments,* Volume 3, Section 6, University of California, Riverside, 1970.

Barrett, LB and Waddell, TB: *Cost of Air Pollution Damage: A Status Report,* Report AP-85, Research Triangel Park, North Carolina, U.S. Environmental Protection Agency, National Environmental Research Center, February, 1973.

Development and Resources Corporation, *Study of Methods of Financing the Cost of Preventing, Controlling and Abating Water Pollution from Non-Point Sources,* Report prepared for Office of Water Programs, Sacramento, U.S. Environmental Protection Agency, April, 1971.

Kneese, AV and J Bower, BT: *Managing Water Quality: Economics, Technology—Institutions,* Baltimore, G Johns Hopkins Press, 1968.

Control of Agriculture-Related Pollution: A Report to the President, U.S. Department of Agriculture and Office of Science and Technology, Washington, January, 1969.

Wadleigh, CH: *Wastes in Relation to Agriculture and Forestry,* U.S. Department of Agriculture Miscellaneous Publication No. 1065, Washington, U.S. Government Printing Office, March, 1968.

Costs of Pollution and Recycling

EUGENE E. ERICKSON, Ph.D.

Pollution control regulations are becoming more strict almost daily, and, even if sights are set on more practical goals than "zero" pollution, costs for pollution abatement will increase greatly. Who is going to pay for this? In most cases the costs will be paid by the customer.

There may be alternatives, however. We have traditionally considered wastes to be useless, or if of any value at all, certainly not to the extent that any recovery effort was justified. Actually, waste is only matter and energy in a less useful form or place than matter and energy we conventionally use. Any potential for reducing the cost of pollution control depends on this fact. Until resources become extremely short, it will cost less to "use" virgin materials than recovered or secondary materials. However, if along with the cost differential for using a secondary material, we also consider the saving of conventional pollution abatement and waste treatment costs, and the savings of resources for future use and more critical needs, resource recycling or waste utilization may look much more competitive. We need to find some practical mechanisms for including the entire system in determining the costs.

Several examples of wastes being matter and energy in less than optimum form or place are:

1. *Municipal solid waste (refuse).* It contains materials of value for recovery, primarily metals and paper. It also contains a considerable heating value as an energy source.

2. *Used tires.* They are good energy sources and can be used, when ground, as a component of asphalt paving. They also break down into useful chemicals and fuels.

3. *Thermal pollution from power plants.* Instead of dumping

49

wastes into a stream, the water might be used to heat soil which would promote both plant and microbial growth.

4. *Animal (livestock) wastes.* They are good sources of nutrient and conditioner for soil. They also are rich sources of carbohydrate and protein.

5. *Food processing wastes.* They are usually high in carbohydrate, and provide useful media for biological growth, particularly for conversion to protein.

In the last two cases, soil application by irrigation may be a suitable use. Direct recovery of protein and conversion of the carbohydrate to a recoverable protein are possible.

TWO APPROACHES TO RESOURCE RECOVERY

It becomes apparent from some of these examples that we need to look at two approaches to resource recovery: (1) direct recovery and reuse, and (2) conversion to other forms. Direct recovery and reuse of materials will become more attractive as further development of resource recovery processes reduces their costs. Markets for secondary materials will develop; this will be a real key to the rate at which direct materials recovery increases. Freight rate structures will change to eliminate penalties that secondary materials may have to pay in relation to virgin materials.

The second type of recovery, involving conversion, is perhaps even more important. Use of the material as an energy source for heat generation may become the largest means of utilizing refuse; it may necessarily be combined, with direct resource recovery. Converting carbohydrates to protein may be a practical approach to some liquid wastes and many agricultural residues.

In addition to new and improved processes, we certainly will have to take a new look at the cost picture. We need not only to consider the market value of the material recovered, but also the cost of alternative disposal or treatment without resource recovery. The comparative net costs will often make the resource recovery option attractive. Legislation may be required to eliminate unacceptable options, as open dumps are being eliminated, or competitive advantages. Further, the value of secondary effects needs to be considered, such as increased value of land and conservation of other resources.

Recovery from Refuse

The best way to discuss resource recovery is by considering specific examples. One that is probably the most universal, perhaps even more so than sewage, is municipal solid waste. We hear a great deal of talk about recycling of refuse, which generally means recovering such materials as metals, glass, paper from refuse, and leaving the rest for conventional disposal—landfill or incineration. In many cases, metals and paper can at least pay for their recovery—the value of glass rarely warrants its recovery. Volume reduction may run well over 50% with paper recovery. Without paper recovery, reduction is small, and the "recovery" step does little to reduce volume—one of the prime objectives of a "treatment" process.

But there may be several other options for resource recovery from refuse. One of the more attractive ones is recovery of energy by utilization as a fuel. Although there usually is not a large enough volume of waste in one location for the sole energy source for a large power generating station, there may be enough for other uses. Solid waste can be mixed with coal, for example, for fuel for large power stations. A new use of wastes that looks particularly attractive is the heating and cooling of building complexes. One such application is fairly well developed in the City of Nashville, Tennessee. Here a central steam generating plant will supply steam and chilled water for use in downtown buildings. Cost savings to users is projected to be 25% to 30% of the cost of running their own heating and cooling facilities.

Waste will be supplied by the city to the plant and the city will retain ownership of waste. Volume will be reduced to 10% of the original volume, and will be landfilled without earth covering. It will also be advantageous to the city if salable products can be produced from the residue. Thus, the heat generating plant receives free fuel, and the city reduces its landfill requirements by at least 90% which reduces its waste disposal costs and problems significantly.

A similar concept is being explored by the gas utility in a large city. The economics of supplying gas for individual buildings has been examined. With the growing shortage of natural gas, and with the requirement for interruptable service for large consumers, a central municipal plant that burns solid waste for steam generation could reduce disposal costs. Assuming that the waste would be delivered free to the plant, which was near the source of the waste; this would save the city hauling and landfill costs. The costs of this operation have been estimated by the gas company to be less in comparison to the use of natural gas. There would be a bonus in the availability of natural gas for other and perhaps more critical uses.

In discussions about using solid wastes as an energy source, it is helpful to compare various methods of conversion and fuel sources. Four methods of energy utilization and the fraction of energy typically recovered from them are:

Conversion to fuel by anaerobic digestion typically used in digestion of solids and sludge from waste treatment plants	27%
Generation of electric energy	40%
Fuel production by pyrolysis of wastes	70%
Generation of steam, with heat recovery	80%

Solid waste varies quite widely in composition, and heating values may range, typically, from about 4,000 to 7,000 Btu/lb of raw, wet waste. If we compare this with coal, we may have three tons of refuse equivalent to about one ton of coal. The value as a heat source will probably be in the range of $2 to $3/ton. For example, on the basis of 30¢/million Btu—typical for natural gas in some areas, waste at 5400 Btu/lb would have a fuel value of $3.24/ton. However, costs of equipment and operation are greater than for natural gas. Comparison with coal (20¢ to 50¢/million Btu) gives a similar figure. Some typical heating values are shown below:

Peat	2,400 Btu/lb
Wood	3,200 Btu/lb
Refuse	3,500-7,000 Btu/lb
Coal	13,500 Btu/lb
#6 Fuel Oil	17,300 Btu/lb
Methane	21,600 Btu/lb

Recovery from Discarded Tires

Another solid waste problem that has received a great deal of attention is that of discarded tires. It serves a good example of problems encountered and of new approaches to waste utilization and economics. Conventional uses account for only a very small part of the supply available, disposal by open burning is no longer permitted, and land filling is generally unsuitable. The annual volume of useless tire casings is estimated at 180 million.[2] This is not only a serious problem, but also a tremendous resource to waste.

Many approaches are being explored by major companies, including use as a fuel for steam supply, pyrolysis or destructive distillation to break the rubber down to useful chemicals and fuels, dumping in the ocean to form artificial reefs for fish spawning and feeding, and grinding to incorporate in asphalt road surfacing. The cost of disposal, even dumping in the ocean, runs from 20 to 40 cents per tire.[2] Many other uses have also been demonstrated, but none has been shown to pay its own way. With the public required to pay the disposal cost in the form of added cost by manufactureres, waste disposal cost in the community, added dealers cost to cover disposal of trade-in; etc, perhaps a more direct "subsidy" should be considered. A "head-end" tax of fee, paid by the original purchaser on each tire—say 25 to 50 cents—at the time of purchase, would provide the funds for private corporations or public facilities to operate plants utilizing the tire casings.

Conversion of Food Wastes

Liquid wastes provide other sources of materials of value, but they are usually so dilute or complex that recovery of materials is not practical. Reduction of pollution of receiving bodies of water has been the only objective of treatment. This treatment has met only the legal requirements of protecting public health and periodically maintaining reasonable relations with neighbors. As requirements for treatment have become more stringent, waste treatment systems have become more extensive, somewhat more sophisticated, but are generally still only aimed at pollution control.

Food processing wastes are examples of liquid wastes that present difficult disposal problems. Food processing industries' wastes are generally high in biochemical oxygen demand (BOD). They usually are amenable to biological treatment, but are difficult to treat to levels required for discharge into a stream. The treatment process may require a "pretreatment" to lower the strength of the waste stream so that it is suitable for further treatment in municipal treatment plants which operate at relatively low BOD levels. Such treatment processes characteristically produce sludges which must be disposed of—actually a "solid waste" problem. In some cases, the sludges are dried and burned; sometimes they are treated in anaerobic digestors to produce gas which may be burned for process energy needs. They may also be land filled or spread on soil. There is usually no attempt at utilization or recycle.

Costs for treatment are often expressed in terms of cents per unit of production or product; for example, cents per case of canned food or per 1000 lbs live weight of livestock killed. Another way of expressing cost, and one that is particularly useful when comparing treatment effectiveness, is cents per pound of BOD removed. Actual costs in canning operations are usually not known. However, 1 to 2 cents/lb of BOD would be very low. Cost may well be several times that amount. Cost per case of corn would probably run considerably greater than 4 cents.

There is growing hope that resources can be recovered from liquid wastes. If a "competitive" treatment process could be used that would not only reduce pollution loads to acceptable levels, but would also produce a marketable product, a big step forward could be made. An example of a process that meets these requirements is one that we have developed through a laboratory and pilot stage. Pilot programs have been operated successfully at the Green Giant corn and pea canning plant in Glencoe, Minnesota, and at the corn wet-milling plant of Penick and Ford, Ltd., at Cedar Rapids, Iowa. Cost estimates for full-scale operation are based on the pilot experience. The process is a biological one in which selected strains of *Fungi Imperfecti* are grown aerobically in the waste. The fungi grow well on carbohydrate solutions under controlled conditions, producing a macroscopic mycelium that is readily screened or filtered from the liquid. The mycelium contains about 50% high-quality, readily accessible protein—protein at least the equivalent of soy meal.

Estimated costs are shown for both operations in Table I[3]; investment cost is based on 10 year amortization at 7%, with 3-month operation at the cannery and year-round operation at the corn milling plant.

Table I—Estimated costs for fungal conversion.

CAPITAL COST	$200,000		$1,150,000
ANNUAL COST	$ 52,400		$ 312,000
COST/LB BOD		4.85c	1.65c
PRODUCT CREDIT/LB BOD		3.25	2.90
NET COST (SURPLUS/LB BOD		1.60	(1.25)
ANNUAL COST (SURPLUS)		$17,300	$ (238,000)

Note CANNING PLANT: 1,000,000 GAL/DAY, 1600 mg BOD_5/l,
90-DAY OPERATION

CORN MILL: 3,000,000 GAL/DAY, 3500 mg BOD_5/l,
12-MONTH OPERATION

The short operating season for the cannery imposes a severe penalty on investment costs—even so, it appears that the cannery could be much better off with this process than with conventional processes. This is apparent if we consider that the present treatment cost may run considerably over 2 cents/lb BOD.

In the case of the year-round operation, we can see that the product recovery can not only cover the cost of the treatment, but can produce a net profit. The profitability of the process, compared with what the waste would cost to treat with conventional processes, become at least twice the surplus shown. Based on an investment cost of $1.15 million, the return on the investment could be over 50%.

As a final example, a projected application of the fungal process mentioned above to a waste that is a combination of liquid and solid presents a major problem. This waste is the rumen contents of beef cattle called "paunch" or "paunch manure". Typically, the contents are about 15% solids, and consist of the partially digested feed in the first stomach, or rumen or ruminants. A 1000 lb animal will contribute 50 lbs to 70 lbs/head, a large plant processing 2,000 head/day, would have 28 million lbs/year to dispose of. The material is to a considerable extent cellulosic and is slow to break down in biological treatment processes. It cannot be handled in conventional treatment plants. It is, in fact, a major unsolved problem of packing plants.

The handling of the waste material by any means leads to a solid waste disposal problem. The solids are sometimes spread on land and ultimately plowed in. This is a good method of disposal and utilization, but is practical only if there is adequate land available very near the plant. Hauling is difficult and landfill is generally unsatisfactory.

A better solution is to convert the material to a useful product. This is being done to a very limited extent by composting. Rumen contents can be converted to an innocuous material which has value as a soil conditioner. The product, however, has sufficient value to make the process useful only in the specialty market for nurseries and small gardens. Any volume large enough to make a significant contribution to the disposal problem would give a product of relatively low market value.

A newer disposal approach has been that of drying the rumen contents and using the product as a component of cattle feed. Very limited work has been done on the process and on feeding evaluation. The material can be dried successfully and fed to the cattle. Feeding results have not been particularly promising, however, and the material, at best, would not have a broad market. A better solution would be the upgrading of the rumen contents in a low-cost process to provide a product of significantly greater value. The process mentioned above of converting the organic content of waste materials to fungal protein appears to be an ideal solution. A feed supplement containing about

25% protein (diluted with the inert material, largely fiber, in the paunch), probably having a value of about $65/ton (based on the price for soy meal of $130/ton) would be obtained from the process.

Projected costs for the process are indicated in Table II, in comparison with paunch dehydration, for a 2000 head/day plant. Investment is based on 10-year ammortization at 7%.

As can be seen from the comparisons, the fungal process can show a profit if the product can be marketed for a price near that expected from its likely protein content. It is assumed that both the products would be marketed through existing channels, and no significant new marketing cost would occur. Thus, at anything approaching the current price of soy meal, the fungal process should more than pay its own way, giving the paunch a positive value as a raw material.

In addition, we should take into account the fact that paunch will incur disposal costs if it is not converted to a useful product. It is reasonable to credit either of the processes with the savings over current disposal costs. A minimum cost for disposal to any packer is about 5 cents/head (about $1.80/ton raw paunch). A more usual cost is probably at least 10 cents-/head ($3.60/ton), and, in some cases, costs may be still higher. The effect of a savings in present disposal costs on the "profitability" of the two operations is indicated for values of current disposal costs in Figure 1. It is apparent that the fungal process offers the greatest advantage over dehydration if current disposal costs tend to be low.

The following assumptions were made in estimating the annual costs:
    Quantity of paunch — 56lbs/head at 15% solids
    Cost of gas (heat) — 40c/million Btu
    Cost of electricity — 1c/kwh
    Selling price for dehydrated paunch — $25/ton
    Selling price for converted paunch — $65/ton
    Plant capacity — 2000 head/day for 250 days/year or
        500,000 head/year.
The same costs are shown on the basis of cents per head in Table III.

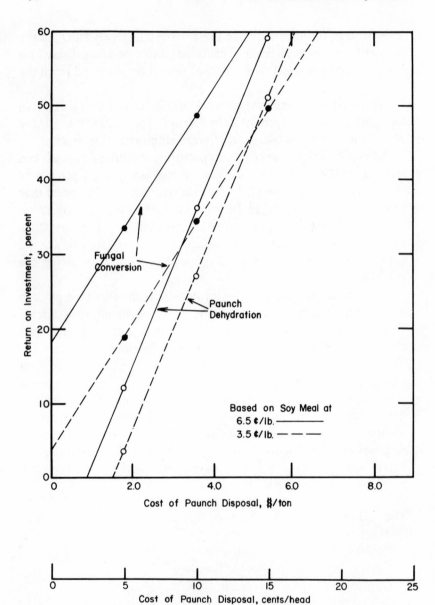

Figure 1.—Projected profitability of paunch utilization.

Table II—Projected annual costs for treatment of rumen contents.

	DEHYDRATION	FUNGAL CONVERSION
CAPITAL COST	$105,200	$162,000
ANNUAL COST		
INVESTMENT	$ 15,030	$ 23,140
OPERATING	41,280	46,280
TOTAL	$ 56,310	$ 69,420
INCOME FROM FEED	$ (43,700)	$ (97,500)
NET COST (SURPLUS)	$ 12,610	$ (28,080)

Table III—Projected unit costs for treatment of rumen contents.

	DEHYDRATION	CONVERSION
INVESTMENT COST	3.01	4.63
OPERATING COST	8.26	9.26
TOTAL	11.27	13.89
INCOME FROM FEED	(8.75)	(19.50)
NET COST (SURPLUS)	2.52	(5.61)

At higher disposal costs, the fungal process loses some of its advantage; however, it is unlikely that current costs would be high enough for the dehydration to be more attractive than the fungal conversion. At lower protein prices, based on the market price of soy meal values of both 6.5 and 3.5 cents/lb are indicated in the figure.

CONCLUSION

The realization that waste is matter or energy, but in a relatively inconvenient form or place can lead to new approaches to pollution control and resource recovery. Utilization of the materials and energy in our waste streams offers the only promise for reducing the burden of the ever increasing costs of pollution control. Further, as we realize many of our resources are far from limitless, conservation of resources through recovery will not reduce the cost of treatment, but conservation will demand it.

We should not overlook new means of financing pollution abatement and resource recovery operations. Because the public ultimately pays the cost when we look at the overall systems, public financing, head-end taxes to the user, subsidies for recovery, and utility-type operations may all have their places. We need to begin to find the ways in which the cost can be minimized within the total framework of abatement of pollution and utilization of our resources.

Acknowledgements

W. Brosz of the Green Giant Company is thanked for his comments.

References

1. Local Trash Cuts Downtown Fuel Bills, *Environmental Science and Technology* 6:780, 1972.
2. *Wall Street Journal*, April 27, 1972, p 34.
3. Church, BD; Erickson, EE; and Widmer, : +: Fungal Digestion of Food Processing Wastes at a Pilot Level, presented at the 72nd National Meeting, A I Ch E, St. Louis, Mo., May 21-24, 1972.

Agricultural Wastes

E. PAUL TAIGANIDES, Ph.D.

The current disposition of our society is one of growing concern with the problem of pollution. Although environmental pollution is a new concern for the majority of the people in the United States, it has been with us from the beginning of time. Pollution could be defined as the result of extreme ecological disruption. Man, animals, and plants have caused ecological disruptions above and beyond those caused by natural floods, droughts, the ice age, etc. What makes pollution by man unique, is that man can prevent or control man-made ecological disruptions.

Man has caused major agricultural disruptions as he evolved from hunter to herder to farmer to industrialist. As a hunter, man's activities produced only temporary disruptions in the ecosystem of the small valleys in which he hunted his prey. When man developed into a herder by domesticating animals, he caused agricultural disruptions of enough local significance to compete with natural changes in the ecosystem. As a herder, man enjoyed a more steady source of food and more leisure time which he devoted to increasing his numbers and to advancing his technology. Population pressures and advanced technology caused the great mass movements from the Indoeuropean steppes into continental Europe and across the Atlantic to America.

As farmer man-made agricultural disruptions became regional in nature, the dust bowl era of the 1930's was the first environmental crisis in the United States. The recognition of the disruptive power of modern farming launched extensive soil and water conservation programs. This environmental crisis occurred at the same time as the economic depression which hastened the pace of industrial development.

Man as an industrialist is causing agricultural disruptions which have global significance. Building a dam on the Nile River to irrigate agricultural land disrupts significantly the fish catch in the Mediterranean Sea, which in turn, globally disrupts protein sources for human consumption and for the preparation of animal feed. The application of large quantities of phosphorus, ammonia, other plant nutrients and pest controlling chemicals is causing changes which go beyond the boundaries of regional ecosystems. DDT sprayed with airplanes over cotton fields and forests may conceivably find its way to the fat tissues of penguins in the Artic.

Industrialization of crop and animal production is the primary effect of recent advances in the science and technology of agricultural production systems. The secondary effect is pollution. Transition from pasture to "factory" production of animals helped meet additional demands for eggs, pork, and milk without increase in the number of hens, pigs, and dairy cows in the United States during the last twenty years while the human population increased by sixty million people.

Today the average daily consumption of animal products in the United States is 1.70 (0.77kg) lbs of meat, milk, and eggs.[1] The amount of manure being generated from the livestock population is 40 lbs (18 kg) per American per day. Thus, for every pound of animal product being consumed by humans, about 23 lbs of manure have to be managed.

The factors that cause or aggravate the problem of animal waste management are the inherent characteristics of wastes and the limitation of the present methods of waste handling and disposal. These limitations will increase and be magnified as industrialization of production continues to grow and as the public continues to become more aware and less tolerant of ecological disruptions.

Food and fiber production generates by far more waste than any other economic sector. Agricultural wastes, however, do not create pollution in proportion to their quantity.

Since 1960 the federal government has been keeping a census of fish kills. In eight years a total of 103,380,000 fish have been reported killed because of water pollution.[2] In 1968, 88% of the fish kills were caused by industrial and city sewage, but agriculture was responsible for less than 3% of the total.

The basic difference between wastes generated by agricultural food and fiber production and the auto, metal, or chemical industries is that the former are natural by-products which can be recycled in the natural cycle, while car exhausts, metals, or plastics undergo little degradation and dispersion by natural processes.

The problem is the great rate of development and application of new technology for the production of food and fiber with little old and no "new technology" for the management of associated by-products or "wastes."

Every day 3.4 million tons of animal manure are produced.[3] If all this manure were to be discharged into our streams and lakes, the resulting water pollution would be equivalent to almost 5 times the pollution load of raw sewage of the total United States population.

However, if the animal production of manure were to be spread on the 400 million acres of cropland in the United States, the average application would be a little over 3 tons per acre.[4] Manures produced in a year's time contain 11.6 million tons of nitrogen, 3 million tons of phosphates, and 3.2 million tons of potassium. Furthermore, they contain all the necessary nutrients for crop production.

On the other hand, municipal refuse contains metals, 8% to 11%; glass about 8% to 11%; paper, 40% to 50%; yard and tree trimmings, 3% to 80%; wood, 3% to 70%; other synthetics, 1% to 20%; and food waste, 10% to 26%.[5]

The industrial revolution is producing materials that are not synthesized by Nature. Nature does not manufacture and does not have an ecological niche for plastics, non-degradable beer cans, or hard pesticides. Metals are a serious threat to environmental quality because all of them tend to accumulate and most of them are toxic at low concentrations. What is probably not known about the impact of heavy metals released into the environment is as foreboding as what can be ascertained.

One of the dramatic effects of space exploration has been the realization that the earth's biosphere is a very thin and limited layer with finite capacity to absorb and assimilate organic waste and no capacity to assimilate synthetic and nondegradable materials. This is helping to bring about a needed change of attitude toward the ecological feasibility of technological innovations introduced in the food and fiber industry and the assessment of environmental impact of the methods of food and fiber production before such methods are introduced and used widely.

Human survival today demands that we grow more food for more people, in less time, on decreasing land areas, and with less environmental degradation. This is a Herculean task that only technology can perform.

This task calls for the science of the future—coprology. (This is a term I have coined from the Greek words for waste, *copros,* and science, *logos.*)

The basic premise of coprology is that there is no such thing as "waste." Wastes are things we have decided to call economically worthless and socially taboo because we were too obsessed with the production of things for our affluent society. Then, we encouraged economists to work out statistics to confirm our prejudice.

Wastes must be defined as resources "out of place" or "out of time." Nature must eventually assimilate everything that is produced, both product and by-product. We must help nature assimilate our wastes. This effort is ushering in the "Age of Coprology."

The notion that we can grow without chemicals the necessary food and fiber for the 3-soon-to-be-6 billion people on the earth is absurd. About one-third of our protein nitrogen intake in this country originated from man-made and applied nitrogen. This figure will continue to increase. What will and should cease to occur is the excessive use of nitrates, phosphates, pesticides, and other chemicals. Chemicals "out of place" are pollutants. Chemicals used at the wrong time, for the wrong plant or pest, at the wrong rate, and so on, become pollutants bringing forth the wrath of the "overnight" environmentalists. Chemical "heroes" can easily become criminals. Pointing to the great contributions of agricultural chemicals to the survival and well-being of the human race does not give us the license to use these chemicals indiscriminately.

We must not waste time and effort denouncing the accusations of the "overnight" ecologists. Instead, we should support educational efforts to make it possible for the average food producer to detect readily the pest or weed that needs to be controlled (not necessarily eradicated) and to select the right pesticide or herbicide. Furthermore, application equipment must be perfected so as to apply chemicals at the right dose, at the right time, to the intended target!

Very little can be disposed in earth's bioshphere without affecting ecology. Disposal, therefore, must be done in such a way and at such a rate that nature will be able to assimilate it. Man must help nature assimilate his wastes, in order to improve our ecological environment.

References

1. Inglett, GE (ed.): Symposium: *Processing Agricultural and Municipal Wastes,* Westport, Conn, The AVI Pub. Co., 1973.
2. Taiganides, EP: Discussion, Cattle Wastes—Pollution and Potential Treatment, by Loehr, R and Agnew, RW, Proceedings. American Society of Civil Engineers 93(SA4), 1967.
3. Taiganides, EP: Agricultural Waste Management, Proceedings SOS/70—Third International Congress/Food Science and Technology, Chicago, Illinois, Institute of Food Technologists, 1971, pp 890-894.
4. Taiganides, EP and Stroshine, RL: The Impact of Farm Animal Production and Processing on the Total Environment, *Livestock Waste Management and Pollution Abatement,* St. Joseph, Michigan, American Society of Agriculture Engineers 1971, pp 95-98.
5. Turk, A et al: *Ecology Pollution Environment,* Philadelphia, Pa, W. Saunders Co., 1972.

The Economic Consequences of Regulation or Prohibition of Agricultural Chemicals in American Agriculture

DUANE CHAPMAN, Ph.D.

Three recent studies (two empirical, one essay) warrant consideration in discussing the regulation on prohibition of agricultural chemicals, both pesticides and fertilizers.

Professors Farris and Sprott, in a theoretical essay on farm programs, pollution, and agricultural chemicals, hypothesized numerous consequences of a more comprehensive chemical regulation. Their suggested consequences are (1) higher costs to producers, (2) poorer quality, (3) higher consumer food costs, (4) a reduction of the incentive to substitute chemicals for land, (5) greater impact in the South than in other areas, and (6) greater impact on agricultural exports than on other markets.[1]

Each of these points deserve consideration. But before proceeding, we need an approximate definition of agricultural chemicals. Let us consider here just those chemicals used in agricultural production: inorganic fertilizers, insecticides, herbicides, fungicides, miticides, nematocides, rodenticides, gastropodicides*, tranquilizers, antibiotics, hormones and growth agents, and vitamins. Excluded from consideration here are chemicals used in food processing and marketing: nitrates to redden meats, orange coloring for oranges, bread preservatives, and so on.

---

* Most elements in this list should be clear, but some explanation might be helpful. The first part of a type of pesticide describes the category of organism the chemical is designed for. The last part of the name is a variant of "-cide", to kill. Thus, miticide is a chemical designed to kill mites (relatives of ticks, and spiders). Nematocides (parasitic worms on plants, particularly potatoes, and on animals), but they find potatoes especially attractive. Rotenticides are aimed primarily at mice, and rats, but also at rabbits. Gastropods include snails and slugs.

The first likely consequence is readily evident. If farmers are following economic principles, they are presently using the least costly methods of production available to them. If effective regulation reduces chemical use, other more costly methods will be employed. The resulting output will be produced at higher unit cost.

The food quality effects of chemical reduction are generally negative with present food preferences, but some limited positive changes could be anticipated. It is certain that fruits and vegetables would experience more bacterial and insect spoilage; obviously, this would be more important for fresh items than canned goods. But the question here is partly genetic. As growers have turned to high-yield varieties, they have unintentionally "bred out" natural resistance in some species.* Pomes (apples, pears, peaches, plums) are particularly prone to pest damage as presently grown. But within this group there is variation: the Northeren Spy apple has some aphid resistance while the MacIntosh does not. Other commodities such as carrots, parsnips, radishes, or turnips remain relatively pest resistant. Generalization is difficult, but four broad responses in fruits and vegetables can be noted if pesticide controls are introduced: a) in crops which retain natural resistance, no effect; b) in crops with both high-yield, pest sensitive varieties and low yield (generally smaller) resistant varieties, there will be greater use of the second type; c) some products may disappear from many markets because they are dependent on pesticides for their present competitive situations; d) some commodities would be marketed with noticeably more "guests."

The quality aspect of cereals as affected by chemical use is probably minimal. If reduction of chemicals meant a return to older varieties or strains, there might be a return to higher-protein cereals.[2] This effect is probably a quality improvement.

The situation regarding meat products is unclear. The present trend in beef, chicken, and pork production has been towards increased use of feedlots. Egg City (Ventura, California), for example, has 2½ million hens and produces 600 million eggs/year. Thus, a single poultry operation can produce about 3 eggs

---

* This and related points were suggested by David Pimental.

per year for each American. Fat City (Gilroy, California) has 60,000 steers and processes 180,000 carcasses per year. Feedlot produced meat is tenderer and has more fat than pasture or range meat. If chemical regulation reduces the relative profitability of feedlots, our meat would simultaneously become tougher, but might also be healthier in the reduction of cholesterol. There is substantial disagreement about the dependence of feedlots on chemicals. Some agricultural economists believe that feedlot requirements of disease control, stress reduction, and growth stimulation can be profitable only through chemicals. Others believe chemicals are not essential to profitable feedlot operation, or that many small feedlots would substitute for todays trend towards large lots.* There seems to be no clear evidence at present, and the effects of chemical regulation on overall meat quality cannot be clearly discerned.

Higher consumer costs would follow from higher producer costs. But the percentage increase in consumer costs would be less than the percentage increase in farm costs. This is because about one-third to two-fifths of the average food dollar is for farm production costs, and the remainder is for marketing and processing costs. The proportion of cotton or woolen clothing consumer expenditures going to farms is substantially less. If farm production costs increase and this cost is passed on to consumers, the percentage increase in consumer costs will be less than the percentage increase in farm production costs. There is wide variation by commodity: most of a farm cost increase in potato growing will appear in a higher fresh potato price, but a farm cost increase in growing wheat would be barely noticeable in retail bread prices.

The fourth point of Farris and Sprott is the suggestion that termination of acreage control programs would reduce or reverse the incentive to substitute chemicals for land. This leads directly to the Langham, Headley, and Edwards study. This latter study is an empirical analysis of the economic consequences of herbicides, insecticides, and other pesticides. Their work provides quantitative information about the land-chemical

---

* Comments offered by Olan Forker and George Casler.

substitutions suggested by Farris and Sprott. Table I is taken from the Langham et al analysis.[3] The estimates for insecticide use in the Southeast are very high; perhaps too high. They should be viewed in the context of the methodology of this kind of analysis. First, the Southeast estimates may not be statistically significant. Second, the marginal rate of substitution is itself a variable. There are no constant values; the estimates in Table I are calculated for then—existing levels of cropland and insecticide use.*

Table I—Substitutability between Cropland and Insecticides by Region, 1964.

Region	Ounces of insecticide reduced per one acre increase in cropland (marginal rate of substitution)	Percentage decrease in insecticides per one percent increase in cropland (elasticity of substitution)
Appalachian	-33.19	-2.70
Corn belt	-10.03	-4.35
Delta	-256.47	-14.89
Lake	-0.80	-8.16
Pacific	-24.06	-6.49
Mountain	-0.97	-7.77
Southeast	-3,257.00[a]	-326.67[a]
South Plains	-547.17	-170.04
United States	-13.24	-6.49

Source: Langham, et al[3]
(Minus sign indicates reduction)

* These definitions can be illustrated algebraically. Suppose $Y = AX_1{}^{a_1} X_2{}^{a_2}$ where Y is agricultural output, X_1 is insecticide use, X_2 is cropland use, a_1 and a_2 are parameters, and A^1 is the use of other factors such as labor and machinery. The marginal rate of substitution is defined as $dX_1/dX_2 = -(a_2 X_1/a_1 X_2)$ for constant output and use of other factors (that is, $dY = 0^2$ and $dA = {}^1 0$). Clearly the marginal rate of substitution will become less negative as insecticide use falls and land use rises. The elasticity of substitution (ES) in the Langham study is $(dX_1/X_1) / (dX_2/X_2)$, or ES = $-a_2/a_1$.

There are wide regional variation: substitutability seems greatest in the South. This is partially attributable to insects finding Southern climate generally more to their liking. But in all regions, the percentage ratios (second column) are greater (more negative) than -1.0, and the elasticity of substitution for the Nation is -6.5. Langham *et al* note "If all of this land (about 40 million acres diverted from production in 1967 under various government land retirement programs) were returned to production, the cropland base currently in use would increase by about 12%. The use of an elasticity of substitution of cropland for insecticides of -6 to -7 for the United States leads to the conclusion that a 12% increase in cropland harvested would reduce insecticide use by 70% to 80% and maintain output." However, another calculation from their data would suggest a 50% reduction in insecticide use would follow from a 12% increase in harvested cropland[3] (see footnote*). In either case, there is a clear indication of the substitutability of land for insecticides.

It is appropriate to turn to the third study for further information. This study (by Leo Mayer and Stanley Hargrove) is addressed to the question of the economic consequences of restricting nitrogen fertilizer use.[4] They began by postulating likely U. S. population and per capita income growth to 1980: 230 million people and $3,250 per capita income in 1970 prices. Another step in their analysis is to draw upon existing studies for empirical estimates of the production relationships and demand for major agricultural commodities. These commodities were corn, soybeans, wheat, cotton, non-corn feed grains, beef, pork, broilers, eggs, milk, and lamb. They established six cases of various types of restriction on nitrogen fertilizer use. In each case they used what is termed a linear programming model to estimate acreages, yields per acre, production levels, at-farm prices, cash receipts, government pay-

---

* The Langham calculation seems to have multiplied the 12 percent cropland insecticide decrease. Another calculation would derive $X_1 = (Y/AX_2 a_2)^1 a_1$ from the preceding discussion. Then if X_2^* (new cropland acreage) is 1.12 of X_2, and ES = - 6.49, the ration of X_1 to X_1^* works out to .48, or a 52% reduction in insecticide use. Regardless of the percent, it is high and land and insecticides are substitutes.

ments, "soil bank"[3] (see footnote*) acres, farm production expenses, net income per farm, retail prices, consumer expenditures, and exports. As is to be expected, their work provides substantial quantitative information of a preliminary nature which is relevant to the points discussed above.

In the six cases of restricted use, one variable is maximum application of nitrogen fertilizer per acre. They chose three possible maximum levels to examine: 100 lbs per crop acre (the average application rate per acre of fertilized corn in 1969), 50 lbs per acre, and complete prohibition. A second variable was the size of the geographic area in which the restriction applied. In one set of 3 cases the restrictions applied only to the State of Iowa, but not to the rest of the country. In the second set, the restrictions applied throughout the Nation. While analysis was made for 150 production regions, results are reported for U.S. totals as in Table II.

Table II—1980 Projections for Alternative Nitrogen Fertilizer Decisions.

Item	Nitrogen use limited to 110 pounds per cropacre	Nitrogen use prohibited on major crops
Soil bank	51 million acres	0
Corn yield	85.8 bu./acre	45.8 bu./acre
Government payments	$3.1 billion	$0.5 billion
Cash receipts	$56.8 billion	$67.8 billion
Farm expenses	$46.1 billion	$49.2 billion
Net income	$8,000/farm	$10,300/farm
Corn price at farm	$1.04/bu.	$2.30/bu.
Consumer purchases	$117.0 billion	$134.0 billion
Wheat exports	600 million bu.	100 million bu.

Source: Mayer and Hargrove[4]

* "Soil bank" is a general term to indicate a variety of government land retirement programs including the Conservation Reserve, feed grain programs for corn and grain sorghum, the cotton program, the cropland conversion program, and the cropland adjustment program.

In Table II, two of the six cases are summarized for 1980 estimates: a National restriction of 110 lbs per acre and a complete prohibition. As suggested in our previous discussion, the soil bank of about 50 million acres was estimated to disappear. This land had been removed from production. So we see the effect of land replacing the chemical: (nitrogen fertilizer here) noted above. Yields decline, as expected. For corn, the decline is 47%. At-farm prices rise: corn price is 121% higher per bushel.

It is interesting to note that although total output and government payments decline and farm expenses rise, net income per farm also rises. This rise in per farm income (29%) is much higher than the rise in farm expenses (7%). It is attributable to the inelasticity of demand for most agricultural commodities. On the whole, agricultural goods are necessities and their consumption is relatively fixed compared to other commodities. Thus, a slightly lower output is sold at a noticeably higher price, and the higher revenue effect of the price increase is greater than the sum of the lower revenue effect of the output decline, the lost subsidy, and the higher production cost.

This inelastic effect is explained in Figure 1. Suppose output is at 100 and price at 1.0. Suppose the average price elasticity for all food is -0.34. (The price elasticity shows the percentage change in sales caused by a small percentage change in price.) Now suppose reduced chemical use lowers output to 95 at Q_2. Price will rise from 1.0 to 1.16, and revenue will increase from 100.0 to 110.5.[5,6] This principle accounts for the net income increase in the Mayer-Hargrove analysis.

It is also of interest to see that consumer expenditures rise proportionally less than farm receipts. Consumer expenditures rise $17 billion, or 14.5%. Farm cash receipts rise $11 billion, or 19.4%. This is because marketing costs, on the average, are about one-third to two-fifths of the food dollar, and since processing and marketing costs rise less (in proportion) than farm receipts, consumer costs rise less than farm receipts.

Incidentally, exports (such as wheat) fall as predicted by Farris and Sprott.[3]

At this point I wish to depart from the summarization of the three studies to introduce other possible economic conse-

quences of reduction of agricultural chemical usage. One subject
raised by George Casler is the probability of increased soil
erosion.[7] This would be caused by the nature of land currently

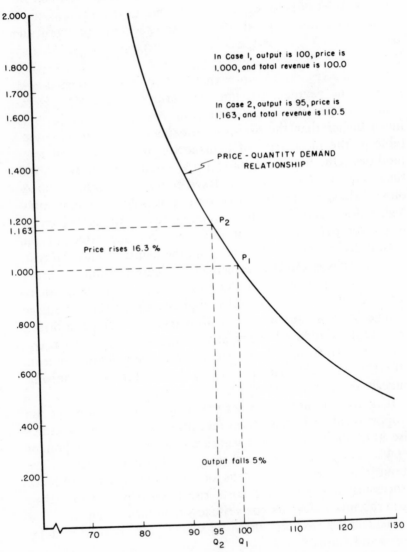

Figure 1.—Illustration of small output reduction causing farm revenue
increase.

in the soil bank. It is generally steeper, and would probably experience greater soil loss per acre than land presently culti- vated. Thus, there could be a 20% increase in soil loss from a 20% increase in cultivated acreage, and the additional loss from the nature of the land brought into production. However, economic conditions would set certain mitigating influences in motion. If chemical pesticides are reduced, we can anticipate that natural methods of pest control become more profitable. Since monoculture encourages pest populations, some shift to increased crop rotation can be expected from this motivation. Similarly, if nitrogen or phosphate fertilizers are reduced, crop rotation for nitrogen fixation and manure spreading for nitro- gen and phosphorus become more profitable. Both of these practices reduce per acre soil loss compared to single-crop cultivation with chemical fertilizers. In summary, the economic influences of chemical reduction simultaneously point towards greater and lesser soil erosion. The average net effect is indeci- pherable.

In the discussion of the three studies we noted the likelihood of increased average net income per farm as a consequence of reducing chemical use. While not specifically cited in these studies, it seems likely to me that this higher net income per farm is an inducement to retard or reverse the decline in numbers of farms and farm operators. And the regulation of chemicals and the growth in acreage combine to make increased farm labor relatively more profitable than it otherwise would be. Thus, a reduction in agricultural chemicals would seem to lead directly to a reduction or reversal in the emigration of the farm population to cities.

However, it must be recognized that the significance of regional variations carry through to the conclusions about net farm income. If we consider solely the possibility of fertilizer and herbicide prohibition or regulation, one effect would be in the corn-soybean areas of the Midwest. As feed corn prices rose, hog prices would rise relative to range fed beef in the West. This in turn would induce some shift from pork to beef products. Some midwestern hog operations that are presently only of marginal profitability might be terminated. The same point can be made more simply with tomatoes: California growers use less insecticides than those in New Jersey. If insecticide use is regulated, average net income for tomato growers may rise, but some growers in New Jersey would probably lose income. Although it seems nearly certain that average net farm income would rise from increased chemical regulation, this average includes losers as well as gainers.

The points made here can be easily summarized. If levels of usage of agricultural chemicals are regulated (or if some or all types were to be prohibited), we can anticipate these economic consequences compared to what the future will otherwise be:

- Reduced government farm subsidies
- Higher average net income per farm, with regional and individual exceptions
- More farms and farm operators
- Increased farm employment
- Reduced or reversed farm population emigration
- Reduced soil erosion from increased crop rotation
- Possible reduction of profitability of feedlots and chicken factories
- Reduction or elimination of soil bank
- Increased soil erosion from hillside cultivation and increased acreage
- Lower yields per acre
- Higher farm prices
- Smaller rise in consumer prices
- Reduced exports
- Reduced quality of fresh produce

In the preceeding discussion we have made no reference to the motivation for chemical usage reduction or mechanisms for regulation or prohibition. Are all or most agricultural chemicals pathogenic to human life? If so, in what quantities? Would the effect of prohibiting some present chemicals cause greater harm than the present usage? How dangerous is nitrogen contamination of water supplies? Can regulatory policies be devised so that the social benefit of regulation exceeds the social cost of regulation? These questions are significant in their own right; here we have only attempted some informed conjecture about the general economic implications of regulation and prohibition. Neither the quantitative nor qualitative conclusions can be clearly shown or proven. The significance is this: as our economic system responds to regulation of agricultural chemical usage, it will induce a variety of results, and these results are positive as well as negative. If we focus upon the negative consequences alone, we lose sight of feasible alternatives.

References

1. Farris, DE and Sprott, JM: Pollution and Agricultural Chemicals, *Amer J Agr Econ* **53(4)**:661-2, 1971.
2. Perelman, MJ: Farming with Petroleum, *Environment* **14(8)**:8-13, 1972.
3. Langham, MR; Headley JC; and Edwards: Agricultural Pesticides: Productivity and Externalities, Kneese, AV and Bower, BT (eds.): Chap.5 in *Environmental Quality Analysis* Baltimore, Johns Hopkins, 1972.
4. Mayer, LV and Hargrove, SH: Food Costs, Farm Incomes, and Crop Yields with Restrictions on Fertilizer Use, CAED Report No. 38, Center for Agricultural and Economic Development, Ames: Iowa State University Press, March, 1971.
5. Brando, GE: Interrelation Among Demands for Control of Agricultural Supplies, bulletin 680, Pennsylvania Agricultural Experiment Station, 1961, pp 15-18.
6. Fox, KA: A Submodel of the Agricultural Sector, Duesenberry, JS et al (eds.): in *The Brookings Econometric Model of the United States,* Chicago, Rand J McNally, 1965.
7. Casler, GL: Comment on Economic and Policy Implications of Pollution from Agricultural Chemicals, *Amer J Agr Eco* **54(3)**:535-6, 1972.

Pesticides in Relation
to Environmental Quality*

FRED H. TSCHIRLEY, Ph.D.

There are a number of definitions for environmental quality. In the following discussion of pesticides and their relation to environmental quality, I shall consider the environment to be the total world in which we live - its physical, chemical, and biological components, including man. Exclusion of man from the environment is artificial; it ignores that component which has greatest potential for affecting the remaining components of an amazingly complex and interdependent system.

TOXICITY AND TRANSPORTABILITY

A primary consideration for all pesticides is toxicity—to the target organism, to the associated fauna and flora, and to man. In that regard, we must recognize that all pesticides are toxic to a greater or lesser degree. Thus, the controlling variables in determining the use of a product are the manner and degree of use rather than relative toxicity per se. Pesticides in use today range from (lethal dose for 50% survival of test group) LD_{50} in the tens upward to several thousand mg/kg body weight. Acute toxicity, expressed in terms of LD_{50}, can be dealt with quite readily. Chronic toxicity, on the other hand, is a much more difficult problem because low dosages are usually involved and the effects are often subtle. Data for acute and chronic toxicity, together with residues that are likely to be found in food and feed, are used to establish tolerances during the registration procedure.

The persistance and transport of pesticides in the environment are also matters of concern. While it is true that any pesticide, or indeed any chemical, may move from one place to another in several ways, the problem is more severe with persistent compounds that tend to concentrate and bioaccumulate than with those that degrade rapidly. DDT and methoxychlor offer a case in point. The compounds are similar in chemical structure, differing only in that methoxychlor has methoxy groups rather than chlorines in the p,p' positions. DDT does not degrade rapidly; methoxychlor does. Because of DDT's persistence, it has become widely distributed throughout the environment. Because of its *lipophilicity* (affinity for and solubility in fat) and resistance to degradation it tends to concentrate (absorption and ingestion by aquatic organisms so that tissue concentration is higher than that in the water) and possibly to bioaccumulate (higher residues in higher trophic levels). The characteristics of persistence, concentration, and bioaccumulation have resulted in some adverse effects on fish and wildlife, particularly among the raptors which are the apex of a food chain.[1] The magnitude of the adverse effects is open to serious question, but there is no denying that some adverse effects have occurred.

EFFECTS OF THE BAN ON DDT

On June 14, 1972, final notices of cancellation were issued for the remaining uses of DDT, except for public health and quarantine purposes and three minor agricultural uses.[2] Those cancellations became final as of December 31, 1972.

With DDT no longer available, a different problem arises. Most of the agricultural use of DDT (roughly 80% of total use in the United States) involved the control of insects affecting cotton. DDT being unavailable, we believe that the principal alternate pesticide will be methyl parathion, a highly toxic organophosphate insecticide. Not only is methyl parathion toxic to a broader range of insects, including beneficial insects, than is DDT, it is also highly toxic to man. Parathion can be and has been used safely, but the margin for error is small. This is particularly true for undereducated users and those farmers whose financial status precludes purchase of the more sophisticated application equipment needed for parathion. The U.S. Department of Agriculture, in cooperation with the Environmental Protection Agency (EPA) and the states have initiated an educational program directed toward users, applicators, and the medical community so that the toxic effects on man can be prevented entirely or at least minimized as much as possible.

Pesticide use has increased dramatically since the introduction of synthetic organic chemicals at the close of World War II. In recent years, the use of herbicides has risen more rapidly than have the use of other pesticides. Despite intensified and accelerated research on integrated and non-chemical methods of pest control, it is unreasonable to assume that there will not be a continuing need for chemical pesticides. Agricultural scientists cannot conceive of producing an adequate supply of food, feed, and fiber on the acreage now used for agriculture, without judicious use of pesticides.

Legislation under which pesticides have been regulated, the Federal Insecticide, Fungicide and Rodenticide Act (FIFRA), is essentially a labelling law. It does not provide for control over end use of a product. Accordingly, there were instances of misues. New legislation was signed by the President on October 21, 1972, that provides the authority for control over end use, among numerous other improvements.

Even though some misuse has occurred, there is no evidence of severe ecological disruption resulting therefrom, nor is there evidence of unreasonable residues in food products. Indeed, pesticide residues in food are generally far below what is specified as an acceptable daily intake (ADI) by the World Health Organization (WHO) (see Table I).

BENEFITS AND RISKS

Despite the generally good picture with regard to pesticide residues, there is no justification for complacence. We cannot assume that pesticide usage will or should continue to increase as it has in the past. As with any other technological improvement there are benefits and risks associated with the use of pesticides. Selected increases and selected decreases will un-

Table I—Dietary intake of pesticide chemicals (3)

Pesticide	FAO-WHO* Acceptable Daily Intake mg/kg/day	mg/kg body wt/day** Total Diet Studies 5-year average 1964-65 − 1968-69	Factor
aldrin-dieldrin	1×10^{-4}	8×10^{-5}	1.25
carbaryl	2×10^{-2}	5×10^{-4}	40
DDT-DDE-TDE***	1×10^{-2}	8×10^{-4}	12.5
Lindane	1.25×10^{-2}	5×10^{-5}	250
Heptachlor &			
H. epoxide	5×10^{-4}	3×10^{-5}	17
malathion	2×10^{-2}	1×10^{-4}	200
Diazinon	2×10^{-3}	1×10^{-5}	200
parathion	5×10^{-3}	1×10^{-5}	500

* Food and Agriculture Organization of the United Nations and World Health Organization.
** Five-year average (1964-1969).
*** DDE is 1, 1-dichloro-2,2-bis (p-chlorophenyl) ethylene and TDE is 1,1-dichloro-2,2-bis (p-chlorophenyl) ethane.

doubtedly occur. The new pesticide legislation will be immeasurably helpful in defining that selectivity and leading us to a situation where agriculture will have available the tools needed for pest control without violating the demands for environmental quality.

The charge is often made that farmers and other users have developed an inordinate dependence on pesticides for the control of their pest problems. There is at least partial justification for that charge, but agriculture is not the sole user of pesticides.[4] Agricultural usage represents only about 50% of the total. Chemicals are effective, easy to apply, and relatively cheap. Thus, there are many attractions to their use. Yet there is ample evidence to show that adverse effects can work against the use of pesticides as a sole method of pest control. Resistance to one or more insecticides has now developed in more than 200 species of insects[5], persistent pesticides can be distributed over the breadth of the earth, and adverse secondary effects may overshadow primary beneficial effects. If chemicals are not the sole answer to pest problems, what is being done in the way of developing alternative methods of pest control?

Host Resistance

Breeding for host resistance has been one of the principal research areas that provide first-line defense against pests. Outstanding success has been obtained in breeding crops resistant to diseases and nematodes, particularly, and to a lesser extent for resistance to insect attack. Better competitive potential of crops with weeds has not been a consideration in breeding programs.

Resistant crop varieties cannot be expected to endure for all time. On the average, resistance is broken in about 5 to 15 years. Sometimes the breaking of crop resistance by means of a mutation in the pest is of major significance. A recent example was the epidemic of southern corn leaf blight which occurred because most of the corn varieties had identical cytoplasm. In other cases, the gene pool of the crop contains sufficient genetic heterogeneity so that resistance is broken gradually and adjustments can be made readily.

Biological Control

Biological control of insects and weeds with insect predators and parasites has been under investigation in the U.S. since 1888 when the Vedalia beetle imported from Australia saved the California citrus industry from destruction by scale insects.[5] There have been other striking examples of success, and examples of lack of success, although the latter are never so well publicized. Our search for parasites and predators that control weeds, insects, diseases, and nematodes should be strengthened to take greater advantage of an obvious potential.

There is a widespread feeling that biological control is the ultimate answer to pest control problems. In simple terms, the feeling is that biological control would preclude the need for pesticides. In addition, there appears to be a general belief that biological control of pests can be developed quickly. Both notions need to be dispelled. In the United States, there are about 10,000 species of insects, 1,500 species of weeds, 500 species of nematodes, 8,000 species of fungi, 250 viruses, and 160 bacteria that are considered pests.[5] Thus, we must deal with about 20,000 species. If biological controls were developed for even 5% of these pests—1,000 species—the task would be enormous. However, there is a good possibility that we can suppress several key pests with non-chemical methods. This would make the management of others considerably less difficult. Biological control of aquatic weeds is particularly important because of the difficulties imposed by the direct application of pesticides into water.

The possibility of an undesirable mutation by exotic fungi, bacteria, and viruses that may be proposed for biological control is especially troublesome. Because of their short life cycle and their evolution in an environment different from that in this country, the potential for an adverse mutation must be seriously considered. The use of a chemical can be discontinued when previously unknown adverse effects are discovered. The same is not true of a pathogen. Moreover, pathogens deliberately used for pest control in the United States must be registered. We have already intensified our efforts in developing data needed for new registrations of *Bacillus thuringiensis,* polyhedrosis viruses, and other pathogens. Others will surely be discovered and we will be involved in developing protocols and data needed for their registration.

Chemical Growth Modifiers

Research is also being conducted on substances that modify growth, development, or behavior. Examples are the juvenile hormones, chemosterilants, and sex attractants. These compounds are no more a panacea than any other class of chemical. We know, for example, that some juvenile hormones are not specific for a single species. Thus, their introduction into the environment could have extreme deleterious consequences. Chemosterilants are highly reactive compounds that have not yet found a place outside the laboratory. Sex attractants are in a much higher stage of development. Their use appears promising. Each of these classes of compounds must be tested for acute promising. Each of these classes of compounds must be tested for acute and chronic toxicity and for environmental safety prior to registration.

Other Pest Control Techniques

Success was achieved with the sterile-male technique for the control of screwworm. Research is actively underway to extend that principle to other pest species.

The attitude regarding pests has changed gradually from the concept of control, which implies the destruction of the pest for a period of time, to a concept of management, which implies the regulation of pest populations at a level that is not economically damaging. With that changing attitude has come the concept of "Integrated Pest Management". This implies the use of a variety of control methods in an integrated manner. Unfortunately, integrated pest management is used almost exclusively for the management of a single class of pests, usually insects. It represents an advance, but is still too narrow in its construction.

Integrated pest management, in my definition, is not limited to the integrated control of weeds only, insects only, diseases only, or nematodes only, but rather an integration of methods for managing all four classes of pests in a systems approach to crop protection.

It is only through such a systems approach that we will be able to manage pest populations intelligently. Unfortunately, we do not now have a cadre of individuals who have the broad training needed for a systems approach. The strictures resulting from specialization in a narrow field are not easily overcome. An academic program that will provide the broad training is urgently needed. Progress has been made in providing the necessary curriculum, but the change in emphasis will not come about overnight.

There have been both benefits and risks associated with the use of chemical pesticides. The use of pesticides will continue and there must be a continuing assessment of the benefits and risks resulting from their use. Systems of pest management and crop protection will receive primary emphasis in the future for the simple reason that any single method of pest control, if used exclusively, is doomed to failure. Thus, there must be a broad array of pest management technology available, and it must be used in a systems approach if we are to accomplish the needs for protection against pests on the one hand, and environmental quality on the other hand.

References

1. *Man's Impact on the Global Environment,* Cambridge, Massachusetts and London, England, The MIT Press, 1970.
2. Federal Register Notice, 37 F.R. 13369, July 7, 1972.
3. Duggan, RE et al: Pesticide Residue Levels in Foods in the United States from July 1, 1963 to June 30, 1969, *Pesticides Monitoring Journal* 5(2):80, 1971.
4. Fowler, DL: *The Pesticide Review,* Agriculture Stabilization and Consumer Service, U. S. Department of Agriculture, 1972.
5. Man in the Living Environment, The Institute of Ecology Report of the Workshop on Global Ecological Problems, 1971.

Fertilizers

OSCAR A. LORENZ, Ph.D.

The great increase in use of commercial fertilizers during the past 20 years has given us reason for concern about their effect on environmental quality. This is not surprising. The use of nitrogen in the United States since 1950 has increased some sevenfold, phosphorus nearly threefold, and the use of potassium has almost quadrupled.[1]

Since there is little or no indication that potassium fertilizers are harmful to soils, foods, or waters, and there is no indication that further additions will enhance algal growth in waters, we can say that they are not of major concern.

We do know that phosphorus can increase algal growth. The addition of phosphorus from other sources, however, seems of more significance than that possible from fertilizer. We know that soils have the ability to fix, absorb, or in some way make the phosphorus unavailable in soils, or to keep it from entering the soil solution. As agriculturists we are more concerned about how to keep it available or soluble, then we are about the opposite. The level of soluble phosphorus in soils is so low as to be of minor consequence: 10 parts per billion is a common level, even less in some cases.

The cases of phosphorus contamination of streams and lakes have practically always been associated with some erosion or runoff of fertilizers rather than with leaching from the soil phosphorus. If we can control the surface runoff from erosion, phosphorus from this source will be of minor concern as a source of environmental pollution.

We said that use of nitrogen had increased sevenfold since 1950. We now apply about 7 million tons a year and this is expected to increase to about 12 million tons by 1980.[2] In addition, this increase has been primarily on land that was already receiving some nitrogen. Much research has demonstrated that plants are not efficient in the recovery of nitrogen applied to the soil.[3] Only about half of the nitrogen applied is actually recovered by the crop. Furthermore, only about 40% of the nitrogen applied is removed from land, an equal amount of the vegetative growth is returned to the soil.

Let us look at what this means. In an average field of vegetables, about 200 lbs of nitrogen would be applied per acre. The crop would remove only about 80 lbs of that, leaving 120 lbs as a possible contaminant, if we like to call it that. What happens to the 120 lbs remaining? We know that some of it has denitrified and returned to the atmosphere as gaseous nitrogen. We do not know to what extent. We do know also that the denitrification process from nitrate to gaseous nitrogen is possible only when there is a source of energy and anaerobic conditions. We know that some of the nitrogen that we apply can go into nonavailable organic forms. We do not know how quickly that nitrogen will be made available again. A third possibility, and the one of most concern, is that any excess nitrogen will be converted to nitrate, and, thus, will appear as a contaminant in our subsurface waters.

We could say that the overall use of nitrogen would be creating no problem, because the crops are removing about 9.5 million tons of nitrogen per year, and we are using only 7 million tons.[4] Thus, the crops are still removing more than we are putting on, so there could be no problem. That is not the case, however. We cannot use the overall and have it mean much. It is estimated that erosion losses are about 3 million tons of nitrogen, and leaching losses are about 2 million annually.[4] Now we are concerned about the nitrate contaminant in our ground waters, and certainly there is evidence to indicate that in many soils there is serious nitrate contaminant in our ground waters, and certainly there is evidence to indicate that in many soils there is serious nitrate contamination.

Conversely, though, it should be emphasized, that in most cases high rates of nitrogen fertilization have not resulted in an appreciable increase in the nitrate content of the drainage waters. In many cases, this is due to the fact that the water application, either from rainfall or irrigation, is enough to dilute the nitrates so that they are below harmful levels. In many other conditions, dentrification accounts for the loss in nitrogen.

Rates of application of nitrogen in California are roughly twice those used in the greater part of the United States due largely to the cropping patterns involved. In many cases we are dealing with high value cash crops. California produces 40% of the vegetable crops in the United States. Cotton and sugar beets utilizing high rates of the fertilizer, are big cash crops in California. In growing citrus, a high rate of nitrogen fertilization is used.

Several examples of problems with nitrate contamination can be examined. Most of these problems originate in our western areas where the water application is at a minimum. In a citrus area in a closed basin near Riverside, California, in an orchard of 1,000 acres, nitrogen application has been about 130 lbs per acre per year; 45% of the applied nitrogen, or 60 lbs per acre per year, has appeared as nitrate in the percolate water.[5]

Another good example is a closed basin in the Arroyo Grande area, near the coast north of Los Angeles, where the land has been cropped to strawberries and vegetables.[6] Nitrogen additions exceeded that removed in the crop by about 75 lbs per acre per year. Nitrate concentrations in the soil solution of 14 ppm to 122 ppm at depths of 10 to 40 feet were measured. The highest concentrations were about three times the standards set for drinking waters by the U.S. Department of Public Health.

Another study, dealt with 9 randomly chosen fields in the Santa Ana drainage basin in Riverside, San Bernardino, and Orange counties.[7,8] The average annual nitrogen application in these fields was about 350 lbs per acre, but varied from a low of 145 lbs to a high of 1200 lbs. Nitrate nitrogen in the drainage water varied from a low of 36 ppm to as high as 119 ppm. In other words, the nitrate level in the subsurface waters of all fields exceeded the Public Health drinking standards from 3 to 12 times. The highest nitrate levels were in the fields which received the largest amounts of nitrogen. There is no doubt that the current fertilization practices are putting large amounts of nitrate in the drainage water.

One point deserves special emphasis. There is an extended time lag, especially with limited irrigation water, between the time when nitrogen is applied to the surface and when it appears in the ground water. Depending upon the soil texture, soil depth, and the amount of water applied, this lag may vary from several years to well over 30 years. If in the 9 fields mentioned earlier, we take transit times to the 50-foot depth, the time lag would have varied from 5 to 22 years. Hence, we may not yet be measuring the effects of any greatly increased use of nitrogen. Problems that we are creating today may not be measured until 1990 or 2000.[7,8]

I would like to emphasize that these examples for California do not represent the average situation in the United States. We do know many, many cases where nitrogen fertilization has not increased the nitrates in the ground water.

Unfortunately, we do not know how much dentrification — the logical way to get rid of excess nitrogen — occurs in our agricultural soils. We do know that in some soils it can be very great. In rice fields which are flooded, for example, it is tremendous. It has been estimated that in many of the midwestern states, about 30% of the nitrogen applied escapes by denitrification; an estimated value for irrigated western soils is about 20%.[9]

Figures collected from fertilization of California vegetables illustrate the significance of nitrogen contamination. After application of 200 lbs of nitrogen per acre, an average crop would remove about 40%, leaving 120 lbs of nitrogen, unused by the crop, and a possible contributor to pollution. If we use 10 acre-inches of water, in excess of the crop need or evapotraspiration to leach down the salts, (and 10 acre-inches is certainly a reasonable amount to use) this 10 acre-inches, with the 120 lbs of nitrogen left by the crop, could result in contamination in the ground water of 240 ppm of nitrate, if no denitrification had occurred. If we then subtract the value given above of about 20% denitrification, we would still end up with 160 ppm of nitrates, which is almost 4 times the level set by the Public Health for drinking water.

The question that naturally follows is "How can nitrate contamination of ground water be avoided or reduced?" "Can growers cut down on their nitrogen application rates and still maintain yields?" The best information from many experiments with vegetables is that if the rates are cut by more than 20%, yields would be reduced. This would still provide a considerable excess of nitrogen beyond crop removal and implies, perhaps, that if growers are to maintain high yields under all conditions, we will have to be content with some nitrate contamination in the ground waters.

Another method for reducing the nitrate concentration is to use more irrigation water and dilute the nitrates. This is a possibility, but irrigation water is costly. Generally speaking, if we add more water, we do more leaching which would result in adding more nitrogen to produce satisfactory yields. In many cases it would be feasible to use dual wells, i.e., use shallow wells with the higher nitrate concentration for irrigation purposes, and use deeper wells for drinking water.

There is the opportunity for greater efficiency in crop utilization of nitrogen fertilizers. This involves proper placement in the soil and repeated applications that parallel crop removal. For example, crops like lettuce make over 80% of their growth and utilize most of the nitrogen during the last few weeks of growth. It follows that there is no need to apply excess nitrogen before it is needed for growth. In some cases it may be possible to use some of the "controlled release" nitrogen fertilizers. Currently the materials with slow-release characteristics include compounds, such as urea formaldehyde, and various types of coating materials such as sulfur, clays, plastics, etc. It is also possible to apply certain biocide materials that inhibit soil microorganisms and prevent the transformation of nitrogen from amino and ammonium compounds to nitrates.

In conclusion, we must address ourselves as to whether or not nitrogen fertilizers are contributing to nitrate pollution of sub-surface waters. It is my conclusion that, in the majority of cases, they are not. In the more arid regions of the country with limited leaching water and high rates of nitrogen fertilization they often cause higher levels of nitrate in the leaching water. We might reconsider the problem of nitrate in drinking waters. "Is the level of 45 ppm nitrate toxic or harmful?" The National Academy of Sciences reports only one case of an infant developing methemoglobinemia as a result of drinking water from a public water supply since 1950.[10] If the permissible level for nitrates were doubled, then certainly many, many more waters would qualify as safe.

References

1. *Agricultural Statistics 1972,* Washington, United States Government Printing Office, pp 569-570, 1972.
2. Ibach, DB: Fertilizer Use in the United States — Economic Position and Outlook, U.S. Department of Agriculture Economic Report No. 92, 1966.
3. Changing Patterns in Fertilizer Use, in Nelson, LB (ed.), *Soil Science Society of America,* Madison, Wisconsin, 1968.
4. Viets, FG and Hagemen RH,: Factors Affecting the Accumulation of Nitrate in Soil, Water, and Plants, *Agriculture Handbook No. 413,* U.S. Department of Agriculture, 1971.
5. Bingham, FT; Davis S; and Shade E,: Water Relations, Salt Balance, and Nitrate Leaching Losses of a 960-Acre Citrus Watershed, *Soil Science* 112:410-418, 1971.
6. Stout, PR and Burau RG: The Extent and Significance of Fertilizer Buildup in Soils as Revealed by Vertical Distribution of Nitrogenous Matter Between Soils and Underlying Water Reservoirs, in Brady, NC (ed.) *Agriculture and Quality of our Environment,* pp 283-310, Washington, D.C., American Association Advancement Science, 1967.
7. Adriano, DC *et al*: Soil Nitrogen Balance in Selected Row-Crop Sites in Southern California, *J Environ Quality* 1:279-283, 1972.
8. Adriano, DC; Pratt, PF; and Takatori, FH: Nitrate in Unsaturated Zone of an Alluvial Soil in Relation to Fertilizer Nitrogen Rate and Irrigation Level, *J Environ Quality* 1:418-422, 1972.
9. Stanford, G; England, CB; and Taylor, AW: Fertilizer Use and Water Quality, Agriculture Research Service Report 41-168, U.S. Department of Agriculture, 1970.
10. Accumulation of Nitrate, Washington, Committee on Nitrate Accumulation, National Research Council, National Academy of Sciences, 1972.

Nitrate Accumulation in Vegetables

O.A. LORENZ, Ph.D.; B.L. WEIR, M.S.

Abnormally high levels of nitrate accumulation in plants have been noted for many years. New interest, particularly with vegetable and forage crops, has been generated since the 1950's, due to the greatly increased use of nitrogen fertilizers. There is also public concern over possible health hazards as a result of nitrate accumulation in certain foods.[1] Methemoglobinemia in infants has been associated with high levels of nitrates in water and foods. The toxicosis results from nitrites produced after nitrate reduction by microbial action, either before ingestion or within the gastrointestinal tract. The nitrate content of foods is a potential index of the amount of nitrite that may be formed.

Some of the effects of nitrates and nitrites on domestic animals are well known. Less well known is the effect on humans. Nitrate poisoning in livestock was reported by Mayo[2] in 1895. Beginning in 1940, Bradley and others[3-6] reported numerous cases of cattle poisoning from nitrates in the Mountain States. Reliable reports indicate that nitrate poisoning was responsible for the loss of 2000 to 3000 cattle in the Salinas Valley of California during the spring of 1952.[5] Reports vary as to the levels of nitrate considered toxic to animals and several factors other than the actual nitrate content must be evaluated. Tucker *et al*[5] in California considered plants containing more than 0.20% NO_3-N (Nitrate-Nitrogen) on a dry weight basis as being potentially dangerous to livestock.

Although no authenticated cases of nitrate poisoning of human adults have been reported, there are reports of young babies being poisoned by eating spinach with a high nitrate content.[1] The Public Health Service has not established standards relating to the nitrate content of vegetables. Standards have been set at 10 ppm nitrate nitrogen (NO_3-N) for drinking water and 200 ppm nitrate (NO_3) or nitrite (NO_2) for certain processed meats. Simon[7] has proposed that spinach for baby food should contain no more than 67 ppm NO_3-N based on fresh weight. Sollman[8] has estimated that a toxic dose for an adult might be 1 gram NO_3-N. Canned acidic vegetables such as tomatoes and beans that contain high nitrates[9,13] often result in excessive detinning of the cans, which can result in extensive economic loss. Under certain conditions as little as 20 ppm NO_3-N, fresh weight basis of tomatoes can cause serious detinning for canned tomatoes.

Vegetable crops receive high rates of nitrogen fertilizers. In California the rates continue to increase and in many instances are double the 1950 rates. We were interested in identifying the crops and plant parts that have the potential for accumulating high levels of nitrate. Our principal concern was in assessing the part of the plant commonly eaten by man, but we also considered the part of the plant which may be trimmed away and have other uses such as cattle feed, for example, the wrapper leaves of lettuce and the tops of radishes and turnips. This was an ideal time for the studies as similar investigations were being conducted by workers in Massachusetts [14-16], New York [12,17] and Indiana.[9] There has been excellent agreement of our findings and theirs.

The environmental conditions associated with nitrate accumulation in plants have been studied by many workers and much information on this was reviewed by Wright and Davison. [18]

We also studied some of the factors associated with high nitrate accumulation. We surveyed about 25 of the important vegetables grown in California. Several distinctive cultivars were included in some crops. The plants were harvested at different seasons of the year to determine the influence of different growing conditions, particularly temperatures, on nitrate accumulation. All plant parts commonly eaten were assessed for potential nitrate accumulation. Samples were taken at prime edible maturity as well as at intervals before and after prime maturity. Nitrogen from NH_4NO_3 was applied at rates of 0 lbs, 200 lbs, and 500 lbs nitrogen per acre. The 200 lb rate approximates a normal application to California vegetables, whereas the 500 lb rate is excessive and often several times that required for maximum yield. Most crops grew very poorly with the zero rate and nitrate accumulation was much less than that required for satisfactory yield.

The particular crop, the part of the plant sampled, and the rate of fertilization all greatly affected nitrate accumulation (Tables I and II). Some plant parts, such as pepper fruits or kernels of sweet corn, accumulated only negligible quantities of nitrate regardless of the rate of nitrogen fertilization. Others accumulated very high levels of nitrate; some by more than 10 times the level considered potentially dangerous for cattle feed. Some turnip petioles accumulated over 3% NO_3-N on a dry weight basis, the highest of any crop. Levels of about 2% were found in petioles of spinach, beet, and kale. The leaf blades of these crops were also high. Roots of radish exceeded 1% NO_3-N while turnips and beets were also relatively high. Carrott roots, potato tubers, and onion bulbs were low. Practically all of the fruit vegetables were very low in nitrate and only a single harvest of summer squash exceeded the .2% NO_3-N level. Some workers have reported zero nitrate in a number of the fruit vegetables (Table I).

The wrapper leaves of cabbage were about three times higher in nitrate than were the head leaves of the same plants. Heavily fertilized Boston lettuce has .602% NO_3-N in the wrapper leaves and only .207% in the head. Crisphead type lettuce showed .496% NO_3-N in the wrapper leaves and .326% in the head. Thus, man's consumption of nitrate could be controlled considerably by observing some ordinary practices, such as discarding the older or wrapper leaves of lettuce and cabbage and the outer petioles of celery. Discarding the petiolar tissue of spinach and turnip and eating only the blade would reduce nitrate consumption by more than half.

As a general rule, nitrates accumulated at the highest levels in the leaf and stem tissues. Petioles and stems had more than did the leaf blades. There was considerable variation in the root crops, but generally the storage roots were lower in nitrates than were the leaves or stems. Fruits and floral parts accumulated only very small amounts of nitrate. Assuming 1 gram of NO_3-N to be toxic to man, an adult to be poisoned would have

Table I.—Range of Nitrate Content in Vegetables Grown at Davis, California—Spring, Summer, and Fall, 1971.

Vegetable	Cultivar	Nature of Sample	NO_3-N % Dry Weight[1]
Bean	Contender	pods and seeds	.047 - .162
Beet	Crosby's Egyptian	blades	.011 - .866
		petioles	.031 - 1.891
		roots	.188 - .680
Broccoli	Calabrese	head	.018 - .232
Cabbage	Copenhagen Market	head	.014 - .207
		wrapper leaves	.002 - .543
Carrot	Imperator	roots	.058 - .183
Cauliflower	Early Snowball	head	.002 - .066
Celery	Tall Utah	petioles	.003 - .203
		blades	.004 - .224
Corn	Golden Cross Bantam	kernels	.008 - .016
Cucumber	Picklepak	fruit	.014 - .144
	Pepino	fruit	.001 - .143
Kale	Dwarf Blue Curled	blades	.002 - 1.564
		petioles	.008 - 1.967
Lettuce	Big boston	head	.059 - .453
		wrapper leaves	.018 - .602
	Paris Cos	head	.141 - .303
		wrapper leaves	.119 - .613
	Great Lakes 659	head	.026 - .363
		wrapper leaves	.012 - .496
Muskmelon	PMR 45	fruit	.018 - .026
	Honey Dew	fruit	.043 - .161
	Persian	fruit	.024 - .103
Onion	Grano	bulbs	.020 - .034
		tops	.003 - .038
	Southport White Globe	bulbs	.068 - .097
		tops	.022 - .043
	Sweet Spanish	bulbs	.022 - .071
		tops	.015 - .210
Parsley	Paramount	tops	.032 - .358
Peas	Progress #9	pods and seeds	.019 - .033
Pepper	Yolo Wonder	fruit	.003 - .005
Potato	White Rose	tuber	.004 - .019
Radish	Crimson Giant	tops	.006 - 1.295
		roots	.046 - 1.086
	White Icicle	tops	.014 - 1.487
		roots	.173 - 1.280
Spinach	Viroflay	blades	.030 - .496
		petioles	.054 - 2.288
Squash	Hubbard	fruit	.003 - .074
	Early Prolific	fruit	.062 - .446
	Zucchini	fruit	.054 - .298
Tomato	M.H. 145	fruit	.012 - .024
Turnip	Purple Top White Globe	blades	.039 - .870
		petioles	.022 - 3.109
		roots	.016 - .877
Watermelon	Striped Klondike	fruit	.018 - .047

[1]Each value represents the average samples from two or more plots.

to consume some 2 lbs of spinach at a single meal, a quantity which is extremely unlikely. On the other hand, all of the leafy vegetables and many of the others had nitrate levels that could result in detinning of the cans of processed vegetables.

Nitrogen fertilization had considerable influence on the degree of nitrate accumulation (Table II). At levels of nitrogen

Table II.—Effect of Rate of Nitrogen Fertilization on Nitrate Composition of Edible Portions of Selected Vegetables.

Crop	Plant Part	NO_3-N % Dry Weight[1] N lb./acre 0	200	500	NO_3-N % of Total N[1] N lb./acre 0	200	500
Beet	petioles	.019	.712	1.598	3.7	61.5	88.4
"	blades	.030	.238	.866	2.4	15.2	38.2
"	roots	.187	.243	.384	14.6	13.6	15.7
Broccoli	heads	.114	.196	.232	3.6	4.6	5.0
Cabbage	wrapper leaves	.051	.316	.524	2.4	9.5	15.2
"	heads	.077	.140	.154	4.3	6.0	6.7
Carrot	roots	.080	.183	.146	11.9	15.9	12.8
Celery	petioles	.004	.010	.203	1.0	2.2	25.3
"	blades	.004	.007	.224	0.4	0.7	13.0
Kale	petioles	.009	1.095	1.396	1.3	38.2	31.9
"	blades	.002	.095	.361	0.1	2.5	6.4
Lettuce, Boston	wrapper leaves	.029	.578	.602	1.3	19.3	17.2
" "	heads	.148	.212	.207	7.0	8.6	7.7
Lettuce, Gt. Lakes	wrapper leaves	.035	.229	.496	2.1	9.3	17.6
" " "	heads	.026	.283	.326	2.4	17.2	19.6
Melon, Honey Dew	fruits	.099	.128	.161	38.7	29.1	30.7
Onion	bulbs	.023	.026	.020	3.8	2.9	1.9
"	tops	.014	.014	.038	0.8	0.7	1.9
Parsley	tops	.032	.094	.267	1.6	3.9	8.9
Radish	tops	.700	.953	1.190	19.2	27.3	31.6
"	roots	.802	.942	1.086	37.3	42.4	45.1
Spinach	petioles	.781	2.160	2.288	41.2	69.3	68.6
"	blades	.153	.380	.496	4.1	9.2	11.9
Squash, Early Prolific	fruits	.186	.366	.446	6.2	16.6	18.6
Turnip	petioles	1.563	3.193	3.109	7.3	31.8	42.2
"	blades	.050	.354	.870	1.8	9.1	16.2
"	roots	.022	.066	.364	1.0	2.5	10.0

[1]Values are averages of samples from duplicate plots.

where growth was restricted, accumulation of nitrate was very low. With increasing levels of nitrogen fertilization the rate of accumulation increased. In an experiment with table beets, fertilization with 500 lb nitrogen per acre, as compared to none, increased nitrate accumulation in the petioles of 70 times, in the blades 30 times, and in the roots 20 times. Equally significant was the increase in NO_3-N as related to total nitrogen with the proportion of NO_3-N increasing from 3.7% to 88.4% in the petioles and from 2.4% to 38.2% in the blades. With practically all crops, as nitrates accumulated, the proportion of NO_3-N to total nitrogen also increased (Table II).

A thorough survey of literature relating to the nitrate content of vegetables was made. The values we obtained agree very well with those reported by other workers. The crops which we found to accumulate high levels of nitrate were also found to be so by other workers. Our value for turnip petioles containing over 3% NO_3-N ranks as one of the highest values reported. There has been no appreciable change in the nitrate content of vegetables since the earliest reported analysis of previous workers.[19-21] This indicates that the increased usage of nitrogen fertilizers has not resulted in significant increase in the nitrate content of vegetables.

It should be emphasized that nitrate accumulation in plants, to a certain extent, is a natural and necessary process. Growers could not attain satisfactory yields without some nitrate accumulation in the product. Most of the samples analyzed had nitrate accumulation only slightly above the concentration required for maximum yield. There is a minimum level of nitrate associated with satisfactory growth. Nitrate accumulation beyond that level may be considered excessive, but in some cases results in greener color and increased succulence of the product.

The source of nitrogen fertilizer can have marked effects on nitrate accumulation. In our source of nitrogen studies with spinach and lettuce, nitrate absorption by the plants was higher from nitrogen applied in the nitrate form than from that applied in the ammoniacal forms. Barker et al [14] reported similar experiments with spinach fertilized at high rates of nitrogen, in which the NO_3-N content of the leaves was 0.40%, dry weight basis, from KNO_3 as compared to 0.28% and 0.21% from NH_4NO_3 and urea.

There were large differences in nitrate content among species in our studies, but the differences among cultivars of the same species were small and inconsistent. Data for lettuce are presented in Table III. Brown and Smith [22] reported similar results with vegetables grown in Missouri. Maynard and Barker [15] found that the petioles and blades of savoy-type spinach accumulated about double the amount of nitrate of the smooth-leaf type (Table III).

There was little effect of time of harvest on nitrate accumulation (Tables III and IV). Plant parts sampled at the time of prime edible quality varied only slightly and inconsistently from samples taken before or after this stage of maturity. Other workers have shown no consistent effect of maturity or nitrate accumulation.

Many cases of high nitrate accumulation in plants, and subsequent toxicity to animals have been related to growth condi-

Table III.—Effect of Cultivar, Age, and Rate of Nitrogen Application on Nitrate and Total Nitrogen Composition of Lettuce Heads. Average of Duplicate Plots.

Cultivar	Harvest Dates	NO_3-N % Dry Weight			Total N % Dry Weight		
		0	N lb./acre 200	500	0	N lb./acre 200	500
Planted 2/9/71							
Big Boston	5/03/71	.070	.351	.326	3.01	4.21	4.31
	5/10/71	.059	.453	.388	2.27	3.15	3.64
Cos	5/17/71	.141	.303	.264	2.64	3.22	3.39
Gt. Lakes 659	5/11/71	.026	.283	.326	1.07	1.63	1.66
	5/18/71	.049	.279	.326	1.85	2.57	3.28
Planted 8/10/71							
Big Boston	10/22/71	.211	.254	.439	2.50	2.70	2.58
	11/05/71	.148	.212	.207	2.09	2.47	2.67
Cos	11/17/71	.194	.215	.275	2.86	3.14	3.25
	11/22/71	.158	.169	.147	2.77	3.08	3.18
Gt. Lakes 659	11/08/71	.100	.178	.161	2.19	2.40	2.66
	11/29/71	.183	.299	.257	2.06	2.50	2.32
	12/10/71	.250	.336	.363	2.17	2.39	2.45

Table IV.—Effect of Plant Part, Age, and Rate of Nitrogen Application on Nitrate and Total Nitrogen Composition of Table Beets. Averages of Duplicate Plots.

Plant Part	Harvest Dates	NO_3-N % Dry Weight			Total N % Dry Weight		
		N lb./acre			N lb./acre		
		0	200	500	0	200	500
Planted 2/9/71							
Blades	5/05/71	.037	.273	.650	2.19	3.88	4.53
	5/12/71	.030	.238	.866	1.27	1.56	2.26
	5/20/71	.011	.197	.673	2.25	3.21	4.60
Petioles	5/05/71	.148	.781	1.286	1.30	2.09	3.99
	5/12/71	.019	.712	1.598	.51	1.15	1.80
	5/20/71	.031	.475	1.289	.98	1.72	2.47
Roots	5/05/71	--	.220	.333	--	2.62	3.56
	5/12/71	.187	.243	.384	1.28	1.79	2.44
	5/20/71	.188	.208	.349	.64	1.28	1.71
Planted 8/10/71							
Blades	10/15/71	.057	.211	.237	2.63	2.54	2.85
	11/05/71	.028	.177	.145	2.88	3.60	3.53
	12/08/71	.055	.128	.140	2.61	3.02	3.14
Petioles	10/15/71	.666	1.891	1.874	1.88	2.72	2.86
	11/05/71	.232	1.598	1.618	1.34	2.83	2.79
	12/08/71	.386	1.139	1.316	1.66	2.37	2.61
Roots	10/15/71	.342	.566	.680	1.82	2.23	2.29
	11/05/71	.221	.466	.524	1.41	2.07	2.31
	12/08/71	.151	.266	.360	1.61	1.83	2.05

tions—particularly a sudden drought. Evidently, there is a cessation in growth which is not accompanied by a corresponding reduction in nitrate absorption and hence the effect is that nitrates accumulate. [18] It is doubtful if such drought conditions would be encountered in vegetable production and they definitely would not occur with vegetables grown under irrigation.

Light very definitely affects nitrate accumulation. [17,23] Plants grown with deficient light, such as during cloudy weather or under short days, are likely to accumulate more nitrate than those grown with ample light. Shading of plants greatly increases nitrate accumulation. Plants harvested in early morning often have higher nitrate content than those harvested near the end of the day. This is due to the fact that the enzyme, nitrate reductase, which is responsible for the reduction of nitrate, is light dependent and is most active under high light conditions.

Temperature has also been shown to influence nitrate accumulation. Plants grown at temperatures where growth is restricted often accumulate nitrates. Tomato fruits grown at 20°C day temperature accumulated nearly five times the amount of nitrate as fruits produced at 30°C. [24] Conversely spinach plants accumulated much more nitrate when grown at 25°C than at lower temperatures. [25]

Several tests investigated the effect of temperature and time on changes in the nitrate and nitrite composition of stored vegetables. These studies, conducted under aerobic conditions, showed no appreciable reduction in nitrates or increases in nitrites, even after extended periods of storage.

Over 25 important vegetables were grown at low to high rates of nitrogen fertilization, and their potential to accumulate nitrates determined. Leaf and stem tissues accumulated the highest levels of nitrate, followed by the roots. Fruits and floral parts accumulated only small amounts of nitrate. Some nitrate accumulation is a natural and necessary process and the levels of nitrate in the plants cannot be reduced much without reducing yield. The stage of maturity of the produce at harvest had little effect on nitrate accumulation. Differences in nitrate levels between cultivars of the same species were small. Nitrate accumulation increased as the rate of nitrogen fertilization increased. Nitrate sources of fertilizer resulted in higher nitrate accumulation than did ammonical sources. Even at the highest rates of nitrate accumulation observed, the possibilities of an adult consuming enough food to cause nitrate toxicosis are exceedingly remote.

References

1. Phillips, WEJ: Nitrate Content of Foods—Public Health Implications, *Can Inst Tech J* 1:98-103, 1968.
2. Mayo, NS: Cattle Poisoning by Nitrate of Potash, bulletin 49, Kansas Agriculture Experiment Station, 1895.
3. Bradley, WB; Eppson, AF; and Beath, OA: Livestock Poisoning by Oat Hay and Other Plants Containing Nitrate, bulletin 241, Wyoming Agriculture Experiment Station, 1940.
4. Gilbert, CS et al: Nitrate Accumulation in Cultivated Plants and Weeds, bulletin 277, Wyoming Agriculture Experiment Station, 1946.

5. Tucker, JM et al: Nitrate Poisoning in Livestock, circular 506, California Agriculture Experiment Station, 1961.

6. Whitehead, EI and Moxan, AL: Nitrate Poisoning, bulletin 424, South Dakota Agriculture Experiment Station, 1961.

7. Simon, C: Nitrate Poisoning from Spinach, *Lancet* 1:827, 1966.

8. Sollman, T: *A Manual of Pharmacology and Its Applications to Therapeutics and Toxicology,* Philadelphia, WB Saunders Co., 1957.

9. Hoff, JE and Wilcox, GE: Accumulation of Nitrate in Tomato Fruit and Its Affect on Detinning, *J Amer Soc Hort Sci* 95:92-94, 1970.

10. Johnson, JH: Internal Can Corrosion Due to High Nitrate of Canned Vegetables, *Proc Fla State Hort Soc* 79:239, 1966.

11. Johnson, JH and Orth, PG: Total Nitrate-N and Solid Content of Processed Tomatoes as Affected by Fertility and Variety, *Proc Fla State Hort Soc* 80:313, 1967.

12. Lee, CY et al: Nitrate and Nitrite Nitrogen in Fresh, Stored, and Processed Table Beets and Spinach from Different Levels of Field Nitrogen Fertilization, *J Sci Food Agr* 22:90-92, 1971.

13. Strodtz, NH and Henry, RE: The Relation of Nitrates in Foods to Tin Plate Container Corrosion, *Food Tech* 8:93-95, 1954.

14. Barker, AV; Peck, NA; and MacDonald, GE: Nitrate Accumulation in Vegetables. I. Spinach Grown in Upland Soils, *Agron J* 63:126-129, 1971.

15. Maynard, DN and Barker, AV: Critical Nitrate Levels for Leaf Lettuce, Radish, and Spinach Plants, *Comm Soil Sci and Plant Anal* 2:461-470, 1971.

16. Maynard, DN and Barker, AV: Nitrate Content of Vegetable Crops, *Hort Sci* 73:224-226, 1972.

17. Cantliffe, DJ: Nitrate Accumulation in Vegetable Crops as Affected by Photoperiod and Light Duration, *J Amer Soc Hort Sci* 97:329-331, 1972.

18. Wright, MJ and Davison, KL: Nitrate Accumulation in Crops and Nitrate Poisoning in Animals, *Advances in Agron* 16:197-247, 1964.

19. Richardson, WD: Nitrates in Vegetable Foods, in Cured Meats, and Elsewhere, *J Amer Chem Soc* 29:1757-1767, 1907.

20. Wilson, JK: Nitrate in Plants: Its Relation to Fertilizer Injury Changes During Silage Making and Indirect Toxicity to Animals, *J Amer Soc Agron* 35:279-290, 1943.

21. Wilson, JK: Nitrates in Food and Its Relation to Health, *Agron J* 41:20-22, 1949.

22. Brown, JR and Smith, CE: Nitrate Accumulation in Vegetable Crops as Influenced by Soil Fertility Practices, bulletin 920, Missouri Agriculture Experiment Station, 1967.

23. Nitrate Accumulation in Spinach Grown Under Different Light Intensities, *J Amer Soc Hort Sci* 97:152-154, 1972.

24. Luh, BS; Ukai, N; and Chung, JI: Effect of Nitrogen Nutrition and Day Temperature on Composition, Color, and Nitrate in Tomato Fruit, *J Food Sci*, 1973, in press.

25. Nitrate Accumulation Grown at Different Temperatures, *J Amer Soc Hort Sci* 97:674-676, 1972.

The Food System and Environmental Quality

WALTER A. MERCER

In America, the food industry is the nucleus around which has developed a vast and complex cluster of American industries that in recent years has come to be called "Agribusiness." The development of the food canning and freezing industry was both the necessary condition and the lever which brought Agribusiness into being.

Agribusiness is the sum total of all farms and ranches, all the industries and businesses that supply goods and services to agriculture; all those businesses involved in the movement, processing, packaging, storing, and distribution of agricultural products, and all the supporting services that this huge complex of activities requires for its maintenance, support, financing, and promotion.

All of the segments of Agribusiness are interdependent. The forces that affect one for better or worse affect the others. If the bell tolls for agriculture, it tolls for all. If the bell tolls for food processing, it tolls for agriculture.

The economic implications of the increasing concern and pressure for improvement of the environment have serious implications for the food processing industry. The food canning and freezing segment of the industry is a major water-user and waste-generator. This is an inevitable consequence of preparing raw, field-grown foods for human consumption.

Of serious economic implication is the fact that the food canning and freezing industry is characterized by its large number of small businesses having low or marginal profitability. Overall, the food processing industry is highly competitive in the market place, operating on a relatively low-profit margin and a low return on investments. These characteristics of the industry are the causes of its economic vulnerability to suddenly imposed crash programs for environmental control.

Notwithstanding, the food processing industry recognizes its responsibility to manage wastes in a manner which improves environmental quality. It will continue to recognize its responsibility for development of solutions to its pollution problems. Any consideration of food waste must include waste produced in growing and harvesting crops, which are transported to food processing plants. Any proposals for reducing or preventing environmental problems must recognize the interdependence of the grower, processor, distributor, and the consumer.

MAGNITUDE OF FOOD PROCESSING
AND WASTE REDUCTION

Food processing plants are located in 49 of the 50 states of this nation. Approximately one-half of the vegetable crops grown and nearly one-half of the fruit production are used for processing.

The importance of food processing to agriculture and to each consumer is further emphasized by these facts:

- More than 70% of all tomatoes harvested in this nation are canned.
- More than 90% of the beets, and 60% of the peas, green beans, sweet corn, are canned or frozen.
- By canning and freezing, about 75% of the production of asparagus, lima beans, and leafy vegetables are preserved for future consumption.

The food processing industry provides the major market for the grower of perishable fruits; about 70% of all apricots, cranberries, and pears, and about 50% of the peaches and cherries are canned. Within the apple growing areas of the nation, about 40% of the apple crop is canned. In California, nearly 90% of the olive production is canned.

The liquid waste from fruit and vegetable processing operations does not constitute a direct public health problem. The wastes contain only fruit or vegetable residues, which are nontoxic in nature. Pesticide residues and heavy metal contaminants are present in such low concentrations as to be insignificant from a public health or an environmental quality standpoint.

Liquid wastes from food processing operations may and do cause situations or conditions which hamper or aggravate pollution abatement efforts by the processor himself, or by the community which is handling and treating his waste materials. These situations or conditions are identified as follows:

- A large volume of clean water must be used by the food processing industry.
- Raw food products must be rendered clean and wholesome for human consumption.
- The food processing plant must be sanitary at all times.

As a result, correspondingly large volumes of waste waters are discharged from the plants. Variations in waste-water strength and volume cause treatment difficulties. The use of water may vary one-hundred-fold among months of the year, and waste-water volume and organic strength vary several fold between months of the operating day. Therefore, the facilities to treat these waste waters must be designed on an unsteady state basis, not on a steady state basis. Present in most food processing waste waters are soluble or organic materials not effectively removed by physical and/or chemical methods, and which must, therefore, be stabilized by microbial processes.

This means that residence time for treatment dictates that the facilities must be adequate from a capacity standpoint. Although food processing waste waters are generally high in pollution strength, the concentration of organic matter is normally dilute to the point that efforts to recover utilizable materials are not economical at this time. Food processing waste waters are highly putrescible in nature, and cannot, therefore, be stored onsite for later treatment in periods of minimal flow. This is in contrast to some other types of waste materials.

INDUSTRY EFFORTS TO ABATE POLLUTION

The industry believes that the most efficient and economical means of developing effective pollution control is through closely coordinated industry-government programs with continuing research at both the laboratory and plant level. As an example, the National Canners Association has directed its Research Laboratories to perform a positive and comprehensive program of research and demonstration projects.

Early in this effort, it was recognized that the most rapid and significant improvement could be accomplished through in-plant changes and process modifications. Significant achievements have been and will continue to be made in the following:

- Reduction of fresh water requirements.
- Segregation of strong wastes for separate treatment.
- Modification of processes to minimize waste generation.
- Education of plant personnel about pollution control.
- Cooperation with government agencies to develop treatment procedures.

The overall effect of the in-plant efforts will be liquid waste flows smaller in volume but higher in organic content. Containment of the organic load in fewer gallons of water will result in more efficient and economical treatment of the waste waters, regardless of whether treatment is in a city or cannery operated system.

Two parameters significantly influence the size of the treatment system. These are: the hydraulic load, and the organic strength of the waste waters.

It follows then that disposal and treatment problems and costs can be reduced by minimizing water use, and reducing the organic load. Reduction of water use through reuse of the same water will contribute significantly to the solution of water pollution problems. Food processing waters cannot be reused indiscriminately, however. Their recirculation in contact with food products must allow satisfactory product and plant sanitation. To give more specific guidance in the use of reclaimed waters, the National Canners Association makes the following recommendations:

1. That the water be free of microorganisms of public health significance.
2. That the water contain no chemicals in concentrations toxic or otherwise harmful to man, and that no chemical content of the water impose the possibility of chemical adulteration of the final product.
3. That the water be free of any materials or compounds

which could impart discoloration, off-flavor, or off-odor to the product, or otherwise adversely affect its quality.

4. That the appearance and content of the water be acceptable from an aesthetic viewpoint.

Making these recommendations for quality standards for recycled process waters is a simple matter. Meeting those quality standards, however, involves complex problems for which complete answers are not yet available.

It is known that regardless of the development of new technology for the treatment of food waste waters, alone or in combination with other wastes, that the most effective means of control can be established inside the food plants. Process modifications must be made to reduce the volume and/or strength of the liquid waste stream. Such modifications should include:

1. Reuse of clear or relatively clean water in appropriate operations.
2. Elimination of hydraulic conveying or reduction of the volume of wastes used for product transport.
3. Removal of solid waste by hand or mechanical means rather than flushing to the gutter.
4. Segregation for separate treatment of disposal of highly concentrated waste streams.
5. Separation of can cooling or other clean waters for disposal without treatment to reduce the volume of waste requiring treatment.
6. Recombination, under appropriate conditions, of clean waters with treated waters to give dilution at the point of final discharge.

IN-PLANT SURVEYS

Before plans are made for the installation of equipment or a system for treatment of cannery waste, the entire operation should be studied. Certain basic evaluations should be made and the following information recorded:

1. Volume, and packing period for all products;
2. Level of soluble, suspended, and setteable solids in the liquid waste stream;

3. Range and average of pH, Biochemical Oxygen Demand (BOD), and Chemical Oxygen Demand (COD) values for the composite waste flow; and

4. The average and peak flow of liquid waste.

Points of concern are the methods of procedures to be used in obtaining the needed in-plant survey data. If the data gathering is not done correctly, its use may lead to costly errors. The methods and frequency of sampling, the analysis done on the samples and the volume of water in which the waste is contained are extremely important if engineering designs for treatment of the wastes are to be based on the results.

DRY-PEELING
OF FRUITS AND VEGETABLES

Surveys of food canning operations and characterization of individual waste streams have pinpointed one or more streams which use relatively low volumes of water but contribute high percentages of the total organic waste load. For example, waste streams that represent no more than 20% of the total volume of waste may contribute as much as 60% of the pollution load from a fruit canning operation.

Of the unit operations in the processing of fruits and vegetables that use water and generate waste, the most notable for magnitude of water use and waste generation is the peeling operation. Whether the product peeling is by water, steam, caustic, or a combination of these, the operation has always generated a troublesome liquid waste because of its volume, organic load, and pH value. For example, approximately 40% of the BOD from peach canning comes from the peeling operation.

In cooperation with the Office of Water Quality Research of the Environmental Protection Agency and USDA research engineers, the industry has demonstrated the feasibility of dry-peeling of apricots, peaches, and pears. Dry-peeling of beets, carrots, sweet potatoes, and tomatoes can be done without doubt.

Dry caustic peeling offers the important benefits of:

1. Significant reductions in water use,

2. Great reductions in the pollutional load of waste waters,

3. The advantage of handling the peeling wastes as a solid, and possibly,
4. Higher product yields of equal quality.

The most extensive experimental operation by the National Canners Association Laboratories has been on dry-peeling of cling peaches. In preparation for peeling peaches, for example, the halved and pitted fruit are fed onto belts with the pit cavity down and the skin surface up. From this operation the peaches pass into a chamber where hot caustic solution is cascaded over the skin surface. After a minute or two the caustic has penetrated and softened the skin. In the conventional peel-removal system, the softened skin is removed with copious volumes of fresh water applied in strong sprays. The peel and underlying skin surfaces become a part of the waste waters leaving the plant.

In the dry-peel process, the sprays for peel removal are replaced with rows of rotating rubber discs. These discs simply wipe the softened peel from the fruit. The peel is accumulated and handled as a solid waste. As the peel is being removed the peaches are moved forward and are finally passed through a rinse tank and light spray wash to remove the bits of peel and traces of caustic.

The most dramatic difference between conventional and dry-peeling is the greatly reduced water use requirements for the dry-peel system. Reductions in the pollutional strength of the composite waste stream are in the range of 30% or more. Other than these significant reductions in water-borne wastes, the dry-peeling experiment indicates a reduction in product peeling losses.

WASTES FROM BLANCHING

The organic load from blanching is a significant portion of the total pollution load in the effluent from vegetable processing. It is known that, in some cases, the blanch waters constitute only 2% to 5% of the total waste water volume, yet contribute to 80% of the composite pollution load.

The national amortized annual treatment facility cost for the organic load from vegetable blanching alone is estimated to be

$24.4 million. The annual maintenance and treatment cost for the pollution load is about $3.0 million. The loss in weight of product due to water blanching is estimated to be $6.0 million annually.

The loss of nutrients from water-blanched vegetables is more significant today from a consumer viewpoint, than ever before. Although it may be necessary to continue water-blanching of certain vegetables, other low-water volume methods of blanching have been investigated.

Experimental data suggest that hot-gas blanching holds considerable promise for excellent enzyme inactivation, with very small volumes of waste water being generated in the form of condensate. For example, in the experimental blanching of green peas, water usage per ton of product blanched was 0.02 gallon for hot-gas blanching and 1,000 gallons for hot-water blanching. The insignificant use of water was reflected in the trace amounts of organic pollutants generated per ton of blanched product. Hot-gas blanching of other vegetables gave equally dramatic results. For example, 341 lbs of green beans were put through the hot-gas blancher in 60 minutes with the formation of only 77 ml of steam condensate.

If the commercial-scale demonstration project now under way confirms the results reported here, the vegetable processors of the Nation will have the means for further pollution abatement measures. The potential for saving in the case of green beans alone is more than one-half million dollars annually, not considering the increased product yields and nutrient retention.

RECOGNITION OF INDUSTRY RESPONSIBILITY

In recognition of the food canning industry's responsibility to manage wastes in a manner that improves environmental quality, the membership of the National Canners Association in business session on January 25, 1971, approved by unanimous ballot the following resolution of Environmental Pollution Control:

"The canning industry continues to recognize its responsibility for the development of lawful solutions to pollution problems, and that a closely coordinated industry effort, including continuing research at both the laboratory and plant level, is the most efficient and economical means of developing effective pollution control. The interdependence of farmers, processors, workers, and the communities in which they reside, the magnitude, seasonal nature, and interstate character of the food industry's pollution problems, and the overriding interest of the consuming public in a wholesome, abundant, and economical food supply make it imperative that Federal, State, and local authorities not only establish realistic guidelines and objectives, but that they also participate actively and substantially in the development of solutions to these problems. In the necessary overall effort to correct environmental problems, the canning industry supports programs to promote recognition by the public and by industry and governmental leaders that effective pollution abatement programs must proceed in an orderly, logical, progressive manner that will afford adequate time for the development and implementation of technology, any additional needed research, pilot-scale testing, treatment plant construction, and economic adjustment.

The industry endorses cooperative efforts to establish standards that are both practicable in each specific problem area and which avoid blanket requirements that may, in their impact be unrealistic, unnecessary, or unreasonable.

The canning industry endorses the establishment of the Federal Environmental Protection Agency as a forward step and pledges its cooperation with that agency. Necessarily, the producers and processors of our food supply must be allowed to continue to expand the production of food for a hungry world, while at the same time adjusting to the demands of protecting our environment."

Uncited Reference
All the Canning, Freezing, Preserving Industries, in The Almanac, ed 58, Westminster, MD, Edward E. Judge and Son, Inc., 1973, 586 pp.

Energy Use and Energy Waste

R. STEPHEN BERRY, Ph.D.

ENERGY ACCOUNTING

The idea that there is a limit to growth is obviously simplistic and, therefore, somewhat misleading. By the same token, there are clearly limits to growth if we persist in the manner in which we have been growing. I would like to term the factors that set these limits, "diseconomies".

Let us just imagine a simple input-output curve for a hypothetical food processing system. The desired product normally follows a linear growth curve as illustrated in Figure 1, perhaps with more of an upward curve (according to the economics of scale), or perhpas with a diminished return (downward curve). If the return is not more or less linear, a different processing system would be chosen. The straight line in Figure 1 is the curve of the economies, the curve for the desired products.

Along with the desired product there are unwanted products, externalities, which should be small as compared with the desired products. These start off along the slowly rising curve. At some point—the cost-benefit analyst would probably say at point "x", where the slopes of the curve and line are the same—the diseconomies of scale outweigh the economies.

Let us go back to the beginning of the hypothetical processing system. We did not adopt this particular process because it was the only possibility. We frequently have two or three alternatives, and we discard all of those that are predicted to have smaller slopes than the desired one. That is, we typically choose the process that has the greatest marginal return, shown as A in Figure 2.

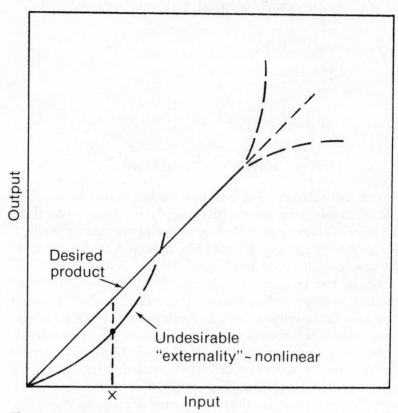

Figure 1.—Input-output curves (schematic) for a desired product and for accompanying unwanted side effects.

What we have come to learn, and what we must assimilate into our analysis, is that if we are required to satisfy the needs of a population, we must reach a high output level at point "y". We may not be able to reach that output level with the selected process A, because the diseconomies of A have equaled the economies. Consider, however, that we may be able to climb part of the way up the curve on the slope in Figure 2 with process A, and part of the way with process B, and part of the way with process C, and maybe we will invent a new process that will give us a new slope, process D. Each one of these has its own unique diseconomies of scale and also satisfy the needs of a population as large as ours.

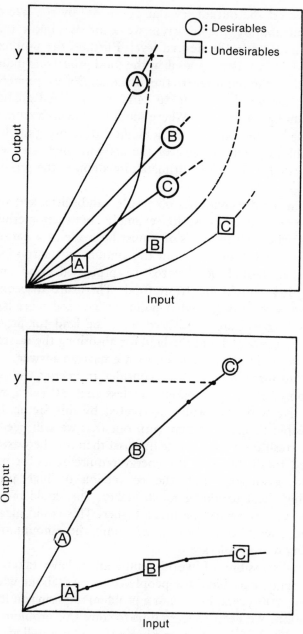

Figure 2.—Input-output curves illustrating the use of several processes to maintain output and minimize undesirables; top separate processes; bottom processes combined.

We have set the output level at point "y" by the size of the population and by the life-style we want. We know that we cannot quite attain the desired level. Further, the problems of liquid and solid waste disposal in the food processing industries have reached the point where the diseconomies are tremendous. We have not yet been able to carry out rational analysis to choose among the options. Where should one switch from doing everything by method A to using method B, to using method C? We *are* able to identify *some* of the diseconomies, and we also know a little bit about the ultimate diseconomy, the production of heat.

Problems of diseconomies obviously can be attacked at plant level, where one chooses, for example, between methods of purifying whey. Other decisions must be made at a national or international level, decisions on the amount of the food supply system that should be devoted to processed food and the amount that should be fresh food. There are diseconomies associated with both. At what point do we need more land for fresh food agriculture, compared with the land for producing food to be processed and the land for absorbing the waste from processing food? The question does not have an answer.

The "ultimate problem" to consider in energy use in heat diseconomy, energy dissipation. In less than 30 years, we will have to live with the problems created by this factor. Here is one possible scenario. It may turn out that we will need more land for fresh-food solid waste disposal than for the waste from processed foods, but that the energy requirements for processing food, associated with the conversion of high potential energy into heat would be much higher. This could mean that heat and energy would be much higher. This could mean that heat and energy consumption will limit the amount of food processing we can tolerate.

Many discussions of world temperature have taken place. This presents a problem for people concerned about what will happen in 200 years, but is not a problem requiring an immediate solution. We need to learn *how* to solve this problem within the next 30 years, however, and begin to evolve a policy.

Our present concern is the problem of regional climate change associated with heat disposal. The best projections indicate that present rates of growth in the use of energy are going to lead to a 5° F annual increase in average temperature in the Boston, New York, Washington metropolitan area between the years 1990 and 2000. Five additional degrees still leaves it perfectly livable, but it does affect the way of life. The estimates may be off a degree or two either way. An increase of more than 5° F begins to cause a little discomfort, and that is the ultimate diseconomy. (For an analysis of this problem, see Theodore Brown, *Energy and the Environment,* Merrill & Company, 1971.)

Let us return for a moment to the broader questions. The public generally has had no way of recognizing where we stand on the curve of undesirable externalities until we are so far along that the level of undesirables approaches the level of desirables.

As part of our adaptation to the complexity and highly consumptive nature of our society, we will have to find ways to make available to the public the kind of information we have been describing. One of the greatest challenges for the next decade or two will be learning how to keep informed, normative decision-making a public process. We cannot expect every voter to read environmental impact statements, but we must find ways to prevent autocratic teams of technocrats from taking over the normative part of making policy.

The evaluation of diseconomics requires two levels of analysis. The first is the physical and biological evaluation, the step in which we quantify the secondary consequences of the processes we use. This step is the one we are learning to do currently, in various ways. The second part of my discussion deals with one particular way of carrying out the physical evaluation, which will be especially powerful in the context of diseconomics when it is applied to consequences such as corrosion, dissipation of materials and resource requirements that arise in order to deal with pollution.

The second level of analysis is normative. Physical and biological analysis can only tell us what does or will occur when we follow a particular policy. We must still choose among alternatives.

The value of the physical and biological analysis lies in their ability to tell us which processes are clearly untenable, and which are clearly advantageous, given *particular systems of values.* Let us look at a rather obtuse example. We might decide that what happens to the human race three generations hence is of absolutely no concern to us. If we chose that particular value, we would find all sorts of policies acceptable that we would otherwise reject, such as using up the world's supply of oil and gas.

The process of converting physical and biological information into human values is the activity of economics. The scales of input and output for Figures 1 and 2 could be presented in physical units, such as energy or mass or man-hours, or in monetary units, dollars of input vs dollars of value of output. The dollar valuation is one measure (some economists say it is the only measure), of preferences for goods, processes and services. The Department of Commerce has produced a giant input-output table for the United States economy based on dollars; Robert A. Herendeen, at the University of Illinois, Urbana, has been translating this backward into energy terms. Eventually, we will have to learn to make translations in the other direction: if we make such-and-such a change in the processes we use, then what physical and biological changes are likely to occur, and then, how would we respond in terms of our own preferences?

In the past, we have been unconcerned about diseconomics until they rise to intolerably high levels. Some economic analysis of the effects of pollution claim that we have let the curve of externalities actually cross the curve of output for the desired product (see Figure 1). Whether or not we have been that short-sighted, it is clear that we frequently have passed the point "x" of Figure 1, where the marginal diseconomics increase faster than the marginal desired return, before we have tried to deal with the diseconomics.

The justification for the physical and biological analysis, expressed in economic terms, is this: we want the information to be able to locate the point "x" before we reach it. An uninformed public cannot possibly realize when that point has been reached.

PRINCIPLES OF THERMODYNAMIC THRIFT

Since I have been involved in discussions concerning the so-called energy problem, I have come to view the use of resources in terms of thermodynamic thrift (or energy husbandry). Any rational policy concerned with development of energy use or energy allocation involves plans for the reduction of energy waste.

First, one must recognize *where* energy use is wasteful. I am going to describe a method of determining energy waste, and illustrate how one can develop policy based on this method. I will use the concept of energy husbandry and develop it, in economic terms, into a quantitative tool for discussing resources. (We have not yet used this method in the area of food production or processing, which will be a much more difficult problem than the example I give here.)

Let me begin by asking the questions the economists ask, "What are our physical resources, or better still, what are the resources that are in shortage? What are the resources with which we must deal when we try to make some kind of reasonable allocation of energy?" There is no substance, no element in the world, that is truly in shortage. As far as we know, we are still far from the point where any element (except those that are artificial) is in shortage in an absolute sense.

Thermodynamic potential—Some forms of energy are obviously very abundant. Solar energy comes to us every day in far larger quantities than we can use. What really is lacking is the capacity to transform matter, the capacity to do work in a desired way at a desired rate. As a reminder, let me point out that one of the central concepts of thermodynamics is that of thermodynamic potential, sometimes called free energy, which, precisely defined, is the stored capacity to do work. Thermodynamic potential is a quantity that contains energy as one of its major parts. It also contains entropy, insofar as it reflects how organization and concentration reflects some stored capacity for obtaining work.

Thermodynamics provides us with a set of rules and recipes for evaluating the amount of stored thermodynamic potential, and the amount used in any process that we choose to analyze.

In some processes, we know how to obtain these values, although it is moderately difficult to get precise values. Moreover, for most of the physical processes that we carry out in our own society, we can determine the thermodynamic potential as accurately as we would like, far more accurately than we would ever need for making policy decisions.

Thus, we have a quantifiable tool to evaluate the amount of thermodynamic potential that we consume in any given process, whether it be a real or hypothetical potential we are considering and might want to adopt. This tool gives us another capacity, and that is evaluation of the ultimate natural limit for a process, if carried out with maximum efficiency.

What can we do with the ability to find these numbers? First and foremost, we can apply a kind of general principle of thermodynamic thrift. That is, we have a certain amount of stored capacity. Given alternative ways of achieving the same end, clearly the alternative that uses up the least amount of the capacity to do work, that uses up the least potential, is the desirable process. This gives us an opportunity to throw out the undesirable, less thrifty processes. I do not mean to say necessarily that we should try to find the one and only path to the good life by using thermodynamics, but I do think it is important in helping us weed out those alternatives that are untenable.

We can select specific ways of applying the principle of thermodynamic thrift to choose among policies. In one project, for example, we were able to evaluate thermodynamic potential precisely enough so that we could advise a public agency, the Illinois Institute for Environmental Quality, on how to cope with one aspect of solid waste disposal. It also gave us a great deal of insight into the analysis of the whole manufacturing sector.

The Study of Automobiles—In order to choose a system for study, we had to delineate the whole life-style of this country, deciding what constituted relatively separable pieces. For example, transportation is one area and manufacturing is another. Human subsistence—feeding, clothing, sheltering, and caring for the health of people—is another area. Serving consumers, getting manufactured goods from the point of manufacture to the consumer is still another. We decided to look at manufacturing first, because of the reliable data already available in this area. The decision was made to analyze the manufacture, discard and recycling of automobiles, evaluating the energy consumption and the thermodynamic potential consumed at each step, with the intention of trying to identify alternative policies.

We did not deal with the automobile as an item of transportation nor did we deal with the problem of keeping people who make automobiles alive, fed, and clothed.

Figure 3 shows the substance of our study at one point along its path.

In a qualitative way, Figure 4 represents the system, beginning with ores going through the process of mining and smelting, to primary materials, refining, through manufacturing. Roughly, the position (qualitatively) on this scale represents the state of thermodynamic potential of each one of these stages. That is, ores represent a very low state of thermodynamic

Figure 3.—The experimental apparatus, well along in the experiment.

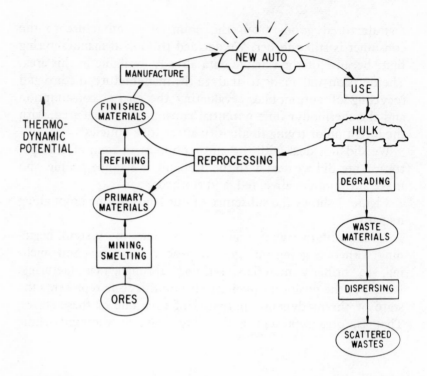

Figure 4.—A schematic representation of the system of manufacture, discard and reuse of automobiles. The vertical position gives a qualitative indication of the thermodynamic potential or value of each stage.

potential, but not as low as the final state of scattered wastes. This is because there is a degree of organization in ore composed 50% of iron that is not found with iron that is scatterd at its level of natural abundance, uniformly distributed over the face of the earth.

One has to break each one of these steps down into reasonably small steps in order to evaluate the process. Figure 5 simply illustrates the complexity of the structure, involving many stages, including the return of scrap. (For example, scrap that is produced in a steel shop is fed back into the furnaces. Some materials get diverted along many different paths.) It is a completely analyzable problem, and we are quite confident now that we have been able to achieve a 10% overall accuracy in our evaluation of the costs of making an automobile.

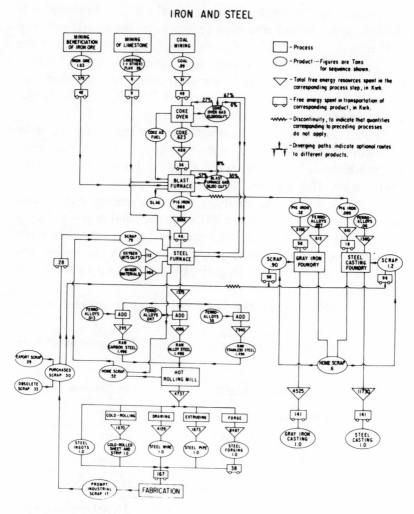

Figure 5.—A detailed breakdown of part of the system.

It turned out that the most useful source of data was the U.S. Census of Manufacturers, and corresponding censuses of transportation and mining. People from the industry were helpful, and the standard industry monographs were useful. The data required checking because of certain gaps and redundancies. For example, in checking data from the automobile industry, we found that in 1967, the year in which we developed our analysis, there were 7.8 million automobiles produced, and only 7.2 million automobile engines, implying that there were 600,000 automobiles on the road with no engines. Taking trucks into account made it worse! It turns out that there are places where the data are not reported. That happens to be the worst single example, but there were others.

Table I shows what it costs with present technology to make an automobile. This is cost, not in dollars, but in energy units, thermodynamic potential, with kilowatt hours (Kwh) as the energy unit. This goes all the way back to primary fuels, so that when we deal with electricity, we are not dealing simply with kilowatt hours of electricity, but with the total primary energy required to generate them. The manufacture of metallics, starting with ores, and continuing up to the point of fabrication and assembly, uses by far the largest part, 26,200 out of a total of 37,000 kwh.

Thus, Table I gives the basic cost for the process as it is

Table I—Free energy consumed in making a typical American automobile, by present practices.

Manufacture of metallics	26,200 kwh
Other materials	900
Fabrication and assembly	9,300
Transportation	900
Total	37,300

carried out now. Let us consider how we can reduce these costs by using alternative policies. We determined that the savings in thermodynamic potential would be 14,500 kwh if aluminum and iron were recovered from scrap, as opposed to using the "new" materials from ore. Then, we learned that the cost of converting an automobile hulk into scrap of the desired quality would be 2,500 kwh. In other words, a net of 12,000 kwh hours per automobile could be saved if we converted automobile hulks to the highest grade scrap that present technology allows. (This is *not* the most common current practice.)

There are two ways of bringing automobiles back into the materials pool after they have been discarded. The most common way still is to squash an automobile to make it into what is called a No. 2 bundle. A No. 2 bundle, apart from being a piece of sculpture, is a very impure block of iron. Unfortunately, No. 2 bundles have to be diluted with pure iron if they are to be useful in making automobiles. In fact, the only practical use for the steel in No. 2 bundles in the impure state is for reinforcing rods. Essentially, the capacity of the automobile industry to absorb No. 2 bundles is very limited. The capacity of the automobile industry to absorb high grade scrap, the kind from a shredder with a separator, is much greater.

We examined a number of recovery policies, using different amounts of automobile hulks and processing them through shredding or through squashing (Figure 6). Figure 6 is essentially two graphs combined. The bottom represents, in black, the fraction of automobile hulks that are squashed into No. 2 bundles. The white represents the number that are just left in junk heaps. The shaded area represents the number that are shredded and segregated. Each one of the bars represents a different recovery policy. In the top graph, corresponding to each one of those policies, we have, on the left side, the savings in kilowatt hours that can be achieved. The policy corresponding to no shredding at all is the one at (a), where the maximum number of automobiles that can be used have been converted into No. 2 bundles. The savings is about 2000 kwh per automobile.

On the extreme right of Figure 6, the policy indicated by (e), representing the recycling of all cars by shredding them, shows a savings of 12,000 kwh per new vehicle. One can do even a little better than that by mining the junkyards.

The reason that junk recovery is not as great as it could be at the moment is that we undervalue the ultimate price of energy, to the point that the cost or the current market price of collecting hulks is too high. In large cities the hulks are brought in with increasing ease and speed, but the rurally disposed cars

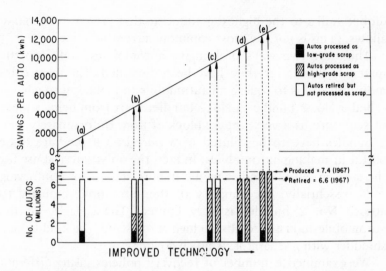

Figure 6—The benefits of various recycling policies. The lower graph shows the policies; each bar represents automobiles discarded in one year (1967), except the pair at far right, which represents that number plus the extra wrecks needed to provide the steel for all the automobiles produced in 1968. Black represents autos processed as No. 2 bundles; hatched area represents shredded and separated hulks, and white represents discarded hulks that are not recycled. The upper part of the figure shows the savings, per new automobile, in kwh, if the recovered materials were used again to make automobiles.

are just being left out in the fields. They would make find raw material, as you can see from this kind of analysis.

The maximum savings nationally from a policy of mining the existing junkyards over a period of 20 years, which we judged as roughly the time when automobile production will level off, based on population projections, would be about 11.5 thousand megawatts each year. That is, the output of about ten large power plants could be saved simply by a maximum recycling policy. This looks like a big savings, but I want to put it in perspective—we have not yet tackled the biggest energy-consuming problems in the society. Auto manufacture requires only one-thirtieth of the energy consumed by the road vehicles each year. Transportation still is a much bigger consumer of energy than manufacturing.

The moral we learned from this is that the chance of finding any single, easy solution to cutting down the national energy budget is nil. All we can really hope to do is chip away at one problem after another, recovering a little energy here and little energy there.

There are two other alternatives that I will mention. One is to extend the life of the vehicle. We found that if the life of the vehicle (presently about 10 years) were tripled, one could expect about a 15% increase per car in the expenditure of thermodynamic potential. That means a saving of, not 12,000 kwh, but about 23,000 kwh per present vehicle lifetime. In other words, we would do almost twice as well, if we triple the vehicle lifetime and persuade people that it is worthwhile to the society to keep a car for 30 years instead of 10 years. The second alternative is the possibility of actually redesigning the vehicle to save energy. Much about this cannot be said because studies of this problem have apparently just started.

We looked very carefully for the processes that really waste thermodynamic potential and energy. We defined this waste in a quantitative way, by looking at the real cost in consumption, and subtracting from it the ideal limit. We looked at both the absolute amount and the relative amount, that is, the ratio of the wasted amount to the real amount. Some of these amounts are shown in Table II which gives some insight into the kind of technology with which we live. Notice in Table II that the ratio of wasted to real-amount is sometimes greater than one. Coking, which has the highest waste, is also the most archaically operated of all of these processes. Aluminum production, which is the most expensive, as you might expect, has the lowest waste ratio. These two are at opposite poles; one has never required energy economics before now, and the other is so energy-intentive that it has always paid off to make it more energy-efficient.

We should be able to *recover* energy from some processes for which we are now *paying* energy. There *are* processes that we can identify, where we can get a great return in energy with relatively small change in the process. We can apply what I believe David Rose of MIT has called Sutton's Law. Willy Sutton robbed banks. When asked, "Mr. Sutton, why do you rob banks?" he said, "Because that is where the money is." *Our*

Table II—The free energy (Thermodynam potential) wasted in preparing materials and manufacturing an automobile by present practices.

PROCESS	Free Energy Waste	$W= \dfrac{\text{Free Energy - Free Energy}}{\dfrac{\text{Free Energy}}{\text{Real}}}$
Cooking	900. kwh/ton	1.13 kwh/ton
Blast furnace	5400.	0.90
Steel furn.	1600.	1.2
Refining		
bauxite	3200.	1.0
Smelting Al	56,000.	0.92
Auto	36,200/car	0.97/car

The first column of figures gives the absolute amount, the difference between the real amount used and the natural, ideal limit. The second column of figures gives the ratio of wasted free energy to the total actually used.

real resource is our thermodynamic potential! If we, as an economic community, had a correct perception of what our thermodynamic potential is, and a reasonably long time period for evaluating energy, we would place higher values on energy use. We might even state it as a theorem: as the time horizon for evaluating use of resources gets longer and we look further into the future, thermodynamic valuation and economic valuation move closer together; ultimately, with an infinite time horizon, they should become identical.

The Philosophy of Acceptable Risk
and the Practicality of Maximum Safety

WILLIAM J. DARBY, M.D., Ph.D.

Some broad issues are ignored by many who zealously advocate ever-increasing constraints upon food production and processing technology without appreciation of their broader impact upon the health and well-being of mankind. I examine these issues as well as certain aspects of the decision-making process, first, however, identifying some of the hazards that exist and then considering the responsibility of scientists and others within this framework.

Only from such a perspective can objective, rational, non-emotional, informed judgements emerge that properly relate risks and benefits so that man enjoys the maximum betterment of health and quality of life attainable from full appreciation of science and technology. Value judgements that determine policy decisions and regulatory actions are not scientific. The perspective, however, from which they are drawn must reflect the multifaceted surfaces of scientific information and advances without exaggeration or distortion.

WORLD FOOD RISKS

The major masses of world population in Southeast Asia, Africa, and Latin America are increasing at rates that exceed the per capita increment of food product in those regions. They subsist at present on some two-thirds of the per capita calorie supply of technologically developed countries of Western Europe and North America. Agriculture is at subsistence level and provides a tuber or cereal-based diet of low nutrient density, especially with respect to protein. Particularly at risk are young children six months to six years of age, teen-agers, and pregnant and lactating women. Not uncommonly half of those born die before school age.

Primitive methods of agriculture, ineffective pest and rodent control, and wasteful methods of harvesting and storage result in low yields and in losses estimated to be 30% to 50% of the harvest. Almost 80% to 90% of these populations are engaged in agriculture, in contrast to 4% to 5% in the United States. The monotony of domestic life and the drudgery of subsistence preclude time or effort for educational pursuits. The quality of life and nutritional health is low. Deficiency disease—pellagra, kwashiorkor, severe anemia, starvation, goiter—are an accepted part of life. The high birth rates of 35 or more per 1000 combined with the high mortality of the young produces an appalling reproductive waste and social loss.

These nations, exporters to the West in the 1930's, now are dependent upon importation of millions of tons of cereal annually from the United States, Canada, Australia, and New Zealand—the technologically advanced countries. Without agricultural technology and applied food science these supplies would not exist.

The increasing needs during the two decades from 1965 to 1985 as estimated by the Panel on World Food Supply of the President's Science Advisory Committee may be illustrated by those for India of a 2-fold increase in calories and 1.6-fold increase in protein—and for Pakistan of a 2.2-fold increase in both calories and protein.

The solution of these problems is dependent primarily upon the application of science to agriculture and food in the developing regions, with continued intensity of production in the current exporting nations.

Clearly, unwise regulatory or legislative constraints that prevent the application of scientific and technologic knowledge to increasing food production and prevention of spoilage or losses can have disastrous world consequences. Such are the risks that should be weighed against whatever cautions arise from laboratory findings in relation to any particularly useful agent.

What are the risks of divesting ourselves of a useful agent? Can we afford them? What are the trade-offs?

Can we justify denying the benefits of use on the strength of the postulated extrapolation of experimental findings to man?

TECHNOLOGY ASSESSMENT AND RISK BENEFIT

The pertinent considerations are numerous: the possibility of human exposure levels in relation to demonstrated levels of toxicity in the test species, the existence or non-availability of alternately effective agents, the relative safety of the alternative or possibility of injury from it to those who work with the chemical or agent.

Such is the concept (applied to nutrition) of technology assessment as defined by the Colloquium of the Committee on Public Engineering Policy. This report states in part:

"Technology Assessment is a systematic process of determining the consequences of various alternative actions involving the application of technology.

As part of this process, the side effects and long-range consequences are evaluated along with the obvious and direct consequences. The result of a technology assessment is information on options, useful to decision makers.

"Benefit-costs . . . refers to an evaluation to all the benefits and costs of proposed action. It is a much broader concept than that of the traditional cost-benefit analysis involving only economic factors.

"Benefit-risk refers to that category of benefit-cost in which risk to life and health are important components of costs.

It is obviously necessary to deal with uncertainty in all of the above analysis. But it should be noted that even when uncertainties, in a statistical sense, are resolved, risks to life and health are present in many of our individual and collective activities.[1]

A consideration in technology assessment is public *benefit* versus *individual* (or private) risk. This consideration is inherent in vastly diverse types of decisions: For example, should we continue smallpox vaccinations? Should boys be vaccinated against chicken pox to protect their mothers from infection during pregnancy? Should iodinization of salt be mandatory?

Should a man's home be destroyed to make way for a new, safer highway? Indeed, the issue recently raised relative to iron enrichment of cereal products was one of public benefit versus postulated individual risk. Analysis of the arguments reveals that the position taken by those opposing increased enrichment would have the effect of maintaining a large segment of the population (women of child bearing age and many teen-agers, especially) on a less-than-recommended intake of iron in order to afford theoretically "protection" to an undetermined small group who might have a rare abnormality of iron metabolism. On considered examination, one finds that many of the currently debated issues of risk/benefit rest on most tenuous grounds. The hypothesized "risk" reminds one of Hellaire Belloc's concluding couplet to "The Microbe." After noting that no one had ever seen a microbe Belloc boldly states:

"Oh, let us never never doubt that which no one knows about!"[2]

SOCIETAL CRITERIA OF
ACCEPTABLE SAFETY

In the above-mentioned symposium, Chauncey Starr presents a thought-provoking essay on "Benefit-Risk Decision Making" in which he examines the problem of societal criteria for evaluating benefits versus costs.

Through an analysis of historical data on accidents weighed by society against economic costs and operating performance he examined the concepts of "traditionally acceptable" or "how safe is safe enough?"

He notes that societal activities fall into two categories—those participated in voluntarily by the individual and those imposed by the society in which the individual lives. Voluntary activities are evaluated by the individual using his own value system. Involuntary activities differ in that the criteria and options are determined by a controlling body, such as a government agency, a leadership group, or "opinion makers."

Starr comments: "In examining the historical benefit-risk relationships for 'involuntary' activities, it is important to recognize the perturbing role of public psychological acceptance of risk arising from the influence of authorities or dogma ... society has generally clothed many of its controlling groups in an almost impenetrable mantle of authority and imputed wisdom. The public generally assumes that the decision-making process is based on a rational analysis of social benefit and social risk. While often it is, we have all seen, after-the-fact, examples of irrationality ..."

Starr's analysis of "How safe is safe" indicates than an initial basis for judicious national decisions on *involuntary* risks associated with our sociotechnical systems may be the following:

1. Rate of death from disease is an upper guide in determining acceptability of risk—somewhat less than 1 to 100 years.
2. National disasters ("Acts of God") tend to set a base guide for risk—somewhat more than 1 in a million years.
3. Societal acceptance of risks increases with the benefit to be derived from an activity (but "benefit" is a movable judgment; thus, the group risk per year from commercial aviation and recreational boating is the same.)
4. The public appears willing to accept voluntary risks roughly 1000 times greater than involuntary exposure risks.

Starr concludes: "Societal policy for the acceptability of public risks associated with sociotechnical systems should be determined by the trade-off between social benefits and personal risks ... the upper bound of such risk is the disease level and the lower bound is several magnitudes below the national disaster level. This provides a trade-off range of one million for societal policy determinations—from an individual risk of one fatal accident in 100 years to one in 100 million years."

He notes that we need much more study of methodology in this area but that we "should not be discouraged by the complexity of this problem—the answers are too important, if ever we want a rational society."

NECESSITY FOR RATIONAL JUDGMENT

The costs of irrationality are tremendous. I have discussed elsewhere this and related matters. [3]

Policy decisions, legislative action, and regulatory measures are politically influenced. Decisions and actions often stem from highly vocal groups who communicate demands to the public official or politician, directly or through various media. Such decisions, made under public pressure, often are reached in an atmosphere of crisis. They may not be scientifically defensible. They also may undesirably and unnecessarily restrict production and distribution of foods, resulting in economic losses that are inevitably reflected in increased cost to the consumer, and prevent future research and development of the application of science.

Unpredictable and often hastily-made restrictions have made it less attractive to invest in development of those pesticides that are highly specific in their action. The volume sales of highly specific pesticides are predictably small and, hence, expected returns to the manufacturers are low. With increasingly extensive demands for safety evaluation and with continued uncertainty about the imposition of restrictive measures, the industry is reluctant to invest in research and development of these useful materials.

The seriousness of interruption of such developmental efforts may be appreciated by some recent information that indicates the average cost of developing a successful pesticide is some $5 million and that it requires about 5 1/2 years to obtain registration and another 3 years for market development. The point at which the company can expect to break even on its investment is estimated to be between 13 and 18 years after the initial discovery. It is evident why companies now are reluctant to invest heavily in the face of such risks and why there is a reduced effort directed to discovery and development of new pesticides. Only the future can tell what the impact of this will be on food production, but the implication is apparent.

Currently, apprehension is being expressed relative to the level of use of nitrates in agriculture. Consideration is being given in several political quarters to the imposition of one or another type of restriction on their use. Without a doubt, more effective and efficient use of nitrates can be devised than is sometimes practiced. Be this as it may, it is appalling to consider the potentially disastrous consequences in terms of food production that could result from unwise restrictive action.

Considered judgments on such crucial matters cannot be reached in an atmosphere of crisis generated by emotionally charged, highly vocal persons who see a problem in limited perspective.

IRRATIONALITY OF SCIENTIST-TURNED-POLITICIAN

Decisions must not be based upon the limited views of one individual laboratory scientist. Decisions must reflect objective, informed, mature understanding of the scope of their effects and must not be forced by public pressure exerted by premature or unwise statements of scientists in the press or on television. It has become increasingly easy for a prominent scientist to undermine the confidence of the public in the safety of its food supply use through statements. To so undermine the confidence of the public is a serious betrayal of the trust that the nation places in its scientists and public health officials. The scientist must act responsibly in relation to issues of public concern.

Evaluation of the desirability of use of various food additives, chemicals or processing techniques demands a specialized background of knowledge and experience without which scientific judgment falls short of what is desirable in the public interest. Public misinformation about food safety is an inevitable consequence of misplaced confidence of scientists in their individual ability and authority to pass opinions on the question of food safety. We as scientists must recognize that, outside our own field or specialized background and knowledge, we too are laymen. We must help, in concert with others of diverse and differing scientific, professional, and public backgrounds, to formulate policy. The individual scientist is unlikely to be so all-wise that he should dictate policy decisions and public positions.

The great French master and teacher, Maurice Arthus, warned that the scientist who publicly adopts a doctrine or dogma based on some arguments of faith accepts or rejects the position for reasons which in most cases are purely personal and are not always exclusively scientific. In accepting such a dogma, he performs an act of faith and, wrote Arthus, ". . . Performing an act of faith . . . involves the entire man, up to and including his conscience; and to persist in one's faith becomes in a sense a question of honor." Arthus notes that having adopted such a public position the protagonist ". . . who is not necessarily a man without scientific merit when he condescends to experiment . . . becomes like the attorney who defends a client in spite of the evidence of his crime, like the politician who exalts his party even for its mistakes and vile actions which he proclaims to be acts of virtue and of courage . . . He . . . automatically sorts the facts newly brought to light. He retains those, even the modest ones that seem to prove him right and neglects the others, even the clearest and most precise and convincing ones if they appear to indict him. Blinded by his passion, that is, by his immoderate love for his theory, he has recourse to all means, honorable or not, in order to defend it, for to him all means have become legitimate. He has ceased to be a scientist and has become a partisan." [4]

"SCIENTIFIC McCARTHYISM"

Had the scholarly Maurice Arthus written today, this distinguished member of the French Academy would certainly have extended his comparison of the partisan to the politician with a warning against the now prevalent tactic of McCarthyism engaged in by some few. By this means, "honorable or not," is being staged an irresponsible effort to impugn the reputation of public servants, scientists, scholarly institutions and societies through innuendoes, through implication that integrity does not exist among one or another group of scientists, and through making deliberately misleading and false statements in Congressional hearings and other situations where a "good press" will be obtained.

Some scientists blame the media for this. I maintain that the primary guilt lies with the scientist-turned-partisan, the theoretician in Arthus' description, who "blinded by his passion . . . by his immoderate love for his theory . . . has recourse to all means, honorable or not, in order to defend it, for to him all means have become legitimate."

Arthus, indeed, also might well have detected the appearance of taints of another political device in the writings and public speeches of some . . . a device resembling the authoritarianism of the Hitler regime. I refer to the pontifical dictates made by scientists outside of their field of competence—relative to many aspects of what should be forbidden or permitted—based upon *their* individual personal bias . . . and made with complete confidence that they possess some superior wisdom because they belong to a chosen, superior, all-knowing segment of the scientific community.

MORE THAN SCIENTIFIC PERSPECTIVE NEEDED

But even a broad, rationally viewed scientific perspective is insufficient to resolve many issues. Scientists alone cannot make decisions and enforce policy. Value judgements seldom if ever are founded upon science and strict logic. They cannot be made solely upon nutritional or, indeed, even, toxicologic considerations. These considerations should enter into formulation of value judgments, but often do not. Value judgments made by individuals or society are composites of attitudes determined by history, by cultural experiences, by religious and ethical influences, by economic forces, and by needs. They vary with social grouping and with time. They determine the personal satisfaction of the individual and condition his way of life. It is only recently that scientific considerations have consciously entered into the making of such judgments.

Accordingly, it is only recently that scientific considerations have entered into formulation of policy and of political decisions. Simultaneously, the nature of forces that influence decisions has dramatically changed because of the immediacy of modern communication media—print, radio, and television.

The complexities of meshing the professional responsibilities of chemists, physicians, food scientists, agriculturalists, industry, economists, consumer spokesmen, politicans, and statesmen, as well as others, are great. They require tolerance, trust, and understanding from all quarters, without which the quality of life open to man through the application of science will not be attained.

SCIENTISTS AND POLITICIANS

It is instructive to consider with C. Kenneth Mees the attitudes and responsibilites of two of these groups, the scientist
and the political leader:
"The cleavage in intellectual outlook and mental habits between the political leader and the scientist, the engineer, or,
for that matter, the industrialist is a very real and fundamental one and is by no means to be dismissed summarily. It
is common for scientists and industrialists to discuss the
methods of the politician as if he were either merely stupid
or deliberately wicked, while the views of the political expert
on the "intellectuals" are often scornful in the extreme.
As long as men's actions are controlled by their emotions, an
objective thinker who discusses every proposition without
emotion can have no part in modern political life, since a
politician must understand the effect of emotional thought
and must be prepared to utilize emotional appeal if he is to
obtain popular support. A successful political leader must
tend, therefore, either to believe his own emotional appeal or
to become a cynic and to some extent a hyprocrite if he
exerts that appeal without belief. It is this difficulty that
makes even the greatest democratic leaders seem insincere in
many of their actions. The appeal to emotion is unavoidable
if popular sanction is to be obtained, and yet their critics and
often they themselves in retrospect feel that appeal to be
false and unwarranted. For this reason alone the political
arena would seem to be unsuitable for the scientific man, and
those who believe most fully in the value of the scientific
spirit should be prepared to understand and sympathize with
leaders who must obtain general popular approval for their
action." [5]

MUTUAL UNDERSTANDING ESSENTIAL

Again, I assert that mutual understanding and respect by all
groups is essential if we are to attain that goal of science
expressed by Francis Bacon who wrote in his organum novum

". . . the real and legitimate goal of the sciences is the endowment of human life with new inventions and riches."

If the scientist today truly is concerned with unfulfilled social and economic needs and if he is to deserve continued support of society, particularly that public support made available by the politician, he must act to restore the confidence of the public and of the political leader in the scientist and in his science by maintaining the objectivity and competence that commands respect.

National leaders, both political and industrial, must espouse sound and truthful positions on issues of great public concern, and these positions must be soundly founded upon the best scientific judgment obtainable. These leaders must not continue to react in haste and fear in such manner as to give the appearance of having a sense of guilt, an appearance that is not infrequently the image, albeit unjustified, in public actions pertaining to chemicals in foods, pesticides and related environmental matters within recent years.

Responsible public officials must discriminate between the voices to whom they listen and react. They must discriminate emotion from logic, bias from objectivity, self-seekers from public spirited persons, and areas of competence and incompetence of their expert advisors. Authority carries with it responsibility for such judgments and the silent public must be protected from the risks inflicted through denying a proper weighing and application of risk versus benefit.

It would be trite to repeat that it is necessary to have a responsibly informed public so that policy decisions are not influenced by ignorance or bias. I seriously raise for consideration whether it is possible to develop a public sufficiently well informed on details of science to make many of the decisions with which we are faced today.

EXAMINE DECISION-MAKING PROCESS

Do we need to examine critically our decision-making process and perhaps devise a new mechanism that will permit such decisions on policy to be formulated in a balanced perspective?

The use of scientific panels and committees in advisory capacity is commonplace. Is there not a role for a tribunal of humanists, philosophers, social scientists, political scientists, and others who become experienced and knowledgeable relative to public issues pertaining to science through working in parallel with conventional biological and physical scientists? Could such scientific and non-scientific groups working in concert evolve more rational policy and regulatory decisions concerning complex matters of health and quality of life? Would such combined groups have a public credibility that would restore the confidence of the public in the correctness of decisions arrived at by their leaders? Would it assure that those dimensions beyond the ken of science, recently termed trans-science, are more properly in perspective?

I cannot answer the question concerning the effectiveness of some such new decision-making process. The concept is intriguing, however, and I propose a serious and full consideration of it.

References

1. Perspectives on Benefit-Risk Decision-Making, Collquium of the Committee on Public Engineering Policy. 1971, pp 3-4, 17-42.
2. Belloc H: The Microbe, in *Cautionary Tales for Children*. New York, Alfred A Knopf Inc., 1941.
3. Darby WJ: Food, Nutrition, and Science. Read as the Kenneth A Spencer Award Lecture, before the Kansas City Section of the American Chemical Society, Feb. 24, 1972.
4. Arthus, M: *Philosophy of Scientific Investigation*. Henry Sigerist (trans), Baltimore, The John Hopkins Press, 1943.
5. Mees CK: *The Path of Science*. New York, John Wiley and Sons, 1946.

Natural Toxicants of Geologic Origin and Their Availability to Man*

HELEN L. CANNON

Legislation to control toxic metals in the environment is being enacted in many areas without the necessary background information that is essential before tolerance limits for contamination can be set and without sufficient regard to the *availability* to man of the metals in the environment. The information presented here is intended to show the range of concentrations that can be expected in the natural environment; a discussion of those concentrations contributed by man's activity has been purposely omitted.

The relationship between the areal distribution of geologic formations and the concentrations of metals in ground water is commonly clean-cut; so, to a lesser extent, is the relationship between the metal contents of soils and plants. A correlation between rocks and disease, however, is not as readily observable, although disease patterns commonly suggest a close correlation with some geologic or geographic attribute of the environment. The total metal content is not as important as the availability of the metals, which is affected by many factors including the conditions under which the rocks are weathered, the climate, the acidity, and the mode of eventual concentration.

The normal levels of toxic metals in unmineralized and uncontaminated areas are discussed in this paper along with some information on the anomalous amounts of metal that may be found in certain geologic environments. Such data for any particular area must be considered before the effects of man-made contamination can be predicted or assessed.

Selenium—Selenium is known to have a marked effect on animals at both toxic and deficient levels and is potentially

---

* Official government material, U.S. Department of Interior. This chapter may be reproduced in part or full.

143

dangerous to man. The normal or average content of selenium in rocks, soils, water, and plants is shown in Table I. The selenium content in igneous rocks, sandstone, and limestone is generally low, but may be enriched in shales that contain volcanic ash layers. Seleniferous shales of anomalous content may extend for several hundred miles; beds containing as much as 675 ppm selenium have been reported by Lakin.[5] On the Colorado Plateau, selenium, along with vanadium and uranium, is concentrated in ore deposits in permeable sandstone beds. The selenium—rich parts of sandstones are, thus, restricted to the relatively small areas that are mineralized. Selenium also occurs in phosphate rocks and in phosphate fertilizer made from these rocks, but the extent of soil enrichment through the use of such fertilizers is not known.[6]

The selenium content may approach toxic levels in waters that are derived from wells drilled through seleniferous shales that contain soluble selenium. Domestic-use water is not usually analyzed for selenium. Recent spot-check analysis by the U.S. Geological Survey revealed seleniferous water on some farms near Denver and as much as 0.21 mg/l selenium in water on a South Dakota Indian Reservation.[7] The presence of selenium in excess of 0.01 mg/l constitutes cause for rejection of the water for use. These findings have been reported to medical authorities. Analysis for selenium should be run on any domestic water that is analyzed for major constitutents for seleniferous areas of the west.

In geochemical behavior selenium resembles sulfur, and is volatile. Selenium and sulfur compounds are emitted as gases during the natural phenomenon of volcanism and during the smelting of sulfide ores and the burning of coal. In soils, selenium generally occurs as relatively unavailable elemental selenium or as ferric selenite, but may occur as the selenate ion in soils that contain oxidizing sulfides. Only where the water-soluble selenate ion occurs in soils can plants take up substantial amounts of selenium. Thus, western Cretaceous shales of relatively low selenium content produce toxic vegetation; yet soils of higher selenium content in Puerto Rico and Hawaii, where the selenium occurs as selenite bound to ferric oxide[5] do not produce toxic vegetation. Selenium may also be complexed by organic matter in peat soils[8], like those in Ireland reported to contain 850 ppm and to produce toxic vegetation.

The predictable uptake of selenium by plants is complicated by a great difference in uptake by various species under different soil conditions. Certain species of *Astragalus,* for instance, utilize selenium in an amino acid peculiar to the species and may absorb many times as much selenium as do other plants growing in the same soil.[9] *Astragalus bisulcatus* (Figure 1) which grows on the Cretaceous shales of Wyoming and neighboring States has been found to contain as much as 10,239 ppm selenium in the dry weight. [10] A content of 8,512 ppm selenium was measured in *Astragalus pattersoni* (Figure 2), which is used as an indicator of uranium deposits on the Colorado Plateau where the two elements occur together. These plants are very toxic to sheep. Although areas of toxic vegetation are generally rather small, they do occur in 15 states of the United States, 3

Table I—Selenium in the Natural Environment (Values in parts per million)

Material	Average content	Range		References
Igneous rock	0.05	—		1
Shale	.60	—		1
Sandstone	.05	—		1
Limestone	.08	—		1
Coal (ash)	3.3	0.46	-10.6	2
Phosphate rock	18.0	—		3
Soils	.1 -2.0	<.04	-1200	3, 4
Surface water	.0002	.0001-	.4	5
Forage grasses	.26	<.01	- 9.0	*
Forage legumes	.2	.075	- .7	*
Vegetables and fruits	.05	.01	- .20	*

*Cannon, HL: Unpublished data.

Figure 1.–Photograph of *Astragalus bisulcatus,* a selenium accumulator plant.

provinces of Canada, and 15 other countries.[5] Subchronic poisoning, in which the animals are weakened and have an increased susceptibility to disease, has been recognized in seleniferous areas of South Africa.[11] Chronic selenium poisoning form seleniferous vegetation occurs in many parts of the world. There is also evidence of industrial contamination in urban areas; for example, in Tokyo local soil contents of selenium may be increasing to near-toxic levels from the burning of coal and oil.[12]

The opposing extreme is shown in figure 3—large rural areas in the eastern and far western parts of the United States are deficient in selenium; this deficiency is now known to cause white muscle disease in livestock. The use of selenium-bearing phosphate fertilizer and of additives in feed has been advised as treatment for the condition. It should be pointed out that the most industrialized parts of our country are in areas of de-

Figure 2.—Photograph of *Astragalus pattersoni*, a selenium accumulator plant.

ficiency and so increments of selenium from power plants and other sources of atmospheric selenium in these areas may not be harmful.

Arsenic—The average and normal range of arsenic is natural materials is given in Table II. Arsenic is commonly concentrated in clays and organic matter. Available arsenic is high in water and soils associated with rocks that contain oxidizing arsenopyrite (FeAsS), and in weathered volcanic rocks. The arsenic content of water is normally 0.01 ppm. In Lane County. Oregon, as much as 1.7 ppm was found in well water from the volcanic Fisher Formation (Figure 4); several cases of poisoning have been reported from this area. [17] Illness and one fatality in a Canadian farm have been reported in a Canadian farm family whose drinking water contained 0.4-10 ppm As_2O_3 [18] and came from a deep well located about 16 km (10 miles) from extensive layers of arsenopyrite.

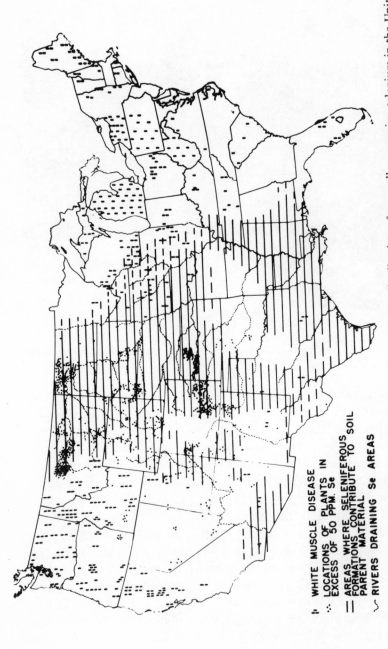

Figure 3.—Map showing relationship of white muscle disease to the distribution of naturally occurring selenium in the United States.

Similar reports of arsenicism have come from Antofagasta, Chile, where the population has for 12 years been drinking water containing 0.8 ppm of natural arsenic [19] —16 times rejection limitations by U.S. Public Health Service (1962). Although arsenopyrite is a common mineral in many mining areas, little attention has been paid to the possibility of arsenic toxicity from vegetation rooted in mineralized ground. In Wyoming, the Atlantic City district, where gold occurs with arsenopyrite, sage was observed by the U.S. Geological Survey to contain 60 ppm arsenic in the dry weight, and a water plant, *Ranunculus aqua-*

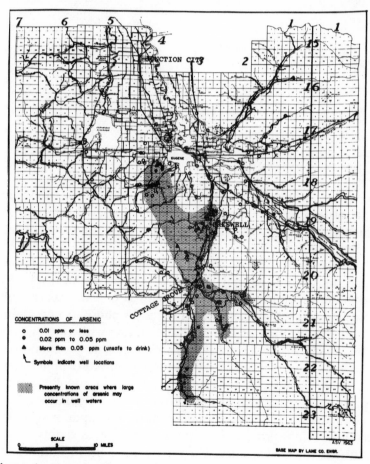

Figure 4.—Map showing arsenic content of well waters in central Lane County, Oregon. [13]

Table II—Arsenic in the Natural Environment. (Values in parts per million)

Material	Average content	Range		References
Igneous rock	2.0	0.2 -	13.8	14
Shale	13	.3 -	900	14
Sandstone	7.0	.6 -	9.7	14
Limestone	1.7	.1 -	8.1	14
Coal (ash)	86	.0 -	700	15
Soils	4.0	1.0 -	>8,000	4,*
Surface water	<.01	<.001-	1.7	16, 17
Forage grasses	.3	.1 -	.62	*
Forage legumes	5.4	.1 -	14	*
Vegetables and fruits	1.0	.07 -	10	*

* Cannon, HL: unpublished data.

tilis, growing in a stream used as a watering place for sheep, contained 180 ppm arsenic. The hazard to stock is greater from legumes than from grasses in which arsenic remains concentrated in the root. [20]

Cadmium—The normal concentrations and range of cadmium found in various natural materials are shown in Table III. Cadmium accompanies zinc geochemically and occurs commonly as a minor element in zinc ores, in phosphorites, and in the organic fraction of shales. It also occurs with zinc in some peats which are under cultivation for vegetable production. [23]

Natural waters normally contain less than 0.001 ppm cadmium. C M Tschanz [24] has reported springs in the Berenguela district of Bolivia which contain as much as 0.58 ppm cadmium, as compared to public health standards of 0.01 ppm. A school is currently using spring water from this district to supply drinking water; the analysis have been reported to health authorities. More than 0.01 ppm cadmium was found [16] in 42 out of 727

Table III—Cadmium in the Natural Environment. (Values in parts per million)

Material	Average content	Range	References
Igneous rock	0.2	0.003- 0.6	21
Shale	1.4	.0 - 11	21
Sandstone	.03	—	1
Limestone	.10	—	1
Phosphate rock	30.0	.0 -170	3
Coal (ash)	.5	.5 - 10.0	15, 22
Soils	.3	.1 - .5	21
Surface water	.001	.001- .58	16
Forage grasses	1.88	.45- 2.4	*
Forage legumes	.04	.04 - .05	*
Vegetables and fruits	.10	.01 - .96	*

*Cannon, HL: unpublished data.

samples of surface water in the United States, but probably most of these cadmium-enriched water samples result from industrial contamination. In an area in Japan where mine water containing as much as 0.225 ppm cadmium was used to irrigate the rice fields, cadmium levels in the soils were as much as 22 ppm and in the ash of rice roots as much as 374 ppm. These high levels were responsible for the development of Itai-Itai disease in the local inhabitants. [25]

Plants absorb cadmium, the amount varying widely between species and between parts of a single plant. As tests for cadmium are relatively new, there are not many analysis available for plants absorbing cadmium from natural materials. Available analysis suggest that the greatest uptake is in vegetation growing in mineralized areas, particularly in areas contaminated by zinc smelters.

Because medically oriented scientists believe that the zinc-cadmium ration may be of greater importance than the actual cadmium levels in the environment, a discussion of the changes in the ratios in an Idaho zinc-mining district may be relevant.[26] Cadmium is more mobile than zinc at high temperatures and it therefore occurs in low concentration in the monzonite (heat source), but forms a wide halo around the monzonite (Figure 5). This halo produces a low zinc-cadmium ratio (50:1 to 99:1) in the soil over a considerable area.[27] Within a radius of 5 miles of a zinc smelter the ratio may be even lower, as the extraction of zinc produces a cadmium-rich effluent. The actual cadmium concentrations are shown in Figure 6; this cadmium is readily available to the vegetation.

Cadmium and lead contents of vegetation collected by the U.S. Geological Survey in a southwest Missouri mining district are shown in Table IV. Similar contents have been found in vegetation near smelters. The ratio of these metals in plants to that in soils suggests that cadmium is more available to plants than lead and is accumulated in considerable amounts by certain species.

Lead—The average concentration of lead in various types of materials is given in Table V. Lead content is higher in organic shales and coal than in other types of rock. It is also concentrated with zinc and cadmium in ore deposits. Because lead is only sparingly soluble at the pH of average domestic drinking water, it is rarely present in detectable amounts. Lead is not particularly available to plants under normal conditions, ranging only from not detected to 18 ppm in 150 background samples, but is absorbed in large amounts by certain accumulator plants that are tolerant of mineralized ground (Table VI). The lead in plants have been shown [34] to become enclosed and immobilized in the cell wall. This enables plants to absorb lead from soils in mineral districts without ill effects. The highest concentration of lead recorded in a living plant is 6,600 ppm lead (dry weight basis) in algae growing in a stream draining a mineralized area in New Hampshire. The most common edible wild plants in mineral districts in the United States are raspberries and blueberries, which are particularly common around lead-zinc mines. Blueberries (*Vaccinium*) collected from tailings of an abandoned

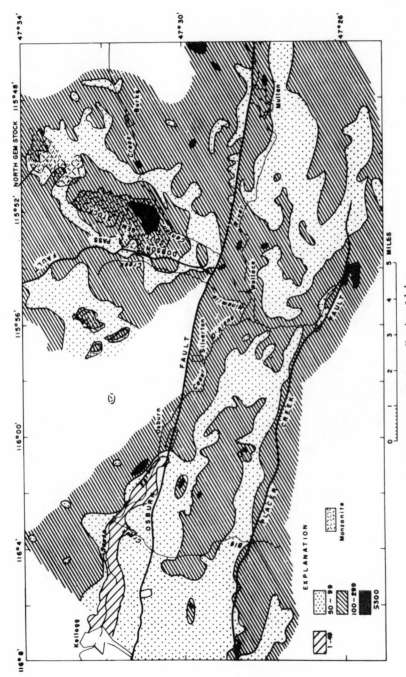

Figure 5.—Zinc-cadmium ratio in soils of the Coeur d'Alene district, Idaho.

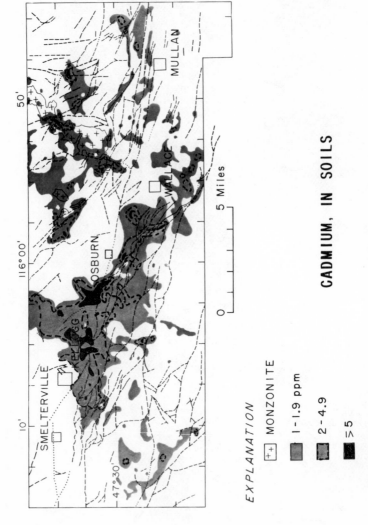

Figure 6.—Cadmium in soils of the Coeur d'Alene district, Idaho.

Table IV—Cadmium and lead in vegetation and soil of Southwest Missouri mining district. (Data in parts per million, dry weight.)

| | Poplar on old mine dumps | | Birch on mineralized ground | |
	Cd	Pb	Cd	Pb
Leaves	40	11	18	22
Twigs	45	45	14	175
Wood	22	17	6.5	14
Bark	37	24	21	73
Soil	18	5000	160	2000

Reference 23

Table V—Lead in the natural environment. (Values in parts per million except as noted. ND, not detected)

Material	Average content	Range	References
Igneous rock	15.0	2 - 30	21
Shale	20.0	16 - 50	21
Sandstone	7.0	<1 - 31	21
Limestone	9.0	—	1
Coal (ash)	62.0	1.0-2000	15
Soils	20.0	10 - 50	**
Municipal water	.0037	ND- .062	29
Forage grasses	1.7	<0.8- 4.0	**
Forage legumes	2.5	ND- 3.6	**
Vegetables and fruits	1.5	<1.5-18.0	**
Air (natural sources)	*.0005	—	30

* In $\mu g/m^3$

**Cannon, HL: unpublished data

mine at Warren, New Hampshire, contained 81 ppm lead (dry weight basis). Lead concentrations in or on plants are raised considerably by air contamination from smelters, along roadsides, and by various types of industrial pollution.

Even in uncontaminated areas, washed forage, green vegetables, and unpeeled fruits contain considerably more lead than peeled vegetables, which appear to be consistently low in lead content. The effect of peeling would be marked in an area of air contamination.

Asbestos—This fibrous type of ultrabasic rock, occurring in several mineralogical forms, is an example of a toxic substance that affects man directly by being inhaled into the lungs. Of particular interest medically is crocidolite, even though the percentage of crocidolite used by the domestic industry is less than 2% of the total asbestos consumption. Crocidolite has been found to contain an amino acid [35] that produces a particular kind of cancer in individuals who mine it or work with a product containing it. [36] It is imported from Africa and Australia and mixed with other kinds of asbestos in the manufacture of fiberboard by several companies on the east coast.

Mercury—The abundance of mercury is shown in Table VII. Mercury content is high in organic shales and was also found to occur in amounts of 0.09 to 2.7 ppm in 83 samples of uraniferous phosphatic strata in Wyoming. [43],[44] It occurs in greater concentrations than normal in mercury ores and also as a companion element in gold, molybdenum, and base-metal ores. [38] During hydrothermal deposition, mercury and its sulfides, in the gaseous state, may penetrate the rock surrounding mineral deposits and produce halos extending hundreds of meters or even a few thousand meters beyond the deposits. [45] This mercury in the rock is given off into the atmosphere by direct volatilization. Initial tests show that mercury levels may be high for a hundred meters (several hundred feet) or more above ore deposits and may measure as much as 20 times the established background of 4.5 ng/m^3 at an altitude of 60 meters (200 feet). An airborne mercury detector has been developed by the Geological Survey [42] for use in prospecting for sulfide ore deposits (Figure 7). The amounts released into the air are affected by temperature and pressure. Mercury is particularly abundant in

Table VI—Lead content of some lead accumulator plants. (Values in parts per million)

Species	Part of plant	Locality	Maximum reported in			References
			ash	dry wt	Soil	
Pseudotsuga taxifolia	tips	Coeur d'Alene, Idaho	–	130	20,000	31
Larix occidentalis	tips	Coeur d'Alene, Idaho	–	100	20,000	31
Equisetum arvense	Above-ground.	Warren, N. H.	420	140	–	32
Vaccinium candense	fruit	Warren, N. H.	238	81	21,000	32
Populus sp.	twigs	Missouri	400	45	5,000	23
Betula lutea	twigs	Joplin, Mo.	4,600	175	2,000	23
Gomphrena canescens	flowers	Australia	–	114	5,000	*
Molina altissima	above ground.	Innerstetal, Germany	35,600	–	–	33

*Written communication by H E King.

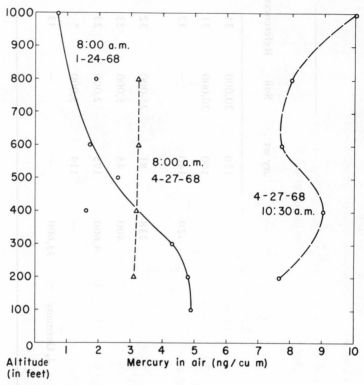

Figure 7.—Mercury in air as a function of altitude.

volcanic gases and is released in quantity from mudflows during volcanic eruptions. But much remains to be learned about this element.

The median content of mercury in municipal water is probably 0.001 and the maximum is 0.0043 ppm.[16] A significant amount of the mercury in stream water occurs in the particulate fraction. Industrial waste water may contain more than 10 ppm mercury.[37]

Collections of soil throughout the United States show an average of 0.083 ppm in western United States and 0.147 ppm in eastern United States.[46] A recent study of the distribution of mercury in soils, stream sediment, vegetation, and water in northern New Mexico shows no significant concentration nor discernible pattern of distribution of mercury that can be attributed to the burning of large tonnages of coal at the Four

Table VII—Mercury in the natural environment. (Values in parts per million, except as noted)

Material	Average content	Range			References
Igneous rock	0.055	0.002	-	0.5	20
Shale	.16	.005	-	1.0	20
Organic-rich shale	.5	.03	-	2.8	20
Sandstone	.05	.001	-	.3	20
Limestone	.04	.01	-	.22	20
Coal	.03	.05	-	13.3	20
Soils	.05	.001	-	.5	20
Surface water (dissolved)	.00001	.00001-		.0043	17, 37
Forage grasses	.025	.025	-	.40	38, 39, 40**
Vegetables and fruits	.025	.01	-	.04	38, 39, 40**
Air (200 ft. above ground).*	4.5	.6		-23,000	41, 42, 43

*In ng/m^3
**Cannon, HL and Swanson, VE: unpublished data.

Corners Power Plant; most of the soils contained 0.07 ppm mercury and all vegetation sampled contained 0.25 ppm[†]. Small increments of mercury are being added to the soils and oceans daily, that until recently were presumed to be harmless since mercury precipitates rapidly. But it is now evident that some of this contribution is converted to methyl mercury, probably through bacterial action under anaerobic conditions[47], and hence is available to microorganisms and finally to the fish and shellfish. A large proportion of the mercury being added to the environment is, thus, from natural sources.

[†]Cannon, HL and Swanson, VE: unpublished data

Table VIII—Nickel in the natural environment. (Values in parts per million; ND, not detected)

Material	Average content	Range		References
Acid igneous rock	4.5	—		1
Ultrabasic igneous rock	2000	—		48
Shale	71	—		48
Sandstone	1	—		48
Limestone	27	—		48
Coal (ash)	200	1 -2000		15
Soils	14	<5 - 700		49
Municipal water supply	<.0027	ND-	.034	28
Forage grasses	3.4	<.2- 23		*
Forage legumes	1.9	<.4- 23		*
Vegetables and fruits	.6	<.04- 6		*

Accumulator plants: *Alyssum bertolonii*, 100,000 ppm NiO in ash[50], *Vellozia*, 270 ppm; Stipa capillata, 6,400 ppm[51].

*Cannon, HL: unpublished data.

Nickel—The content of nickel varies greatly in different rock types (Table VIII). Sandstone contains only 1 ppm and perido-tite or serpentine (ultrabasic igneous rocks) averages 2,000 ppm. Moreover, serpentine rocks also contain very high chromium, and high magnesium and iron, but low calcium; so the growth of plants thereon is seriously affected. These rocks have unusual endemic floras of only a few species; plants that can tolerate these soils commonly absorb large amounts of nickel. The ash of leaves of endemic *Alyssum bertolonii* has been reported to contain 10% NiO from serpentines in Italy. Fortunately, on a worldwide level, serpentine, the silica, iron, and magnesium have been leached by ground water, leaving a nickel-rich residue that is actually mined as ore. The nickel is concentrated at or slightly above the interface of the fresh and weathered source rock and is mined in shallow open pits. Plants growing in lateritic soil absorb large amounts of nickel. Studies by the U.S. Bureau of Mines[52] have also shown that, geographically, the nickel content of coal varies significantly. The nickel content of western coals averages 262 ppm in the ash and that of eastern coals only 55 ppm. Nickel is rarely detected in ground water because the nickel is associated with insoluble hydrolyzate minerals. A median value of 2.7 ng/l and a maximum of 34 ng/l in municipal water supplies has been reported[29]; the high values probably reflect industrial pollution.

In conclusion, we must bear in mind that many of our toxic metals, and perhaps we will discover eventually, that all of our toxic metals, are essential in small amounts and that large areas of deficiency for each or many metals may exist throughout the world. In these areas, contamination from industry or the fortification of foods may be beneficial to animals and man; in areas of natural excess, contamination or the abnormal accumulation of metal by certain species may increase the possibility of toxicity. Let us first establish the background levels of metals that occur in various segments of the environment and then strive to achieve the proper balance in order to improve the health of both stock and mankind.

References

1. Turekian, KK and Wedepohl, HH: Distribution of the Elements in Some Major Units of the Earth's Crust, Geological Society America Bulletin 72 (2):175-192, 1961.
2. Pillay, KKS; Thomas, CC; and Kaminski, JW: Neutron Activation Analysis of the Selenium Content of Fossil Fuels, *Nuclear Applications and Technology* 7:478-483, 1969.
3. Gulbrandsen, RA: Chemical Composition of Phosphorites of the Phosphoria Formation, *Geochim et Cosmochim Acta*, 20:769-778, 1966.
4. Swaine, DJ: Trace-Element Content of Soils, in *Commonwealth Agri Bur Soil Sciences Tech Commun* No.48, Harpenden, England, 1955.
5. Lakin, HW: Selenium Accumulation in Soils and Its Absorption by Plants and Animals, in Cannon, HL and Hopps, HC (eds.), *Geochemical Environment in Relation to Health and Disease*, Spec Paper 140, Geological Society America, 1972, pp. 45-54.
6. Selenium in Nutrition, National Academy of Sciences, Subcommittee on Selenium, 1971.
7. U S Public Health Service, Drinking Water Standards, 1972 Publ 965, U S Public Health Service, 1962.

8. Fleming, GA: Selenium in Irish Soils and Plants, *Soil Science* **94** (1):28-35, 1962.

9. Shrift, Alex: Aspects of Selenium Metabolism in Higher Plants, *Ann Rev Plant Physiology* **20**:475-494, 1969.

10. Trelease, SF and Beath, OA: *Selenium—Its Geologic Occurrence and Its Biological Effects in Relation to Botany, Chemistry, Agriculture, Nutrition and Medicine,* N Y, pub by authors, Box 42, Schermerhorn Hall, Columbia Univ, 1949.

11. Brown, JMM and de Wet, PJ: A Preliminary Report on the Occurence of Selenosis in South Africa and Its Possible Role in the Aetiology of Tribulosis, Enzootic Icterus and Some Other Disease Conditions Encountered in the Karroo Areas, *Onderstepoort J Veterinary Research* **29**(1):111-135, 1962.

12. Hashimoto, Yoshikazu, Hwang, JY and Yanagisawa, Saburo: Possible Sources of Atmospheric Pollution of Selenium, *Environmental Sci and Tech* **4(2)**:157-158, 1970.

13. Muth, OH and Allaway, WH: The Relationship of White Muscle Disease to the Distribution of Naturally Occurring Selenium, *J Amer Veterinary Medical Assoc* **142(12)**:1379-1384, 1963.

14. Onishi, H: Arsenic, in Wedepohl, HH, (ed.), *Handbook of Geochemistry,* Berlin-New York, Springer Verlag, vol II-1, 1969.

15. Peterson, MJ and Zink, JB: A semiquantitative Spectrochemical Method for Analysis of Coal Ash, Report of Investigation No 6496, pp 8-10, U S Bureau of Mines, 1964.

16. Durum, WH, Hem, JD, and Heidel, SG: Reconnaissance of Selected Minor Elements in Surface Waters of the United States, October 1970, Circular 643, U S Geological Survey, 1971.

17. Goldblatt, EL; Van Denburgh, AS; and Marsland, RA: The Unusual and Widespread Occurrence of Arsenic in Well Waters of Lane County, Oregon, Eugene, Oregon, Lane County (Oregon) Health Dept, (Open-filed by U S Geological Survey), 1963.

18. Wyllie, J: An Investigation of the Source of Arsenic in Well Water, *Canadian Public Health J* **28**:128-135.

19. Borgono, JM and Greiber, Rosa: Epidemiological Study of Arsenicism in the City of Antofagasta, in Hemphill, DD (ed.), *Trace Substances in Environmental Health—V,* University of Missouri, 1971, pp 13-24.

20. Jones, JS and Hatch, MB: Residues and Crop Assimilation of Arsenic and Lead, *Soil Science* **60**:277-288, 1945.

21. Fleischer, M: Natural Sources of Some Trace Elements in the Environment, in *Cycling and Control of Metals: Proceedings Environmental Resources Conference,* 1972, Cincinnati, Ohio, Natl Environmental Research Center, 1973.

22. Swanson, VE, (compiler): Compostion and Trace-Element Content of Coal and Power Plant Ash, pt 2 in *App J of Southwest Energy* Study (U S Dept Interior, Report of Coal Resources Work Group) 1972.

23. Cannon, HL and Anderson, BM: The Geochemist's Involvement with

the Pollution Problem, in Cannon, HL and Hopps, HC, (eds.), *Environmental Geochemistry in Health and Disease,* memo No. 123, Geol Soc America, 1971, pp 155-177.

24. Tschanz, CM: U S Geology Survey, (written communication), 1970.

25. Kobayashi, J: Relation Between the "Itai-Itai" Disease and the Pollution of River Water by Cadmium from a Mine, *5th International Water Pollution Research Conference (San Francisco) Proceedings,* Pergamon Press, pp 1-25/1-1-25/7, 1971.

26. Gott, GB and Botbol, JM: Zoning of Major and Minor Metals in the Coeur d'Alene Mining District, Idaho, U S A in Jones, MJ (ed.), *Geochemical Exploration 1972,* London, Institute Mining and Metallurgy, 1973, pp 1-12.

27. Gott, GB: U S Geological Survey, (oral Communication), 1972.

28. Gott, GB et al: Geochemical Abundance and Distribution of Nine Metals in the Coeur d'Alene District, Shoshone County, Idaho, U S Geological Survey Open-File Report, 1969.

29. Durfor, CN and Becker, E: Public Water Supplies of the 100 Largest Cities in the United States, 1962, U S Geol Survey Water-Supply Paper No. 1812, 1964.

30. Patterson, CC:Contaminated and Natural Lead Environments of Man, *Arch Envir Health* 11:344-360, 1965.

31. Kennedy, VC: Geochemical Studies in the Coeur d'Alene District, Shoshone County, Idaho, with a section on Geology by Hobbs, SW, Bulletin 1098-A, U S Geological Survey, 1961.

32. Cannon HL; Shacklette, HT; and Bastron, Harry: Metal Absorption by *Equisetum* (horsetail), Bulletin 1278-A, U S Geology Survey, 1968, pp A1-A21.

33. Thyssen, Stephen von: Geochemische unnd Pflanzen Biologische Zusammenhange in Lichte der Angewandten Geophysik*Beitr angew Geophysik* 10:35-84, 1942.

34. Miller, RJ: The University of Illinois, (oral Communication), 1973.

35. Harrington, JS: Natural Occurrences of Amino-Acids in Virgin Crocidolite Asbestos and Banded Ironstones, *Science* 138:521-522, 1962.

36. Hardy, HL: Asbestos-Related Disease, *Amer J Medical Sciences* 250(4):381-389, 1965.

37. Jenne, EA: Mercury in Waters of the United States, U S Geological Survey Water Resources Division Open-File Report, 1972.

38. Warren, HV and Delavault, RE: Mercury Content of Some British Soils, Oikos (Copenhagen) 20(2):537-539, 1969.

39. Warren, HV; Delavault, RE; and Barakso, John: Some Observations on the Geochemistry of Mercury as Applied to Prospecting, *Econ Geology* 61(6):1010-1028, 1966.

40. Wallace, RA et al: Mercury in the Environment—The Human Element, Oak Ridge National Laboratory-National Science Foundation Report ORNL NSF-EP-1, 1971.

41. Williston, SH: Mercury in the Atmosphere, *Geophys Research* 73(22): 7051-7055, 1968.
42. McCarthy, JH Jr; Vaughn, WW; Learned, RE; and Meuschke, JL: Mercury in Soil Gas and Air—A Potential Tool in Mineral Exploration, Circular 609, U S Geological Survey, 1969.
43. Eshlemann, A; Siegel, SM; and Siegel, BZ: Is Mercury from Hawaiian Volcanoes a Natural Source of Pollution?, *Nature* 233:471-472, 1971.
44. Love, JD: U S Geology Survey, (written Communication), 1971.
45. Saukov, AA: "Geochemistry of Mercury" (In Russian), *Akad Nauk SSSR, Inst Geol Nauk* 78:Mineral-Geokhim, ser. no. 17, 1946, p 129.
46. Shacklette, HT; Boerngen, JG; and Turner, RL: Mercury in the Environment—Surficial Materials of the Conterminous United States, Circular 644, U S Geological Survey, 1971a.
47. Wood, JM; Kennedy, FS; and Rosen, CG: Synthesis of Methyl-Mercury Compounds by Extracts of A Methanogenic Bacterium, *Nature* 220:173-174, 1968.
48. Turekian, KK and Carr, MH: The Geochemistries of Chromium, Cobalt, and Nickel, in Part I, Proceedings of Section 1, *Geochemical Cycles,* Copenhagen, 21st International Geological Congress, p 14-26, 1960.
49. Shacklette, HT et al: Elemental Composition of Surficial Materials in the Conterminous United States, Prof. Paper 547-D, U S Geological Survey, 1971b.
50. Minguzzi, C and Vergnano, O: The Content of Nickel in the Ash of *Alyssum bertolonii* Desv (In Italian), *Soc Toscana Science Naturali Atti Mem* 55:1-58, 1948.
51. Malyuga, DP: On Soils and Plants as Prospecting Indicators for Metals (In Russian), *Izv Akad Nauk SSSR Ser Geol* 3:135-138, 1947.
52. Abernathy, RF; Peterson, MJ; and Gibson, FH: Spectrochemical Analysis of Coal Ash for Trace Elements, Report of Investigation No 7281, U S Bureau of Mines, 1969.

Naturally Occurring Toxicants in Foods

J. M. COON, Ph.D.

Toxic substances present naturally in foods include the normal genetically determined components of foods (among these are goitrogens, estrogens, solanine alkaloids, oxalates, cyanogenetic glycosides) and also contaminants from natural sources. This second group of naturally occurring toxicants may be of microbiological origin, as staphylococcal enterotoxin, botulinum toxin, seafood toxins, mycotoxins; or they may be of nonmicrobiological origin transmitted through natural feed of food animals, for example, or in uptake from soil and water. It is recognized that the contamination may be frequently aided and abetted by man's activities, carelessness, or ignorance, as in the case of the bacterial toxins, nitrates in soil, and mercury in water.

The natural components of foods of man constitute the major part of his chemical environment. They contribute both the greatest amount and the widest variety of chemical substances consumed by man during his lifetime. No single food from a plant source has been characterized chemically as well as the air we breath and the water we drink, even when these are polluted. The potato, usually thought of as a relatively simple food, is a complex chemical mixture. About 150 distinct chemical substances have been identified in this natural product; among them are the solanine alkaloids, oxalic acid, arsenic, tannins, nitrate, and over a hundred other items of no nutritional significance to man.[1] All vegetables and fruits and other natural food products are similarly complex. Although many chemical components of natural food products have been identified it is likely that a larger number have not.

TOXICITY vs HAZARD

Relatively few of the specific chemical substances that are naturally present in our foods have been evaluated toxicologically. Furthermore, if almost any one of these many chemical substances were tested in laboratory animals by today's standards of safety evaluation, it would be shown to have some toxic property. Thus, in the natural foods of our daily diet there are thousands of toxic substances. This does not imply, however, that a hazard exists in this situation. The "toxicity" of a substance is its intrinsic capacity to produce injury when tested by itself. The "hazard" of a substance is its capacity to produce injury under the circumstances of exposure. In connection with the safety of natural food products, our concern is not directly with the intrinsic toxicity of their chemical components, but rather with the potential hazards of these materials when the foods in which they are present are eaten. For example, arsenic, lead, mercury, and fluorine have high intrinsic toxicities, but no hazard is associated with their natural presence in foods. Oxalate is toxic, but its presence in spinach is not considered a hazard.

In spite of the many toxic substances naturally present in foods there is little evident hazard involved in the normal diet as consumed by normal healthy individuals. There are several explanations for this.

First, concentrations of most of the toxic substances in commonly accepted foods are so low that consumption of a grossly exaggerated quantity of a food - usually over a long period of time - is required before the toxicity of any single substance becomes a hazard. Such a situation has resulted, for example, from the goitrogenic substances in the turnip, rutabaga and possibly cabbage when these foods have constituted a large proportion of the diet for a long time,[2] or from lycopene following the daily consumption of a half gallon of tomato juice for several years.[3] If one's diet contains a reasonable diversity of foods and no extraordinary amount of any specific food, then no single chemical is likely to be consumed in a toxic amount.

Second, the toxicities of the thousands of different chemicals present in our diet each day are not usually additive. If they were it could be speculated that a single day's normal menu would not be tolerated without adverse effects. The human body can readily tolerate small amounts of many different chemicals taken simultaneously, even though each one of them might be harmful in a somewhat larger amount.

Third, there are many antagonistic interactions between chemical components of the diet. This appears to be an important aspect of the balance of nature. Thus, the toxicity of one element may be offset by an adequate amount of another,[4] or of one amino acid by the presence of another amino acid.[5] Iodine inhibits the action of some goitrogens. Many other antagonistic interactions among chemicals, including pesticides and drugs, and even some carcinogens, are known.

SAFETY IN NUMBERS

The frequency of these antagonisms supports the concept of safety in numbers as applied to the chemical components of the diet. The wider the variety of food intake, the greater will be the number of different chemical substances consumed, and the less will be the chance that any one chemical will reach a hazardous level in the diet. This principle applies also to food additives and pesticides. The Joint FAO/WHO Expert Committee on Food Additives has stated:[6] . . . an increase in the number of food additives on a permitted list does not imply an over-all increase in the (total amount of) additives used; the different additives are largely used as alternatives . . . From the toxicological point of view there is less likelihood of long exposure, or of high or cumulative dose levels being attained if a wide range of substances is available for use. Similar considerations apply to pesticides."

ROLE OF TECHNOLOGY

Food technology has contributed to man's protection against the potential hazards of the natural composition or contamination of his foods. Heating or other processing methods destroy or remove, for example, the cyanogenetic glycosides and some of the goitrogens. Refrigeration, canning, packaging, and other preservation measures suppress contamination by microbial toxins and chemical changes in foods that might generate toxic materials. Further, the widespread geographical distribution of food products area of foods produced in a variety of other areas. This largely obviates the hazards that might arise from geochemical imbalances or other localized environmental factors if a population consumed only those foods produced in its own area.

ABNORMAL CIRCUMSTANCES

We have explained why a normal healthy individual consuming a reasonably varied diet composed naturally of thousands of toxic chemicals is not poisoned by it. However, there are abnormal circumstances under which injury has been caused by the chemicals that occur naturally in foods:

1. Seafood and microbial toxins are categorized as abnormal thorough natural contaminants that adversely affect the normal consumer eating normal amounts of the food in question.
2. Goitrogens, lathyrogens, cyanogenetic glycosides, and avadin are normal constituents of foods and have caused disease in normal people consuming abnormal amounts of the foods in which they are present.
3. Numerous normal components of foods consumed in normal amounts are harmful in abnormal individuals who have increased susceptibilities due to diseased states, malnutrition, allergic sensitivities, inborn errors of metabolism, or nonspecific intolerances.

Even ordinary dietary levels of sodium are undesirable in hypertensive patients. Lactose intolerance, gluten sensitivity, and favism are related to genetic defects in metabolism in which the afflicted individuals cannot tolerate a normal quantitive range of intake of specific foods. Thus, it is apparent that either abnormal contaminants, abnormal levels of intake, or abnormal health or physiological make-up of the individual consumer can bring to light the toxic potential of numerous natural chemical components of foods.

DELAYED EFFECTS

Some plants and animals that have served historically as sources of food for man were not designed by nature for that purpose. It was necessary for man to discover for himself, by trial and error, what he could eat with safety. He discarded things that tasted bad or made him sick. Undoubtedly, most of his decisions to discard were based on what we would now call acute experiments; the injurious effects occurred so soon after eating that there was little doubt as to their cause. However, long-delayed harmful effects of chronic consumption of certain natural products remained a mystery for centuries. The relationships of goiter, lathyrism, favism, and ergotism to their specific dietary causes were slow in coming to light. The problems of establishing the causes of slowly developing or long-delayed effects have recently increased in number and complexity as new suspicions have arisen in the light of new knowledge. It is suspected that dietary sodium and excessive dietary cadmium play roles in the pathogenesis of hypertension. Numerous substances that occur naturally in plant foods are known or suspected to be carcinogenic in animals. There is further suspicion that undiscovered carcinogens still lurk among the chemical compounds that occur naturally in foods. In the complex chemical context of our total food supply, attempts to unravel the cause-effect relationships in respect to carcinogenesis will be extremely difficult. Identification of a carcinogen in a food may be simple, but establishing its carcinogenicity under the conditions of consumption of the food in which it is found will probably be impossible in most cases. Similar difficulties will be encountered in identifying specific dietary causes, if any, of reproductive disorders, genetic abnormalities, and various cardiovascular, endocrine, and mental diseases.

CONSIDERATIONS FOR THE FUTURE

Public educational programs in nutrition should stress a diverse and balanced diet as the basic approach to avoiding toxicologic hazard as well as to acquiring the nutritional essentials. It would be hoped that such teaching might reach those, among others, who have been misguided into the hazards of the so-called Zen macrobiotic diet in which a sequence of regimens progresses to a 100% cereal diet. This is the antithesis of the diet considered optimum on the basis of sound nutritional and toxicologic principles. It is not surprising that such states of malnutrition as scurvy, anemia, hypocalcemia among others, and even death have been reported in the followers of this dangerous dietary philosophy.[7]

The varied diet, however, does not under all conditions provide the maximum safety. In certain instances the margins of safety of natural components of foods are not wide enough to allow for even normally varied patterns of consumption, as in cases of inborn errors of metabolism, allergic sensitivities, individual non-specific intolerances, and various disease states. Under such conditions it may be necessary to restrict the diversity of the diet, thus offsetting some of the advantages of a widely varied diet as consumed by individuals in good health and of normal constitution.

An obligation of the food and agricultural industries in their development and production of new or modified food products is to take into account the known chemical composition of the products they work with, especially in regard to those components that have known toxic properties. The importance of this is illustrated by the recent finding that a new variety of potato, possessing improved chipping and browning properties, unfortunately contained an increased concentration of solanine alkaloids that prevented its further use.[8]

It seems reasonable and advisable, however, to resort to methods of selective breeding to reduce the levels of toxic substances in plant food sources where hazards are known to exist. By such methods toxic erucic acid has been practically eliminated from rape seed oil produced in Canada,[9] and in addition, cottonseed free of gossypol[10] and a lima bean with relatively low cyanide generating capacity[11] have been developed. In selective breeding procedures of this kind it is obvious that attention should be given to any possible changes that might occur in the food product to increase the content of other toxic components or decrease the nutritional quality.

In the processing of agricultural food products it is unlikely that it would be either feasible or beneficial to attempt to extract from foods such toxic components as goitrogens, cyanogenetic clycosides, oxalates, solanine alkaloids, safrol, toxic amino acids, and fatty acids. Such procedures would undoubtedly often reduce the consumer acceptability, induce chemical changes that might introduce other toxic substances or reduce the nutritional quality, and necessitate extensive animal studies to establish the safety of the resulting products for prolonged consumption.

When viewing in perspective all chemicals that are present in our food supply - the natural components, agricultural chemicals, food additives, and natural and man-made contaminants - it becomes clear that the greatest area of the unknown involves the natural and normal components of our foods. To achieve a better balance in the effort applied to the evaluation of the safety of foods in general, at least as much attention should be given to the additives, pesticides, and other man-made environmental contaminants that enter the food supply. It is not suggested, however, that less attention be given to the latter in comparison to the former. In fact, consideration should be given to the potential problems that might arise from the simultaneous presence of both naturally occurring and synthetic chemicals and the potential chemical and toxicological interactions among them.

In the final analysis, however, the major hazards of the dinner table are what people do that cannot be eliminated by science or controlled by law. These may be listed as follows:

1. Plain old-fashioned over-eating, leading to excessive caloric intake;
2. Unbalanced or fad diet, leading to malnutrition or toxicity of specific components; and
3. Careless handling of foods, leading to food poisoning from microbiological contamination.

References

1. Talburt, WF and Smith, O: *Potato Processing,* 2nd ed., Westport, Conn, The AVI Publishing Co., 1967.
2. Van Etten, CH and Wolff, IA: Natural Sulfur Compounds, Chap 10 in *Toxicants Occurring Naturally in Foods,* 2nd ed., Washington, D C, National Academy of Sciences Publication No. 2117, 1973.

3. Reich, P; Schwachman, H; and Craig, JM: Lycopenemia: A Variant of Carotenemia, *New Engl J Med* **262**:263, 1968.

4. Underwood, EJ: Trace Elements, Chap 3 in *Toxicants Occurring Naturally in Foods,* 2nd ed., Washington, D C, National Academy of Sciences Publication No. 2117, 1973.

5. Harper, AE: Amino Acids of Nutritional Importance, Chap 6 in *Toxicants Occurring Naturally in Foods,* 2nd ed., Washington, D C, National Academy of Sciences Publication No. 2117, 1973.

6. WHO Scientific Group, Procedures for Investigating Intentional and Unintentional Food Additives, WHO Technical Report Series No. 348, 1967.

7. Council on Foods and Nutrition: Zen Macrobiotic Diets, *J Am Med Assoc* **218**:397, 1971.

8. Nishie, K; Gumbmann, MR; and Keyl, AC: Pharmacology of Solanine, *Tox Appl Pharmacol* **19**:81-92, 1971.

9. Stefansson, BR; Hougen, FW; and Downey, RK: Note on the Isolation of Rape Plants with Seed Oil Free from Erucic Acid, *Canad J Plant Sci* **41**:218, 1961.

10. Singleton, VL and Kratzer, FH: Plant Phenolics, Chap 15 in *Toxicants Occurring Naturally* in Foods, 2nd ed., Washington, D C, National Academy of Sciences Publication No. 2117, 1973.

11. Conn, EE: Cyanogenetic Clycosides, Chap 14 in *Toxicants Occurring Naturally in Foods,* 2nd ed., Washington, D C, National Academy of Sciences Publication No. 2117, 1973.

Unintentional Additives in Food

H. F. KRAYBILL, Ph.D.

A wide array of chemicals is encompassed within the class of unintentional additives. Some are of natural origin and others are the result of contamination from industrial uses and technological advances. My discussion will be confined to those additive contaminants, mostly synthetic chemicals, which find their way into the food chain and are identified and monitored. A few of these chemicals might be enumerated by class or individual compound such as (1) pesticides, (2) polychlorinated biphenyls, (3) chlorodioxins, (4) estrogens, (5) heavy metals (industrial origin), (6) radioactive compounds (tritium and fallout radionuclides), (7) azobenzenes from pesticides, (8) ethylene thiourea from fungicides, (9) phthalates, (10) asbestos particles in talc, (11) nitrates - nitrites from fertilizer, including polycyclic hydrocarbons from oil spillage, and others too numerous to mention.[1,2]

DETERMINATION OF HEALTH SIGNIFICANCE

The safety or hazard of an environmental chemical is sometimes deduced from epidemiologic evaluation (retrospective or prospective) on the general population (cigarette smoking - lung cancer) or observations related to occupations or accidental exposure where there is abnormal concentration leading to increased incidence of disease [dioxins - chloracne, PCB's - "Yusho" disease (Japan), pesticides - aminoaciduria and CNS effects, estrogens - cancer, heavy metals - Minamata Disease (Hg), plumbosis and encephalopathy (Pb), "itai-itai" disease in Japanese women (Cd)].

More commonly, the mechanism for appraisement of hazards is by systematic toxicity testing in experimental animals (acute, subacute, and chronic) or biological test systems or organisms (cell culture, bacterial, yeasts, etc.). This involves a search for aberrant metabolism, biochemical lesion, teratogenic, mutagenic, reproductive, and carcinogenic effects and any potentiation of other toxicants or shortening of life span.

For assessment of the hazards of chemicals to man, hazards that are extrapolated from animal studies, there may be three concerns. Firstly, the animal may over-state the risk; secondly, the assay may understate the risk; and thirdly, the animal species selected may not relate well to man in the response. There is no answer to this dilemma, but certainly it is preferable to adhere to a conservative approach in cases where the public is to be protected.[3,4] A positive toxicological observation in more than one tissue, in more than one species, and in more than one laboratory, is convincing documentation of potential hazard to man. One of the critical needs of our time is a better understanding of the comparative metabolism of food contaminants in various animal species which will provide a better selection of species more closely related to man. Furthermore, an evaluation of safety is based on extrapolation from high dosage levels or the aspect of metabolic overloading. As to the latter, high dosing may achieve a response by one metabolic pathway with a toxic metabolite, which is not reflected at lower dose levels or exposure which represent present exposure situations (see Figure 1).

In Figure 1, the various metabolic pathways for methyl parathion (pesticide) are shown.[15-16] It is evident that at a low dose given to the rat, 53% of a metabolite indicated as compound A is produced. At a higher dose of the pesticide, close to the LD_{50} dose, the level of this metabolite in the urine is markedly reduced. Also shown are percentages of compound A elaborated for the pesticide sumithion given at a high and low dose. In this instance, the high dose produces a marked decrease in the level of metabolite dimethyl phosphoric acid. These are quantitative data on influence of low and high dose administration on metabolic pathways. Qualitatively, we may ultimately indicate that at high dosing (overdosing), a metabolite is produced which is a proximate carcinogen not built up by adminis-

EFFECT OF DOSE IN METABOLIC PATHWAYS

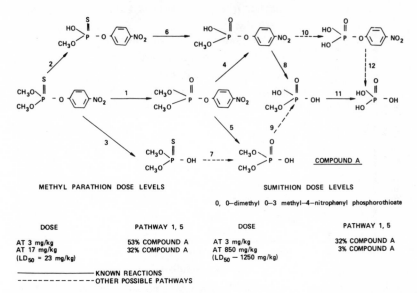

Figure 1.—Influence of dose of chemical administered on level of metabolite excreted and effect of alternate pathways (rats).

tration of the test chemical at a low dose more relevant to typical human exposure events.

In the case of melengestrol acetate (MGA), a dose of 50 μg of this compound appears to be the starting point for elaboration of serum prolactin. It is not until a level of 400 μg of MGA is reached that mammary carcinomas are induced in C_3H mice. Carcinomas are not produced at lower levels of serum prolactin secreted by the challenge of MGA at doses below 50 μg. The hypothesis is advanced that serum prolactin is the etiologic agent for the carcinoma induction and that cancers are not evident by low dose challenge of MGA which will not induce the secretion of serum prolactin (Figure 2).

There are two more illustrative cases on the influence of high and low dose on tumor production. In Figure 3, it is shown that high doses of aflatoxin are ineffective in producing primary liver cancer in the monkey and the over-dosing results in lethality. Conversely, at the lower dose approaching environmental levels,

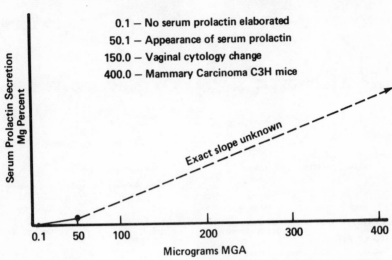

Figure 2.—Influence of MGA dose administered on elaboration of serum prolactin and carcinoma induction (mice).

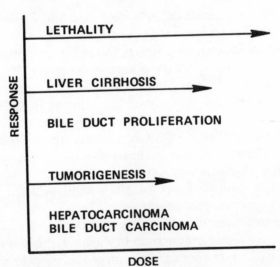

Figure 3.—Demonstration of the significance of dose of aflatoxin administered with respect to potential for tumor induction or lethality (non-human primates).

the hepatocarcinomas may be induced from aflatoxin challenge. Selenium (Se) also presents an interesting case in that some investigators claimed tumorigenic response in rodents to a dose of 5 ppm of selenium in the diet. However, at doses below the toxic level of 5 ppm, this element has been well established as essential in proper functioning of the hematopoietic system. There is still some debate as to the tumorigenic properties of Se (Figure 4).

In essence, the significance of overdosing must not be over-looked and the amount of test compound given influences reaction kinetics and as far as metabolism and metabolic path-ways are concerned, one may have a first order or second order reaction. When the response is carcinogenic, present knowledge on carcinogenic mechanisms makes it difficult to identify inef-fective pathways at low levels of exposure. However, at higher doses (overdosing), such altered pathways or ineffective path-ways may be predominant.[5]

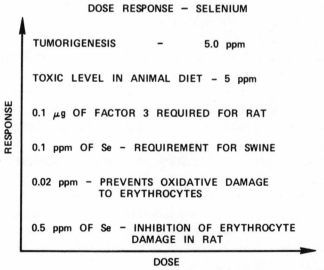

Figure 4.—Demonstration of the relevance of dose to adverse effect and physiological requirement (rats and swine).

In appraising safety, other factors are considered such as (1) excretion in less toxic forms; (2) conversion to toxic or carcinogenic metabolites; (3) evidence of non-absorption; (4) activation by host enzymes to primate carcinogens; (5) property of alkylation or electrophilic reactant in carcinogenesis; (6) storage in tissue; (7) half-life; (8) membrane transport; (9) potential for antagonism of synergism; (10) effect of stress conditions (diet, environment, geriatrics, or disease); (11) sex; (12) and effect on the neonate.

The inadvertent food additive presents a different situation than the intended additive with respect to assessment of risk. In the latter case, the judgments are quite stingent in permitting this agent in the environment; whereas, for the unintentional additive, uncertainties must be balanced against benefits and societal impact.[6,7]

The proposal for considering toxicological insignificance with respect to levels of chemicals in foods, where a ratio of 1:100 is usually applied as a safety factor, may be relevant in demonstrating non-carcinogenic responses (reproductive effects, biochemical lesions, etc.), all of which may be reversible in mammalian systems. However, in a carcinogenic expression, where there is the element of irreversibility, no such thresholds or insignificance can be delineated.

It is in the area of low level exposure that hazard or safety is difficult to assess. The response is usually not acute or dramatic, and chronic testing is required and subsequently is not always successful if experimental conditions are not adequately planned to demonstrate a subtle effect. Many of the chemicals previously enumerated in the opening remarks would fall into this class. Determination of their health significance is dependent on large-scale experimental animal studies, delineating all possible observations in responses in our toxicological armamentarium. This includes the use of many species and large animal populations in several laboratories, and in addition to confirmation, if possible, by human population or epidemiological experiences. This procedure may add an element of assurance in safety evaluation.[8]

For carcinogenic compounds, the aspect of a body burden (i.e., SR-90) as well as the irreversibility of the carcinogenic cellular response, their cumulative nature, and synergistic properties or interaction, present special problems for appraisement. The assessment of health significance for carcinogenic additives as low levels of exposure is difficult, requiring long term observations. For noncarcinogenic additives the problem is one that may lend itself to easier resolution.[5,9]

LEVEL AT WHICH SIGNIFICANT
HAZARD MAY OCCUR

The unintentional food additive may fall into two classes; those that are non-carcinogenic and those that are carcinogenic. These considerations encompass regulatory aspects where tolerances or guidelines are set under legislative mandate. Similarly, in the area of occupational exposure, threshold limit values are set.

Intentional additives exhibiting a biological effect other than carcinogenesis will have a threshold from which tolerances are derived (legally established limits for the concentration of such chemicals allowed in food) or acceptable daily intakes (ADIs) which are not to be equated with tolerances. For unintentional additives, the same procedures are applicable. Toxic effects of an unintentional additive on cells at higher doses may be lethal, whereas, at lower doses an effect may not be as apparent, at least on an acute basis. Indeed, the cells may, be repeated challenge, acquire an increased resistance through adaptation by the microsomal enzymes to the imposed stress. An exception to this may be the induction of carcinomas (see Figure 3).

The carcinogenic expression, however, is irreversible. As the dose rate of a carcinogin increases the latency period decreases and the incidence of tumors increases. With lower doses, the latency period will be extended and, at very low levels, this period may be so extended as to make it difficult to reach the tumor stage under certain experimental conditions. It would appear that there may be a threshold and such an "apparent" threshold may be demonstrated under particular conditions of a certain strain of animal, diet, environment, etc. Alteration of these conditions may elicit a positive tumorigenic response. A carcinogenic cellular imprint prevails subject to the effects of

future exposures or influence of other carcinogens or poten-
tiators in the *milieu*.[9]

Thus, toxicity in its broader sense, based on response to
various treatments with an observed threshold, does not re-
semble the unique properties of a carcinogenic action. The
cancer risk from doses of an inadvertent additive are reflected
even at low level exposure by the persistent cumulative exposure over a long period of time. At the present time there is
no accepted procedure for assessing an absolute safe dose for a
carcinogen (i.e., threshold). Furthermore, until such procedures
and data are developed, it is not feasible to prove or disprove
the presence or absence of a threshold dose through downward
extrapolation from the dose response curve in regions of detect-
ably significant dosage. [5,6,7]

Admittedly, some inadvertent additives may be harmful at
high concentrations and yet beneficial at lower doses. The
action of selenium is a case in point. Some inadvertent additives, therefore, when controlled in the food supply, do not
present a case for absolute elimination. Here, one may appreciate the importance of scientific rationale in making a societal
decision relevant to judgment of safety and permissive levels to
the general population.[6]

Investigators are compiling more and more evidence that
would indicate certain unintentional additives induce or
proceed along certain metabolic pathways at high dose as con-
trasted with low dose. The metabolites may be entirely different and the residence time, the cellular insult and target organ
response, may be quite different at low dose and high dose
administration. Furthermore, the arbitrarily selected massive
dose scheduling may in no way simulate actual exposure conditions for the human population. High dosage may invoke a
biological injury causing death, whereas low dosage, although
not significantly affecting life span, may allow a sufficient time
interval (induction period) for production of an effect (i.e., a
carcinogenic response).

There is a general view that the dosing schedule or exposure
levels applied in many testing protocols are many orders of
magnitude beyond the general population exposure. Indeed,
maximum exposure levels that an animal receives, equated to

man, are far beyond the exposure level man would receive, even in occupational situations. This would be relevant occupational exposure and hazard, but certainly not for evaluation of an inadvertent additive under environmental conditions as a stress to the general population. Accordingly, safety decisions based on such protocols and the data forthcoming from such protocols are being questioned for many non-carcinogenic additives.[10] The same principles may apply in testing compounds proven to be carcinogenic.

When an additive is tested at extremely high dose, the cells may be swamped, precluding the possibility of recovery. Cellular mechanisms for detoxification become inoperable and normal pathways of metabolism are essentially non-existent (example - methyl parathion). Protocols should be planned with these considerations in mind and previous experiments should be re-examined for their biochemical and metabolic validity in design.[5]

Another concept advanced in terms of food additives safety evaluation is that of estimating "toxicologically insignificant" levels of chemicals in food without direct experimental toxicological evaluation. Briefly stated, this approach is practically inapplicable and readily refuted with respect to carcinogenic additives.[9]

Recent proponents of a threshold dose for additives have attempted to demonstrate mathematically for various compounds that such values are absolute. For example, of mathematical formulation on the order of 10^x molecules per kilogram of body weight or a concentration of 10^{-x} molar where x is a discrete number for various compounds, for even a compound classified as a carcinogen have been proposed. Such an approach is currently unacceptable with respect to a carcinogen on the basis of many of the factors previously cited where one must appreciate the irreversible and delayed toxic effects occurring in the carcinogenesis process.[10,11,12]

From all this emerges the concept of virtual safety since complete safety is untenable. Determination of "thresholds" for carcinogens may be made if we knew more about the mechanism of carcinogenesis. Additionally, as previously indicated, the impact of a co-carcinogen on a "threshold" that could increase the hazard level is another aspect which introduces difficulties in such an assesment. [10]

As indicated, the carcinogenic response is unique in contrast to other biological responses in terms of assessment of a safety dose. Calculations, estimates or educated guesses of the safe dose for unintentional additives in relation to carcinogens is unattainable unless we consider some "acceptable" level of risk.[6,7]

Therefore, the alternative that science can recommend is to estimate the upper probable limit of risk. The concept of a safe dose for man, as applied to carcinogenic, unintentional additives, should be replaced by the concept of a "socially acceptable level of risk." Based on the best scientific information one can muster forth, the task of selecting socially acceptable levels of human risk rests with regulatory bodies, society, and perhaps political leaders. [13]

These decisions proceed stepwise with the interaction and contribution that each segment of our society may offer. The cancer investigator provides the information as to whether the compound is a carcinogen or non-carcinogen, using statistical approaches to buttress experimental findings in order to arrive at a dose compatible with some "acceptable" level of risk (i.e., a carcinogen). More assurances on any extrapolations from animal to man in the area of low dose response may be forthcoming through extensive testing, large animal populations, or even epidemiological findings, if available. From this point onward, the decision makers enter the scene, utilizing the concept of a "socially acceptable level of risk." After a decision has been made, one can then arrive at an acceptable dose for a certain risk involved, balancing out benefit and risk in such a societal decision. It is axiomatic in the scientific deliberations that the biochemical, physiological, metabolic behavior of an additive be considered. If the additive is a carcinogen, or even a non-carcinogen, we must consider its half-life or residence time, whether it is rapidly excreted or metabolized and what interaction and injury to cells occurs. In addition, its solubility in aqueous solution and its accumulative distribution or favorable partition ratio in fat and water in the cells for a long residence time and latent effect are of paramount importance.[4]

Tolerance levels or Acceptable Daily Intake (ADI's) can be

ascribed for non-carcinogenic inadvertent additives. This is accomplished in regulatory bodies and international groups such
as FAO/WHO. For some additives, the calculation of a threshold presents certain complications which must be resolved. For
example, thresholds among individuals of varying age, sex, genetic background, and illnesses are to be considered. For any dose,
even minimal, one individual may have a threshold which is still
lower than that of other members of the population. In societal
decisions such factors are considered in judging safety in making
extrapolations from test animals to man as selected doses where
such exposures may or may not be significantly relevant to
human health. Some estimated safe doses of some unintentional
additives are given in Table I as promulgated by regulatory
bodies and FAO/WHO. [14]

Table I—Some Safety Doses for Unintentional Additives
(General Population)

1. ^{90}Sr (FALLOUT RADIONUCLIDE)   73 $\mu\mu$c/day

2. PCB's
    Action Levels - Eggs = 0.5; Poultry = 5.0
    (in ppm)   Fish = 5.0; Milk   = 0.2

    Range of Safety
    150-300 μg/day for 500 days; 500 days then 50 μg/day

3. MERCURY

Guideline	From Diet	In Blood
0.5 ppm	0.06 mg/day	10 μg/100 ml

4. LEAD   40 μg/100 ml

5. SOME PESTICIDES*   mg/kg/body wt/day

Carbaryl	0.02
Lindane	0.0125
Malathion	0.02
Parathion	0.005
Diazinon	0.002

*WHO/FAO Maximum Acceptable Daily Intake (14)

References
1. Atkins, H: Shreds of Evidence — The Sciences, *12, N Y Acad of Sci Publication,* March 1972.
2. Boylard, E: Natural Estrogens and the Safe Level of Estrogen Intake, *Tumori* 53:19-28, 1967.
3. Barnes, JM and Denz, FA: Experimental Methods Used in Determining Chronic Toxicity, *Pharmacol Rev* 6:191, 1954.
4. Gillette, R: DDT: Its Days Are Numbered Except Perhaps in Pepper Fields, *Science* 4041:1313, 1972.
5. Kraybill, HF: Scientific Criteria, Evaluation of Safety of Carcinogens, Mutagenic and Teratogenic Agents, FDA unpublished report, Feb 20, 1971.
6. Mantel, N and Bryan, WR: Safety Testing of Carcinogenic Agents, *J Natl Cancer Inst* 27:455-470 (Nov), 1961.
7. Hueper, WC: Public Health Hazards From Environmental Chemical Carcinogens, Mutagens and Teratogens, *Health Phys* 21:689-707, 1971.
8. Weil, CS: Guidelines for Experiments to Predict the Degree of Safety of A Material for Man, *Toxicol Apply Pharmacol* 21:194-199, 1972.
9. National Academy of Sciences — NRC, Food Protection Committee, Evaluating the Safety of Food Chemicals, NAS/NRC Publication 1859, Washington, D C, 1970.
10. Tenth International Congress on Pharmacology, Abstracts of Invited Presentations, San Francisco, California, July 23-28, 1972.
11. Rossi, HH and Kellerer, AM: Radiation Carcinogenesis at Low Doses, *Science* 175:200-202, 1972.
12. Dinman, BD: 'Non-Concept' of 'No-Threshold': Chemicals in The Environment, *Science* 175:495-497, 1972.
13. National Cancer Institute ad hoc Committee on the Evaluation of Low Levels of Environmental Chemical Carcinogens, (Saffiotti, Falk, Kotin, Lijinsky, Schneidermann, Shubick, Weinhouse and Wogan), Evaluation of environmental carcinogens, Hearings before the U S Congress (Subcommittee on Executive Reorganization and Government Research of the Committee on Government operations), U S Senate, April 6-7, 1971.
14. FAO/WHO, 1970 Evaluations of Some Pesticide Residues in Food, Rome, 1971.
15. Menzie, C: Metabolism of Pesticides, Special Scientific Report, *Wildlife* No. 96, May 1966, Patuxent Wildlife Research Center, U S Department of the Interior.
16. Fukato, TR and Metcalf, RL: Metabolism of Insecticides in Plants and Animals, International Symposium on Biological Effects of Pesticides, *Ann N Y Acad Sci* 160, Art 1, 97-111, 1969.

Phthalates: A Story in the Making

The objectives of this presentation are to provide specific aspects of plasticizer technology and market data necessary for environmentalists and toxicologists to understand the possible points of entry of phthalate esters into the environment or the human body: the esterification process; the ester process; ester transport; polymer plasticizer process; incidences; and natural sources.

Modern plasticizer technology, although rooted in the art of primitive people in their search for materials based on natural products, is now based on a broad spectrum of scientific principles utilizing a vast array of synthetic and naturally occurring compounds.[1] The first commercially significant plasticizers were discovered shortly after the development of cellulose nitrate in 1846. Caster oil was patented for this use in 1856.[2] In 1870 camphor became the plasticizer of choice for cellulose nitrate.[3] Celluloid remained the major thermoplastic material until shortly before World War II. The introduction of phthalate esters in the 1920's overcame the excessive volatility and undesirable odor of camphor. However, the commercial availability of poly(vinyl chloride) in 1931 and the synthesis of di-2-ethylhexyl phthalate (DEHP) in 1933 quickly shifted emphasis away from cellulose nitrate and started the rapid growth of the flexible poly(vinyl chloride) industry.[4] Today, this industry comprises thirteen major suppliers of phthalate plasticizers. Approximately 1 billion pounds of some 20 different phthalate compounds (Figure 1) were manufactured in 1972.[5] In addition, about 350 million pounds of other plasticizer types are used for special purposes such as high permanence, flame retardance, and low-temperature performance. These include adipates, azelates, phosphates, epoxides, polyesters, and trimellitates.

185

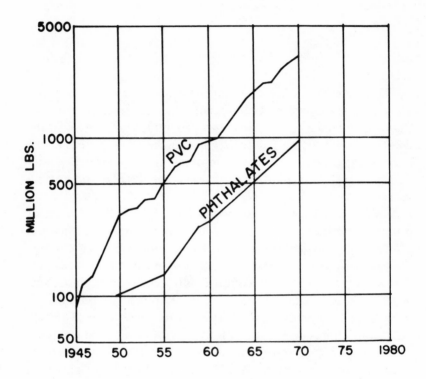

SOURCE: U.S. TARIFF COMMISSION

Figure 1.—PVC - Phthalate Sales History

SOME THEORETICAL ASPECTS
OF PLASTICIZATION

Plasticizers are interfused with high polymers to increase flexibility, extensibility, and workability. This is achieved by lowering the glass transition temperature to below room temperature. The polymer is changed from a hard glass-like solid to a flexible, tough elastomer. Poly(vinyl chloride) is unique in its acceptance of plasticizers. Its polarity, helical structure, and balance of amorphous and crystalline regions in its molecular geometry provide compatibility for a large number of plasticizer structures over relatively wide concentrations of plasticizers to poly(vinyl chloride) actually making the system more rigid. This phenomenon is called "antiplasticization". Using x-ray diffraction, Horsley[6] has shown that these embrittled systems are more ordered (crystalline) due to the increased freedom of motion when a low concentration of plasticizer is present. Higher levels of plasticizer redissolve these crystallites and effect plasticization. Figure 2 is a graphic description of the antiplasticization - plasticization transition.

PHYSICAL PROPERTIES

Figure 3 depicts the physical property changes when the concentrations of a series of typical plasticizers are varied over the range of zero to 40%. The addition of low levels of plasticizer causes the modulus to increase. Modulus is a measurement of the flexibility of a system. The higher the modulus, the more flexible the system. As the level of plasticizer is increased, the modulus is decreased and hence, the plastic composition becomes more pliable. Tensile strength reflects the intermolecular strength of the material. The higher the tensile strength, the more it will withstand external stress. Again, antiplasticization affects higher initial tensile strength. Elongation is the measure

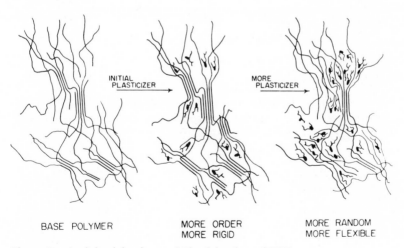

Figure 2.—Antiplasticization and Plasticization of PVC

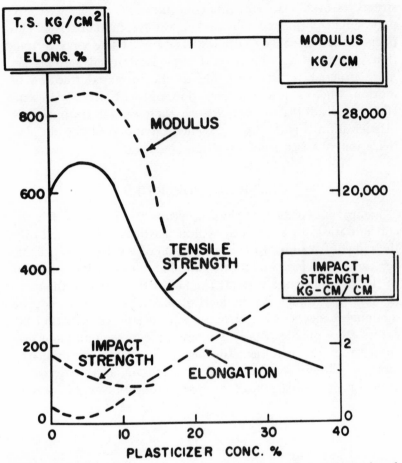

Figure 3.–Effect of Plasticizer Concentration on the Physical Properties of PVC

of extensibility of the resin-plasticizer matrix. As the plasticizer level increases, the composition becomes more extensible and the elongation under stress increases.

Indicated in Figure 4 is the fact that not all plasticizers are equally efficient in changing these physical properties. Di-2-ethylhexyl adipate (DOA) being a linear aliphatic-type ester, tends to impart a higher degree of flexibility (lower modulus) and more extensibility than DOP (di-2-ethylhexyl phthalate). On the other hand, dicyclohexyl phthalate (DCHP), being a

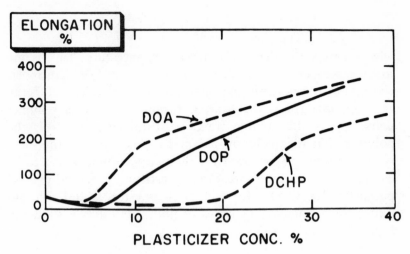

Figure 4.—Effect of Plasticizer Type on Tensile Elongation of PVC

bulky dialkyl phthalate, is considerably less efficient than di-2-ethylhexyl adipate or di-2-ethylhexyl phthalate. One must add significantly more of DCHP than di-2-exthylhexyl phthalate to achieve a given degree of flexibility. Less di-2-ethylhexyl adipate can be added to obtain equivalent flexibility with di-2-ethylhexyl phthalate.

Compatibility

The first consideration in the selection of the optimum plasticizer for any use is its compatibility with the polymer. Incompatibility can result in either an obvious, unsightly phase separation (exudation, crystallization) or a more subtle loss of long-term permanence.

Among many theories of plasticizer compatibility, the following is most frequently used to predict or to measure compatibility of plasticizers with poly(vinyl chloride) and other resins.

Flory-Huggins Interaction Parameter

In this theory[7] the polymer—diluent interaction parameter χ is calculated from the equation:

$$\frac{1}{Tm} = \frac{1}{Tm^O} + \frac{RVu}{HuV_1} \quad (U_1 - \chi U_1^2)$$

where Tm is the depressed melting temperature; Tm^O is the melting temperature of pure polymer; Vu and V_1 are molar volumes of the polymer unit and diluent, respectively; R is the gas constant; Hu is the heat of fusion per mole of polymer units; U_1 is the volume fraction of diluent; and χ is the polymer-diluent interaction parameter. According to the theory, χ must be 0.5 or lower for the polymer-diluent pair to be compatible. The phthalate esters, particularly di-2-ethylhexyl phthalate. The χ value for each of these esters is -0.-5. The chi values for a homologous series of phthalate esters is shown in Figure 5.

Solubility Parameter

The cohesive-energy density (CED) measures the strength of interactions in a pure liquid or solid. The solubility parameter δ is obtained from the equation[8]

$$\delta^2 = \frac{\Delta E}{V} = \frac{\Delta Hv - RT}{V} = CED$$

where E is the molar energy of vaporization; Hv is the heat of vaporization per mole; V is the molecular volume; R is the gas constant; and T is the (absolute) temperature. The use of the solubility parameter to predict plasticizer compatibility assumes that some overall intermolecular interactions are present in the plasticizer as well as the polymer. This empirical method does not distinguish between types of attractive forces between organic molecules such as dipole-dipole, dipole-induced-dipole, or hydrogen bonding. The solubility parameter in conjunction with the dielectric constant provides an excellent prediction of plasticizer compatibility.[9] Phthalate plasticizers have solubility parameters between about 8.4 and 11.4 and dielectric constants between about 4 and 9. Poly(vinyl chloride) has a calculated solubility parameter of about 9.6 by the method of Small.[10]

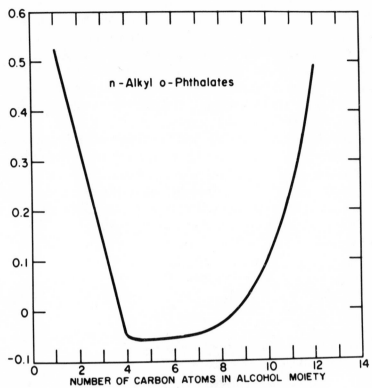

Figure 5.—Chi Values for a Homologous Series of Dialkyl Phthalates

Permanence

Plasticizer Migration—If a plasticized poly(vinyl chloride) surface is placed in contact with other materials, the plasticizer may migrate or extract from the polymer matrix. When the environment (air, oil, water, blood, etc.) has a very high affinity for the plasticizer, the migration rate is dependent upon the ability of the plasticizer to diffuse through the resin matrix to the attracting media. This is matrix controlling.[11]

$$\frac{Q}{S} = 2.26 \sqrt{\frac{Dt}{L^2}}$$

where Q is the weight (grams) of plasticizer lost in t hours; S denotes total weight (grams) of plasticizer in film; D is the diffusion constant (cm/hr); and L is film thickness (cm).

The diffusion constant depends upon the plasticizer molecular weight, modulus of the system, the compatibility of plasticizer, plasticizer viscosity, and the affinity of environment for the plasticizer.

When the resistance to loss from the surface is high compared to the resistance of the sheet itself, the migration is controlled by the surface resistance and is proportional to the first power of the thickness. This is the case when the environment has little affinity for the plasticizer, such as air. Migration rate is directly dependent upon temperature in both cases. The higher the temperature, the higher the rate of extraction or migration.

From a practical standpoint, the migration of a plasticizer to an adjacent surface would depend upon the following:

I. Interaction of Plasticizer and Resin Matrix
   A. Diffusion Constant
      1. Modulus of System
      2. Compatibility of Plasticizer
      3. Plasticizer Viscosity
      4. Plasticizer Molecular Weight
II. Interaction of Plasticizer and the Environment
   A. Solubility of Plasticizer in Blood, IV Fluid or Food
   B. Absorption Rate Plasticizer
   C. Compatibility of Plasticizer with Adhesive or Other Environment

PLASTICIZER VOLATILITY

The volatile loss of plasticizer during use is an important consideration in the study of possible environmental hazards. Table I exhibits data from an accelerated test designed to compare several plasticizers in their tendencies to volatilize from a flexible poly-(vinyl chloride) surface such as upholstery. A stream of air was blown over a film 10 ml thick and having an exposed surface of 240 cm^2. The film contained phr (parts per hundred parts of resin) plasticizer. The temperature was maintained at 83°C (185°F). The flow rate was 250 cm^3/min. These

Table I.—Plasticizer Volatility from PVC Film at 83° C*

Plasticizer	Plasticizer μg/Liter of Air	μg/Hour
Di-2-ethylhexyl	3.4.	51
phthalate	2.3 ⟩2.7	36 ⟩44
	2.5	39
	3.3	49
Linear Phthalate:	0.75 ⟩.70	11.3. ⟩10.6
Tri(C_7-C_9-C_{11} Alkyl)	0.65	9.9
Di-Undecyl Phthalate	⩽.005	⩽0.22
Tri (alkyl) trimellitate	<.0009	<0.04

* Measured in a circular flow cell, 240 cm^2 film area, 70 PHR plasticizer, flow rate 250 cc/min.

results indicate that the linear alkyl phthalate ester is a vast improvement over DEHP. Further improvement can be achieved through the use of diundecyl phthalate or trialkyl trimellitate.

An analysis of the atmosphere inside a new automobile discloses a concentration of organic material to be about 12 ug/l. Over 60 different organic compounds were detached. The phthalate portion of this organic mixture was found to range from 0% to 6%, depending upon temperature conditions. At the lower temperatures, the phthalates were undetectable. Some of the other organic materials found were: C_2-C_5 alkylbenzenes, C_9-C_{18} alkanes, higher alkanes, naphthalene, phenol, and ditert-butyl cresol.

The automobile studied was new. It was driven approximately 2000 miles, during which time no smoking, dining, or storage of materials was permitted.

PLASTICIZER SYNTHESIS TECHNOLOGY

Chemistry

Phthalate esters are prepared from phthalic anhydride and the appropriate alcohol. Equations (1) and (2) show typical

$$\text{Naphthalene} \xrightarrow[V_2O_5]{O_2} \text{Phthalic Anhydride} + 2(CO/CO_2) + H_2O \qquad (1)$$

$$\text{O-Xylene} \xrightarrow[V_2O_5]{O_2} \text{Phthalic Anhydride} + 2(CO/CO_2) + H_2O \qquad (2)$$

$$\text{ASSAY SPEC.} \quad 99.5\% \quad - \text{Phthalic Acid}$$
$$0.5\% \begin{cases} - \text{Isophthalic Acid} \\ - \text{Terephthalic Acid} \\ - \text{Maleic Anhydride} \end{cases}$$

commercial processes for phthalic anhydride from either naphthalene or o-xylene as basic raw materials. Phthalic anhydride from modern processes assays above 95.5%. The remaining 0.5% could be phthalic acid, isophthalic acid, terephthalic acid, and maleic anhydride.

The alcohols are manufactured by two basic processes: The Ald-Ox process and the Oxo process. [12] 2-Ethylhexanol is produced from the Ald-Ox process using propylene as the starting material to form C_4 aldehyde. An aldol condensation produces C_8 aldehyde, which is hydrogenated to 2-ethylhexanol. Butyl alcohol is also made as a by-product in this process. The Oxo process is used to produce both essentially linear and branched chain alcohols from olefins. The olefin is reacted with CO and H_2 to form an aldehyde which is then hydrogenated to an alcohol. Linear alcohols are made from linear olefins produced by the Ziegler process starting with ethylene. Branched chain alcohols are prepared from branched olefins which occur in refinery operation. Both the Ald-Ox and the Oxo processes are typified in Figure 6.

The esterification process is shown in equation (3). The purity of esters from modern esterification processes range from 99.70% to 99.97%.

I <u>ALD-OX PROCESS</u>

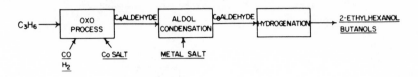

II <u>OXO PROCESS</u>

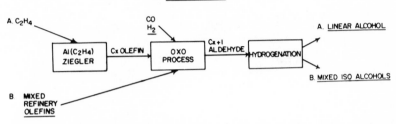

Figure 6.—Typical Alcohol Processes

ESTERIFICATION PROCESS

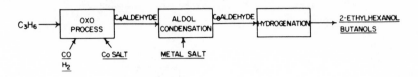

R = 2-ETHYLHEXANOL   (3)

POLYMER–PLASTICIZER PROCESS

In almost all applications of flexible poly(vinyl chloride), heat must be employed to obtain the necessary degree of fusion between the plasticizer and the resin.[13] Figure 7 shows three typified processing routes commonly employed in the manufacture of flexible poly(vinyl chloride).

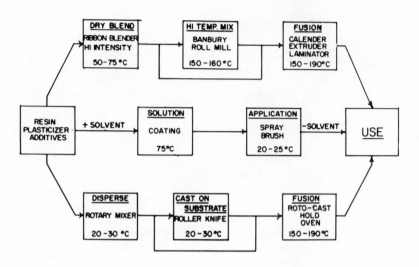

Figure 7.—Processing of Plasticized PVC

A wire insulation compound would follow route at the top of Figure 7. The resin, plasticizer, stabilizer, and filler would first be mixed in a ribbon or high-intensity blender. The temperature of the blend could increase to 50 to 75°C; however, the compound is not fused at this point but rather emerges as a free-flowing powder. The powder is usually masticated on a hot-roll mill at 150 to 160°C and formed into a fused sheet. The sheet is pelletized and forced through a hot extruder to form the insulation around the metal wire. The ribbon blender, high-intensity mixer, and the extruder are closed systems. Roll milling is an open process, but is generally equipped with an exhaust system to prohibit emissions escape into the plant environment.

Flexible poly(vinyl chloride) film is also usually prepared from the route at the top of Figure 7. If it is extruded, the process is quite similar to that described for wire insulation. Poly(vinyl chloride) film is often calendered. When this process is used, the dry blend is masticated in a closed Banbury mixer at 150 to 160°C. The calendering process forms the uniform film. It operates at fusion temperatures and is an open, but usually exhausted process. Incineration of the vapors can be employed. An example of the process shown on the bottom of Figure 7 is the manufacture of leatherlike fabric for upholstery. A special type of poly(vinyl chloride) is dispersed in the plasticizer using a rotary mixer. This dispersion, called a plastisol, is cast on a web of fabric by using a knife or a roller coater. Both of these operations are performed at room temperature. The plastisol-coated fabric is passed through an oven where it fuses at temperatures ranging from 160 to 180°C. Modern ovens are equipped with exhaust systems to vent the volatilized vapor which in some instances is incinerated. Certain poly(vinyl chloride) copolymers can be dissolved in solvents containing phthalate and other plasticizers to form lacquers and other solution coatings. These coatings are applied by spray or brush; the solvent is evaporated providing functional surfaces for a number of of substrates. Very little heat, if any, is required for fusion. This process is also depicted in Figure 7.

PLASTICIZER USES AND MARKETS

No single plasticizer exhibits the perfect balance of properties for every application. Each end-use will demand certain essential properties. To achieve this balance some properties of lower importance must be sacrificed to some extent. In the judicious selection of the "proper" plasticizer system for a given application, the first consideration would be compatibility. Then, depending upon the specific application, other criteria relating to processing, performance, and permanence properties would be obtained. A partial checklist might be as shown in Table II. Toxicity is first on the list of end-use criteria.

It should also be remembered that for each application, the desirable balance of properties must be achieved within a prescribed cost framework.

Table III lists selected performance criteria for a number of plasticizer types, including both branched-chain and linear phthalates. The results from the permanence property evaluations were obtained by using standard accelerated testing procedures. These data compare classes of products and are not meant to characterize individual plasticizers within these classes.

Table II.—Critical Properties of Plasticized PVC

PROCESSING	PERFORMANCE	PERMANENCE
Roll Milling	Toxicity	Migration Resistance
Calendering	Color	Volatility
Dry Blending	Odor	Extraction Resistance
Banburying	Flexibility	Outdoor Aging
Extrusion	Softness	Light Stability
Solution	Mechanical Prop.	Heat Sensitivity
Foaming	Electrical Prop.	Fungal Resistance
Heat Sealing	Flame Retardance	

The measurement for each property (H_2O extraction, volatility, oil resistance, and migration) is expressed in terms of per cent weight loss. Therefore, the higher the number, the poorer the performance. The low-temperature efficiency value is the temperature at which the modulus of rigidity is 135,000 psi, making those systems with the lowest values the most efficient in flexibilizing poly(vinyl chloride) at low temperatures. The room temperature modulus is the flexibility of the system at room temperature. Again, the lower the modulus, the better the performance.

The adipates, being linear aliphatic esters, are used primarily for their plasticizing efficiency. They flexibilize poly(vinyl chloride) well at both room temperature and extremely low temperature. This efficiency is obtained at the expense of permanence. The aliphatic structure leads to poor hydrocarbon resistance, and the relatively low molecular weight causes high volatility. The adipates are used in food wrap film, garden hose, and other applications where low-temperature performance is needed.

The phthalate esters give a good overall balance of properties. They are not as flexibilizing as the adipates, but are more permanent. They can however, have poor hydrocarbon or fat resistance. This probably explains the presence of DEHP in blood after storage in poly(vinyl chloride) bags. The linear

Table III.—Performance Criteria for Selection of Plasticizers

| | PERMANENCE PROPERTIES | | | | EFFICIENCY | |
	H2O	VOL	OIL	MIG	LOW TEMP	R.T. MODULUS
ADIPATE	0.10%	14%	70+%	21%	-66°C	630 psi
PHTHALATE (BRANCHED)	0.03	5	34	4	-39	830
PHTHALATE (LINEAR)	0.02	2	44	2	-48	850
PHOSPHATE ESTER	0.02	7	7	9	-39	700
TRIMELLITATE	0.01	1	82	2	-42	850
POLYMERIC ESTER	0.10%	2%	2	0.4%	-20°C	1300 psi

40% PLASTICIZER IN PVC

phthalates, except for hydrocarbon resistance, are more efficient than DEHP or other branched chain phthalates. As a class, the phthalates are the most widely used plasticizers. DEHP is regulated by the FDA for use in the packaging or storing of high water content food.

The trimellitate plasticizer is just becoming a commercially important system because of its extremely low volatility and high aqueous medial resistance. The trimellitates are used in wire insulation and certain automotive uses where high-temperature performance is required.

The phosphates are used generally to provide flame retardance. The polyester polymeric plasticizer is a reasonable alternate to phthalates for certain critical applications where a high degree of permanence is required. A polyester plasticizer based on butylene glycol, adipic acid, and natural fatty acid (Santicizer 334F) was introduced for these critical uses in 1971. The high molecular weight of this polyester (MW = 2000) provides the excellent permanence in both hydrocarbon and aqueous environments. This polyester is regulated under Food and Drug Administration (FDA) 121.2511 (*Plasticizers for Polymeric Substances*). The following biologic safety tests were obtained on Santicizer 334F:

Chronic Feeding	2 Year Rat & Dog
Metabolism	Oral and Intravenous
Reproduction	3 Generation
Implant	USP
Acute Toxicity	Oral and Intraperitoneal

PLASTICIZER MARKETS

The major market categories accounting for over 90% of the plasticizer uses of phthalate esters are listed in Table IV. Tables V-IX provide further breakdown in each of these major market classifications. [14]

There are several known nonplasticizer uses of phthalate esters. These are shown in Table X. The total sales volume is a rough estimate of 50×10^6 lb in 1972. These numbers are not generally reported making it difficult to pinpoint how much phthalates are used in each area. Since the esters are not bound

Table IV.—Plasticizer Uses of Phthalate Esters

USE	PHTHALATE USAGE, $\overline{M}$ LBS.
BUILDING AND CONSTRUCTION	387
HOME FURNISHINGS	203
TRANSPORTATION	114
APPAREL	72
FOOD SURFACES AND MEDICAL PRODUCTS	46
TOTAL	1022

Table V.—Building and Construction Uses

USE	PHTHALATE USAGE, $\overline{M}$ LBS.
WIRE AND CABLE	185
FLOORING	150
SWIMMING POOL LINERS	20
WEATHERSTRIPPING	13
WINDOW SPLINES	10
OTHER	9
TOTAL	387

Table VI.—Home Furnishing Uses

USE	PHTHALATE USAGE, $\overline{M}$ LBS.
FURNITURE UPHOLSTERY	90
WALL COVERINGS	38
HOUSEWARES	30
GARDEN HOSE	15
APPLIANCES	10
OTHER	20
TOTAL	203

Table VII.—Transportation Uses

USE	PHTHALATE USAGE, $\overline{M}$ LBS.
UPHOLSTERY AND SEATCOVERS	80
AUTO MATS	15
AUTO TOPS	12
OTHER	10
TOTAL	114

Table VIII.—Apparel Uses

USE	PHTHALATE USAGE, $\overline{M}$ LBS.
FOOTWEAR	45
OUTERWARE	20
BABY PANTS	7
TOTAL	72

Table IX.—Food Surface and Medical Product Uses

USE	PHTHALATE USAGE, $\overline{M}$ LBS.
FOOD WRAP FILM	18
CLOSURES	7
MEDICAL TUBING	15
INTRAVENOUS BAGS	6
TOTAL	46

Table X.—Non-Plasticizer Phthalate Uses

PESTICIDE CARRIERS

COSMETICS

FRAGRANCES

MUNITIONS

INDUSTRIAL OILS

INSECT REPELLANT

TOTAL SALES: ESTIMATED 50M̄ LBS.

by a resin matrix, as in plasticization, it would appear that some of these uses would provide a direct route into the environment.

BIODEGRADATION OF PHTHALATES

The laboratory data in Table XI compare the biodegradability of DEHP and butyl benzyl phthalate with a biodegradable detergent, linear alkylbenzene sulfonate. The results were obtained by using a semicontinuous activated sludge at a feeding rate of 5 mg/48 hrs. These results show that phthalate esters do undergo biodegradation. They are not in the same class with

Table XI.—Laboratory Biodegradability Study

	AMOUNT DISAPPEARING IN 48 HRS.	REFRACTORY RESIDUE
LINEAR ALKYL BENZENE SULFONATE	99+%	NONE
DI-2-ETHYLHEXYL PHTHALATE	91 %	NONE
BUTYL BENZYL PHTHALATE	99 %	NONE

SEMI-CONTINUOUS ACTIVATED SLUDGE AT 5 mg/48 hrs

compounds such as DDT which resist degradation and leave considerable levels of refactory residues. For a more complete summary of phthalate biomagnification see Reference 37.

Table XII.—Naturally Occurring Phthalates Reported in the Literature

Source	Type of Phthalate	Reference
Vegetation		
Poppies	Phthalic acid	(16,17)
Cranberries		(18)
Eucalyptus oil	Phthalate, mp 200°C	(19)
Olive oil[a]		(20)
Japanese Canadences	DMP, DIAP, DHP, DOP	(21)
Cigar smoke	Phthalic	(22)
Tobacco leaves	Phthalate esters, trimellitates	(23)
Grapes	DBP	(24)
Kewda	Phthalate ester	(25)
Oxidized corn oil	DOP	(26,27)
Animal		
Atolla jellyfish	Phthalic acid	(28)
Humans[b]	DOP	(29)
Bovine heart, pineal gland	DOP	(30)
Milk[c]		(31)
Fish meal lipids[d]		(32)
Fungus		(33)
Amer. Cockroach	DBP	(38)
Mineral		
Soil		(34)
Crude oil		(35)
Shale		(36)

[a] 1.2-6.4 ppm in 16 samples, Naples, Italy.
[b] Source probably artificial.
[c] Source probably tubing.
[d] Could be artifact.

NATURAL OCCURRENCE OF
PHTHALATE MOIETY

A recent literature search [15] has revealed a number of possible natural sources of the phthalate moiety (Table XII).

Some questions relating to possible phthalate contamination from the equipment and instruments employed in these analysis have arisen. However, several of these procedures were carefully reviewed to assure the absence of poly(vinyl chloride) tubing or other artificial sources of phthalate ester. It is interesting that Paul Karrer's textbook [16] was published prior to the emergence of flexible poly(vinyl chloride) as a major commercial plastic material.

References

1. Darby, JR and Sears, JK: Plasticizers, in Mark, HF; Gaylord, NG; and Bikales, N (eds.): *Encyclopedia of Polymer Science and Technology*, New York, Interscience, 1969, vol 10, pp 228-306.
2. Pellen, M: Brit Pat 2,256, (Mar 1856).
3. Hyatt, JW and Hyatt, IS: U S Pat 105, 338 (July, 1870).
4. Kyrides, LP (to Monsanto), U S Pat 1,923,938 (Aug 1933).
5. Hall, Alan: A Modern Plastics Special Report in Chemicals and Additives, *Modern Plastics* 48:58 Sept, 1971.
6. Horsley, RA: in Morgan, NP (ed.), *Progress in Plastics*, London, Illiffe and Sons, 1957, pp 77.
7. Flory, PJ: *Principles of Polymer Chemistry*, Ithaca, New York Cornell University Press, 1953.
8. Anagnostopoulos, CE and Coran, AY: *J Polym Sci* 57:13, 1962.
9. Darby, JR; Touchette, NW; and Sears, JK: SPE Tech Papers 13, 1966.
10. Small, PA: *J Appl Chem* 3:71, 1953.
11. Quackenbas, HM: Plasticizers Migration, *Ind Eng Chem* 46:1335 1953.
12. Stanford Research Institute, Oxo Alcohols, Report 21, (November 1966).
13. Graham, PR and Darby JR: Effect of Plasticizers on Plastisol Fusion, *SPE J* 17:91, 1961.
14. U S Tariff Commission Report on Plasticizers, 1971.
15. Raizman, P and Graham, PR: Monsanto Literature Search on Phthalate Esters, 1971.
16. Karrer, P: *Organic Chemistry*, English ed 3, Elsevier, New York, 1946, p 518.
17. Klaus, A and von Sydow, E: Aroma of Cranberries, *Acta Chem Scan* 21:2076-2082, 1967.

18. Haagen-Smit; Hirosawa, FN; and Wang, TH: Volatile Constituents of Zinfandel Grapes, *Food Research* 14:472-80, 1949.
19. Dhingra, SN; Dhingra, DR; and Gupta, GN: Essential Oil of Kewda, Perfurmery Essent, *Oil Record* 45:219, 1954.
20. Jaeger, RJ and Rubin, RH: Plasticizers from Plastic Devices: Extraction, Metabolism, and Accumulation by Biological Systems, *Science* 70:460, 1970.
21. Schmid, IH and Karrer, P: Water Soluble Extractives of Papaver Somniferum L, *Helv Chim Acta* 28:722, 1945.
22. Proenca da Cunha, A: Analytical Study of the Essential Oil of Eucalyputs Punctata of Angola, *Garcia Oria* 14:3, 1966.
23. Ranaudo, C and Schettino, O: Colormetric Determination of Phthalates in Olive and Olive Husk Oils, *Rassegna Chimica* 21:171-73, 1969.
24. Shuichi, H et al: Phthalate Esters of Cryptotaenia Cadadenses DC Var Japonica Makina (umbelliferae), *Tetrahedron Lett* 50:5061, 1967.
25. Mokhanachev, IG and Astakhova, LG: Water Soluble Di-and Tri-Carboxylic Acids in Tobacco Smoke, *Tabak* (Moscow) 29:3, 31:4, 1968.
26. Swain, AP; Rusaniwskj, W; and Stedman, RL: Hexane Soluble Substances of Tobacco Leaves, *Chem* & *Ind* (London) 14:435-6, 1961.
27. Perkins, EG: Formation of Non-volatile Decomposition in Heated Fats and Oils, *Food Technology* 21 (4):611-16, 1967.
28. Perkins, EG: Characterization of the Nonvolatile Formed During the Thermal Oxidation of Corn Oil II. Phthalate Esters, *J Amer Oil Chemists Soc* 44 (3):197-9, 1967.
29. Morris, Robert J: Phthalic Acid in Deep Sea Jellyfish. Atolla, *Nature* 227:5264, 1970.
30. Taborsky, PG: Isolation Studies on a Lepoidal Portion of the Bovine Pineal Gland, *J Agr Food Chem* 15 (6):1073-6, 1967.
31. Cerbulis, J and Ard JS: Method for Isolation and Detection of Dioctyl Phthalate from Milk Lipids, *J Ass Offic Anal Chem* 50(3):646-50, 1967.
32. Cross, BE et al: New Metabolites of Gibberella Fujikuroi II. The Isolation of Fourteen New Metabolites, *J Chem Soc* 2937-43, 1963.
33. Cifrulak, SD: Spectroscopic Evidence of Phthalates in Soil Organic Matter, *Soil Sci* 107:63-9, 1969.
34. Hayashi, T and Nagai, T: Components in Soil Humic Acids VIII, *Nippon Dojo-Hiryogaku Zasshi* 31:197-200, 1960.
35. Kokurin, AD and Galutkina, KA: Neutral Oxygen Compounds of Heavy Tar of Bituminous Shale, *Zh Prikly Khim* 40:887-90, 1967.
36. Breger, IA and Phillips, HF: *Geochim et Cosmochim* 15:51, 1958.
37. Saeger, VW and Tucker, ES: Biodegradation of Phthalate Esters, Paper presented to Regional Technical Conference of the Society of Plastics Engineers, Monticello, N Y, March 23, 1973.
38. Jones, WA; Warthen, JD; and Jacobson, M: The Occurrence of Dibutyl Phthalate in American Cockroaches, *Environmental Letters* 4(2):103-107, 1973.

Toxicology of Phthalic Acid Ester*

SAMUEL I. SHIBKO, Ph.D.

Man may be exposed to phthalic acid esters from various sources including (1) direct migration into foods, when used as plasticizers in food packaging material having direct contact with food, (2) direct entry into foods, especially fish, as a result of general contamination of the environment, (3) medical treatment with equipment containing PVC plastics, (4) pharmaceuticals, e.g., tablet coatings and time release composition may contain cellulose acetate phthalate plasticized with diethyl phthalate, or (5) the use of phthalate in cosmetics (perfumes, lotions, deodorants).

Although possible effects on human health will result from a summation of these exposures, this presentation will be concerned with man's exposure through diet. In order to evaluate the hazard associated with this exposure, it is necessary to consider (1) the available information on the toxicity of the phthalic acid esters, and (2) the amounts and types of phthalates that man may be exposed to through the diet.

The available toxicity data must first be considered. For safety evaluation of substances that may enter the diet, emphasis must be placed on the results of oral toxicity studies.

Acutely, phthalate esters administered orally show a low order of toxicity (Table I). In experimental animals, poisoning is characterized by central nervous depression as well as kidney and liver injury. A single report of toxicity in humans relates to a case in which a worker swallowed 10gm dibutylphthalate. Keratitis and nephritis developed, but recovery was complete within 14 days. No after effects were observed.[1]

---

* Official government material, U.S. Department of Health, Education, and Welfare. This chapter may be reproduced in part or full.

Table I.—Acute oral LD $_{50}$ values for phthalate esters in the rat

Phthalate ester	gm/kg body wt
Di-(2-ethylhexyl) phthalate	31
Diethyl phthalate	9.5-31
Butyl phthalyl butyl glycolate	7
Butyl benzyl phthalate	18
Dicyclohexyl phthalate	>40
Di-n-hexyl phthalate	29.6
Diphenyl phthalate	8
Dibutyl phthalate	8-16
Diisobutyl phthalate	15
Diisodecyl phthalate	64
Dimethyl phthalate	6.9

SUBACUTE AND CHRONIC TOXICITY STUDIES

Subacute toxicity studies, that is, studies in which experimental animals were fed test diets containing the phthalate ester for up to 13 weeks, have been reported for 13 phthalate esters. In addition, chronic toxicity studies, studies in which experimental animals were fed the test diets for up to two years (in the case of rodents, essentially lifetime studies), have been reported for some of these esters: diethyl, dibutyl, methyl phthalyl ethyl glycolate, ethyl phthalyl ethyl glycolate, and di-(-2-ethylhexyl) as well as dimethyl and dicyclohexyl phthalate. Table II presents a summary of "no effects" levels (the highest level of exposure to the phthalate esters at which no adverse effects were observed in various species) in the ranges of the compounds tested. [2-11] The studies with dibutyl phthalate, diisodecyl phthalate, di-(2-ethylhexyl) phthalate and ethyl phthalyl ethyl glycolate provide information on the most widely used plasticizers and present a reasonable toxicity profile for the phthalates presently regulated by FDA for use in food packaging materials.

Table II.—Available data on "no effect" levels (mg/kg of body weight/day) of phthalates for rats and dogs (oral administration)

Phthalate	Subacute		Chronic	
	Rat	Dog	Rat	Dog
Dimethyl	—	—	1000(104)[2]	—
Diethyl	2500(6)	1250	1250(104)	625(52)
Dibutyl	50(16)[3]	—	125(52)[4]	18(52)
Dialkyl 7-9	60(13)[5]	—	—	—
Di-n-hexyl	50(13)	125(13)	—	—
Diisobutyl	50(16)	25-500(8)	—	—
Diisooctyl	100(4)	100(4)	—	—
Diisodecyl	150(13)	75(13)	—	—
Diphenyl	1000(13)	500(13)[6]	—	—
Dicyclohexyl	—	—	27(104)[4]	14(52)
Methyl phthalyl ethyl glycolate	240(4)	—	750(104)	—
Ethyl phthalyl ethyl glycolate	500(17)[7]	—	250(104)[7]	250(52)[7]
Butyl phthalyl butyl glycolate	—	—	450(104)	140(104)
Di-(2-ethylhexyl) phthalate	200(13)[8]	500(13)[9]	65(104)[10]	60(52)[10]
Di-(butoxyethyl) phthalate	500(4)[11]	—	—	—
Butyl benzyl phthalate	500(13)[6]	250(13)	—	—

Numbers in parentheses represent duration of study in weeks. Superscript numbers indicate references (2-11); other data taken from FDA files.

In the case of dibutyl phthalate, when rats were dosed twice weekly with dibutyl phthalate (50% in oil) 1 ml/kg body weight, for a period of six weeks, no adverse effects were reported.[4] Another group of rats was maintained on this regimen for 1-1/2 years without any adverse effects on the parameters studied, which included hematology, pathology of tissues, and organ weights.[4] In another study[3], there was no effect on growth or survival when rats were maintained for one year on diets containing diisodecyl phthalate for 14 weeks established a "no-effect" level of 0.1gm body weight for both species.[12] At the highest levels fed (1%), a slightly elevated liver/body weight ratio was noted in all male dogs and in two-thirds of the females. Pathological examination revealed swollen and vacuolated hepatocytes in the livers of these animals. Livers of rats, particularly males on diets containing 1% of the phthlate ester, were markedly heavier than those of controls. No histological changes were observed. Subacute and chronic feeding studies in rats have indicated a "no effect" level of 60 mg/kg body weight/day. At higher dose levels 400 mg/kg/day, depressed growth rates and enlarged livers and kidneys were reported.[9] In a study with guinea pigs maintained for one year on a diet containing 0.04% to 0.13% of the phthalate, the only effect noted was increased liver weight in females.[9] Since the effect was not dose related and no histopathological lesions were observed, the significance of this effect is not known.[9] In another experiment[9] dogs were dosed with 0.03 ml/kg body weight/day of the phthalate 5 days a week for a total of 29 doses and then with 0.06 ml/kg body weight/day for a total of 240 doses; a single dog received doses of 0.09 ml/kg/day (77 doses at 0.06 ml/kg body weight/day; 169 doses at 0.09 ml/kg body weight/day). All dogs showed satisfactory weight gain. Hematologic and biochemical tests including liver function test were normal. The single dog maintained on the high dose level showed some histologic changes in the liver and kidney. These were reported as congestion in the subcapsular area of the liver and moderate congestion of the kidney with cloudy swelling. However, the significance of this effect in a single test dog cannot be evaluated.

In studies with ethyl phthalyl ethyl glycolate (EPEG), rats were maintained on diets containing up to 5.0% EPEG for two years.[7] Rats in the 5% group showed retardation in growth and longevity, none of the males surviving the 55th week of feeding nor the females the 72nd week. Hematological data were normal with the exception of a slight anemia in the 5% group. Elevated sugar levels were observed in the urine in the 5% group only, although not at lower dose levels. Histopathological studies indicated marked changes in the kidneys of rats in the 5% group. The changes consisted of crystalline masses of calcium oxalate in the renal tubules. The origin of the calcium oxalate crystals was attributed to the metabolism of the ethyl glycolate moiety. Dogs dosed daily with EPEG at dose levels up to 0.25gm/kg body weight/day for a period of one year showed no compound-related effects. Specifically, oxalate crystals in the renal tubules or other kidney lesions did not appear.[7]

Evaluation of effects of reproductive performances are important in assessing the safety of substances that may enter the diet. Multigeneration reproduction studies in rats have been reproted for di-(2-ethylhexyl phthalate) and dibutyl phthalate. Rats fed dietary di-(2-ethylhexyl) phthalate (DEHP) up to levels of 0.4% were bred, and the F_1 generation offspring were maintained on the test diet for one year. The parent group P_O was maintained for a total of 425 days on the test diet. Comparison of reproductive performance (litters born, total number of pups born, mean size of litters, maximum number of litters by any female, pups stillborn) showed that the only valid change among the di-(-2-ethylhexyl) phthalate-dosed rats was a decrease in the mean number of litters per female among the F_1 first generation rats at the 0.4% level. The decrease was not present among the P_1 parent rats at the same dosage level. Both parental and first filial generation maintained on the 0.4% dietary DEHP showed increased liver and kidney weights. However, no significant histopathologic effects were observed.[9]

Three-generation reproduction studies have been reported for dibutyl phthalate[4] (daily dosing of female rats with 1 ml/kg body weight of 50% solution) and dicyclohexyl phthalate (daily dosing of female rats with 2 ml/kg body weight). After 6 weeks of treatment the female rats were paired with untreated males. Offspring were bred to produce 2 additional generations. Details of treatment of offsprings are lacking. There was no impairment of reproductive performance. The average weights of endocrine organs of F_1 rats at day 71 of the test were within the range of normal values. In addition, the first incidence of estrous was normal. Development, growth, and fertility throughout the 3 generations studied were normal. Reproduction studies for other phthalates are not available.

Special studies to explore the "subtle" effects of the phthalic acid esters including their teratogenic and mutagenic potential have been reported. McLaughlin *et al* [13] reported that undiluted di-(2-ethylhexyl) phthalate did not have any effect on the development of chick egg embryo. It is possible that in this study the undiluted phthalate failed to diffuse to the developing embryo.

In another study [14], eight esters of phthalic acid (dioctyl, butyl benzyl, *n*-octyl, *n*-decyl, dibutoxyethyl, diethyl, di-2-methoxyethyl, and octyl isodecyl esters) were studied in the chick embryo test. Dibutoxyethyl phthalate appeared to be the most teratogenic, causing malformations or neuromuscular defects. The malformations included crania bifida, anophthalmia, exophthalmia and hemorrhage, and impairment of corneal development. Neuromuscular defects were noted in chicks hatched from eggs treated with dibutoxyethyl phthalate, as well as octylisodecyl, *n*-octyl, and *n*-decyl phthalates. A marked malformation of the leg was reported in 1 of 10 chicks surviving treatment with diethyl phthalate. No neuromuscular defects or malformations were reported for control chicks. Phthalic acid, a possible metabolic product of the phthalates, produced a low incidence (3.1%) of specific malformations in the chick embryo test.

Teratogenicity of phthalate esters in rats has been reported by Singh *et al.* [15] This study involved eight phthalates (dimethyl phthalate, dimethoxyethyl phthalate, diethyl phthalate, dibutyl phthalate, diisobutyl phthalate, butoxymethyl phthalate, dioctyl phthalate and di-(w-ethylhexyl) phthalate). Treatment consisted of intraperitoneal injection on the 5th, 10th, and 15th days of gestation. The six more toxic phthalates were administered at 1/10, 1/5, and 1/3 of the acute LD $_{50}$ at each of the three injections. The two other phthalates (dioctyl phthalate and di-(2-octylhexyl) phthalate) were administered at dosage levels of 5 and 10 ml/kg body weight. At day 20 of gestation, adverse effects were investigated. These included embryo or fetal toxicity as evidenced by resorption and stillbirths as well as malformations, e.g., gross external malformations of fetus, skeletal malformations, and fetal size. The course of treatment did not affect fertility, since the ratios of corpora lutea to implantation sites were similar for test and control animals. All phthalates used in this study caused some resorptions, the highest incidence occurring with the dose level of dimethoxyethyl phthalate. Di-(2-ethylhexyl) phthalate showed greater activity than dioctyl phthalate.

Dead fetuses were observed only in groups treated with dimethyl, dimethoxyethyl, and diisobutyl phthalate. Teratogenicity in terms of gross abnormalities was not uniformly distributed, but seemed to be related to certain phthalates, and showed a dose-related response pattern. The greatest number of gross malformations were observed with dioctyl phthalate, with lesser numbers for dimethoxyethyl phthalate (probably due to high rate of resorption), and dimethyl phthalate. Abnormalities reported included absence of tail, anophthalmia, twisted hind legs, and hematomas.

Skeletal abnormalities were observed with dimethyl, dimethoxyethyl, diethyl, dibutyl, diisobutyl, and butyl carbobutoxy methyl phthalates. No skeletal abnormalities were observed with dioctyl and di-(2-ethylhexyl) phthalates. The skeletal abnormalities reported included elongated and fused ribs, absence of tail bones, abnormal or incomplete skull bones, and incomplete or missing leg bones.

Fetuses from all groups of treated rats were smaller than controls.

Of the phthalate esters studied, the least soluble, dioctyl and di-(2-ethylhexyl), exerted the least deleterious effect on embryo-fetal development.

In another study[16] large quantities of DEHP (12.78-25.56ml/kg body weight) and dimethoxyethyl phthalate (DMEP) (1.19-2.38ml/kg body weight) were administered intraperitoneally (i.p.) to male mice before they were mated with untreated females. The result was a significant reduction both in the number of embryos implanted per pregnancy and in the number of live fetuses per pregnancy. This was interpreted as being consistent with the hypothesis that these phthalates produced dominant lethal mutations in mice.

In attempting to evaluate the significance of the teratogenic and mutagenic studies, particularly in relation to ingested phthalates, it is important to determine if the phthalate esters are absorbed unchanged, because the adverse effects noted were observed following intraperitoneal injection of high doses of the phthalate. Preliminary *in vitro* studies have shown that dibutyl phthalate is hydrolyzed by pancreatic lipase as rapidly as triolein[3], the author suggested that phthalates may be transported and metabolized via the same pathways utilized in normal fat metabolism.

Limited metabolic studies have also been reported in dogs, rabbit, rat, and men.[8] Dogs dosed with di-(2-ethylhexyl) pathalate (DEHP), approximately 0.2 gm/kg body weight, excreted phthalate equivalent to 2.0% to 4.5% of the dose in the urine in a 72-hour period subsequent to dosing.

In a study with rabbits dosed with approximately 1-0.6 gm/kg body weight of DEHP, 26% to 65.4% of the administered dose was excreted in the urine.[8] No increase in urinary excretion of glycuronic acid, ethereal sulfate, or conjugated amino acids was observed in rabbits and rats in these studies, although a large increase in the urinary excretion of fatty acids was observed. The significance of the increased urinary fatty acids is not known.

In another study[6], dogs administered a single oral dose of either diphenyl phthalate or butylbenzyl phthalate (5 gm/kg body weight) excreted 90% of the dose unchanged in the feces. No unchanged phthalate ester was present in the urine. When diphenyl phthalate was administered, 34% of the phenol arising from the diphenyl phthalate was excreted in the free form, 21%-28% as the glycoside and 38% to 44% as the ethereal sulfate. Approximately 90% of the absorbed phthalate was excreted as phthalic acid in urine within 72 hours of dosing. With butyl benzyl phthalate, the urinary metabolites arising from the benzyl alcohol consisted of approximately 94% as the glycoside and the remainder as hippuric acid. The formation of butyl alcohol was not established. Most of the phthalic acid was excreted in the urine within 72 hours after dosing. Humans administered 5 g or 10 g of diethylhexyl phthalate excreted approximately 4% to 5% of the dose in urine in a 24-hour period postdosing. Most was excreted 5 to 7 hours after dosing. In the case of rabbits and possible other species, it is likely that the phthalate content of the urine is a measure of the intestinal absorption of the phthalate ester. However, when dibutyl and diethyl phthalate were given orally to rats, they excreted in the urine, with monobutyl and monoethyl esters as the principle metabolite and phthalic acid as the secondary metabolite. [17]

Recently, Schulz [18] has studied the metabolism of DEHP administered to rats both intravenously and by stomach tube. In both experiments, metabolism and excretion were rapid. Ninety percent of the intravenously injected DEHP was disposed of by the animal within 24 hours. The metabolism of the DEHP that had been administered by stomach tube was so fast that negligible quantities were found in the tissues. In these experiments, the water-soluble products that appeared in the urine and feces could not be identified as the products of simple ester hydrolysis to phthalic acid and the appropriate alcohol.

Hydrolysis of the phthalate esters may not occur in liver. Studies in which isolated rat livers were perfused with solutions containing either butyl glycolybutyl phthalate or di-(2-ethylhexyl) phthalate showed that, whereas, the butyl glycolybutyl phthalate was hydrolyzed to give rise to glycolyl phthalate, the DEHP was not metabolized and accumulated in the liver, primarily in unmetabolized form. It has been established that spleen, liver, lung, and abdominal fat from patients that had received blood transfusions contained DEHP from 0.025 mg/gm (dry wt) in spleen to 0.270 mg/gm (dry wt) in abdominal fat. [19] Although the intracellular localization of DEHP in liver and the other tissues has not been established, Nazir *et al* [20] showed that normal beef, rat, rabbit, and dog heart muscle contained DEHP that was localized in the mitochondria. They were unable to demonstrate the presence of DEHP in other tissues in these species. The absence of DEHP in organs other than the heart in these species raises the question as to whether or not the deposition of phthalate in these tissues in man represented a species difference or was due to the use of blood containing extracted residues of phthalate. The origin and significance of phthalate residues in tissues is not known. The available toxicity data reviewed indicate that all phthalates studied have a low order of acute toxicity. The "no effect" levels of phthalates based on chronic toxicity show ranges from 65 to 1625 mg/kg body weight/day for rats, with similar values for dogs. In general, no specific lesion has been identified with the feeding of the phthalate esters. Effects may be due to ester moiety, as in the case of ethyl phthalyl ethyl glycolate, where the specific tissue damage observed, namely, crystalline masses of calcium oxalate in the renal tubules, could be attributed to metabolism of the ethyl glycolate moiety. No cases of unusual incidence of carcinogenesis in the chronic feeding studies with phthalates have been reported.

In general, good metabolic data on the phthalate esters is lacking. It would be extremely desirable to carry out studies to determine the extent of absorption and subsequent metabolism in species, such as the dog, which are known to metabolize the phthalate moiety in a manner similar to man. Although it has previously been assumed that the phthalate esters would be hydrolyzed to free phthalic acid and the alcohol in the gut, and the products of digestion absorbed, more recent information suggests that some phthalate may be absorbed unchanged, and metabolism in rats may not proceed greatly beyond the non-ester stage. It is not known if phthalates absorbed via the respiratory route or injection are metabolized in the same way as dietary phthalates. Metabolism via these routes needs adequate study if these are important routes of exposure.

These limited studies do not indicate any marked effect on the reproductive process. Teratogenic studies using the chick embryo test, as well as the i.p. study with rats, are difficult to relate to possible effects that may occur following oral ingestion. Because of the large doses (i.p.) required to produce effects in the rat studies, the small amounts of phthalates ingested via the dietary would not be expected to cause a problem. However, it would be desirable to carry out teratogenicity studies using phthalates administered orally. Dose levels should be related to expected dietary intakes in man.

And now the second question in our evaluation: What is known about dietary intakes and types of phthalates that may enter the diet? As I have previously indicated, phthalic acid esters may be used as plasticizers in food packaging materials that may have direct contact with food. Under normal conditions of use only small amounts of the plasticizers would be expected to migrate into the food. The safe use of the phthalic acid esters under these conditions is based on available toxicity data, as well as on regulations which control the maximum extractable fraction of plasticizer that may enter food.

Prior to 1958 (i.e., before the enactment of the food additive amendment to the Federal Food, Drug and Cosmetic Act), sanctions were granted for the use of five phthalates in food packaging material (diethyl phthalate, diisobutyl phthalate, ethyl phthalyl ethyl glycolate, diisooctyl phthalate and di-(2-ethylhexyl) phthalate), with the limitations that they be used in accordance with good manufacturing practice for food packaging materials, as well as that di-(2-ethylhexyl) phthalate and the diisooctyl phthalate be used with foods of high water content. An additional 19 phthalate esters have now been regulated and are listed in the Code of Federal Regulations, Title 21, Food and Drugs. The regulated uses of phthalates may be classified into three categories that reflect the possible levels of direct migration to foods, namely: significant, slight, and essentially zero. Table III lists regulated uses that could result in migration of phthalates to foods. The uses listed in this table include (1) those that will be major contributors of phthalate migration to foods (includes prior sanction), and (2) uses that will result in slight migration to foods. Regulated uses that under normal conditions would not be expected to result in migration to foods are listed in Table IV.

Phthalate esters that are regulated for uses that would be expected to result in migration to foods are listed in Table V. Each of the esters may have several uses that would result in migration to foods, as well as other regulated uses that would not be expected to result in migration to foods. Some phthalate esters are regulated only for uses that would not be expected to

Table III.—Regulated* uses of phthalate esters that could result in migration into foods. †

121.2001	Substances employed in manufacture of food packaging material (prior sanction).
121.2511	Plasticizers in polymeric substances.
121.2514	Resinous and polymeric coatings.
121.2526	Components of paper and paperboard contact with aqueous and fatty foods.
121.2550	Closures with sealing gaskets for food containers.
121.2531	Surface lubricants used in the manufacture of metallic articles.
121.2569	Resinous and polymeric coatings for polyolefin films.
121.2507	Cellophane

*Code of Federal Regulations. Title 21. Food and Drugs. Jan. 1, 1972.

† Order of listing reflects possible level of migration into foods (i.e., 121.2001, 2511, 2514, 2526 and 2550 will result in greatest migration; 121.2531, 2569, 2507, only slight migration).

Table IV.—Regulated* uses of phthalate esters that under normal conditions of use would not reasonably be expected to result in migration to foods, based on available scientific information and data.

121.2577	Pressure sensitive adhesives.
121.2562	Rubber articles intended for repeated use.
121.2571	Components of paper and paperboard in contact with dry food.
121.2519	Defoaming agents used in the manufacture of paper and paperboard.
121.2520	Adhesives.

*Code of Federal Regulations. Title 21. Food and Drugs. Jan. 1, 1972.

Table V.—Phthalate esters regulated* for uses that could result in migration to foods.

Diisooctyl phthalate[†]	Di-n-hexyl phthalate
Ethyl phthalyl butyl glycolate[†]	Diphenyl phthalate
Di-(2-ethylhexyl) phthalate[‡]	Dibutyl phthalate
Diethyl phthalate[‡]	Diisobutyl phthalate
Butyl phthalyl butyl glycolate[‡]	Diisodecyl phthalate
Butyl benzyl phthalate	Dimethyl cyclohexyl phthalate
Dicyclohexyl phthalate	Dihydroxy abietyl phthalate

Castor oil phthalate, hydrogenated

* See Table I for regulated uses. Note: Esters usually have one or more regulated uses. Most of these esters are also regulated for uses which would not be expected to result in migration to foods.

[†] Prior sanction for foods of high water content only.

[‡] Prior sanction.

result in migration to foods under normal conditions of use (Table VI), e.g., adhesives. The use of adhesives is based on the requirement of a functional barrier between the adhesives and the food to prevent any migration of the adhesive.

In the case of phthalate esters approved by prior sanction, theoretically all the phthalate esters (except those intended for use with foods of a high water content) used in food packaging material could migrate into fatty foods held for a period of time in the package. The amount available for migration will be limited by good manufacturing practice for food packaging materials, which include restrictions to insure, for example, "that the quantity of the substance used shall be reduced to the least amount reasonably possible" (21 Food and Drugs, CFR 121.2500). In addition, if all the phthalate esters were to be leached out of the plastic packaging material, the material would no longer be functional. Since levels of migration of these phthalate esters to food might be high, chronic toxicity data were obtained for four of the five phthalate esters whose use was authorized by prior sanction (diethyl phthalate, ethyl phthalyl ethyl glycolate, and butyl phthalyl butyl glycolate).

Table VI.—Phthalate esters regulated for uses* that under normal conditions of use would not reasonably be expected to migrate into foods.

Di-(butoxyethyl) phthalate

Di-(2-ethylhexyl) hydrophthalate

n-Octyl-n-decyl phthalate

Dioctyl phthalate

Butyl octyl phthalate

Dimethyl phthalate

n-Amyl-n-decyl phthalate

Methyl phthalyl ethyl glycolate

---

*See Table II for list of regulated uses.

The source and level of phthalates migrating into foods resulting from their regulated uses is relatively well defined by food additive and supporting data submitted to the FDA. In general, the possible levels of migration have been derived by using the standard petition extractive tests as outlined in the FDA 1966 guidelines. The safety basis for phthalate esters whose regulated use would not result in migration to foods, e.g., in adhesives, may be based primarily on lack of migration rather than detailed toxicity studies.

The major migration of phthalates from packaging material will occur with fatty foods. Fatty foods usually constitute about one tenth of the diet in the United States; thus, the level of phthalates present in the total diet will be reduced. In addition to concern for the type of food that may contain phthalate residues as a result of migration from packaging, it is important to consider the section of the population that may be exposed to the phthalate esters. There is particular concern for young infants, e.g., 21 Food and Drugs, Code of Federal Regulations (CFR) 121.2562(h). Rubber articals intended for repeated use specifically exclude rubber nursing bottle nipples.

Because of the low order of toxicity of the phthalate esters, the low levels of phthalates in the diet from authorized sources do not pose any toxicological hazard.

Another possible source of entry into the diet is through possible food chain accumulation, or accumulation in various foods, as a result of a general contamination of the environment. Since persistent man-made chemicals used in large amounts eventually enter water courses, fish and other aquatic species provide an excellent indicator of the degree of environmental contamination. Meyer *et al* [21] have measured levels of phthalates in fresh water species from various areas (Table VII). The phthalates may be derived from contamination of the lakes, or in the case of pond-reared fish, from contamination of fish feed, possibly through the use of storage bags lined with plastics containing phthalate ester plasticizers. Although the levels may appear relatively high compared with other contaminants that may be present in fish, it is of interest to compare toxicity of phthalate (chronic oral) with that of some pesticide and other residues that may also be present (Table VIII). In all cases, there is a difference of at least an order of magnitude in the "no effect" level. Further, it is likely that the levels of phthalates that may be expected to be present in fish are probably limited, because the rather short biological half life of phthalates in fish would tend to limit the level of accumulation. At present, FDA is planning a modest survey of commercial fish for levels of diethylhexyl phthalate, diisooctyl phthalate, and diisodecyl phthalate, in order to determine if there is a general problem of contamination of this food source. However, the data of Meyer *et al* [21] suggest that the level of phthalates in fish will not result in a significant increase in dietary phthalates.

In summary, the available information indicates that the levels of phthalates that may occur in the diet do not pose any toxicological hazard. In view of the low order of toxicity of phthalates and the absence of any specific lesion in experimental animals administered extremely high doses of these substances, the problem may best be summarized by the recent statement of Dr. Lloyd Tepper, FDA Associate Commissioner for Science, who characterized the present situation relating to phthalates as "an etiology looking for a disease."*

---

* Phthalic Acid Esters Meeting Pinehurst, North Carolina (Sponsored by NIEHS, Sept. 1972).

Table VII.–Phthalate ester, polychlorinated biphenyl, and insecticide residues found in selected samples from North America

Source	Sample type	Residue (ng/g)			
		DNBP	DEHP	PCB	Insecticide
Mississippi and Arkansas (agricultural and industrial areas)	Channel catfish	Trace	3,200	400	DDT-300 dieldrin-40, endrin-30, toxaphene-2200
Fairport National Fish Hatchery, Iowa (water supply from industrial area of Mississippi River)	Channel catfish	200	400	700	—
	Dragonfly naiads	200	400	700	—
	Tadpoles	500	300	1,000	Dieldrin-10
Black Bay, Lake Superior, Ontario (rural and industrial area)	Walleye	—	800	1,300	DDT-120
	Water	—	300	—	—
	Sediment	100	200	40	—
Hammond Bay, Lake Huron, Michigan (forested area)	Water	0.040	—	0.003	—
Lake Huron, Michigan	Water	—	5.0	0.02	—
Spirit Lake, Iowa (agricultural area)	Yellow perch	—	—	—	DDT-160, dieldrin-120, chlordane-30

Clover Leaf Lake, California (10,300 feet elevation)	Brook trout	—	—	—	DDT-110
Missouri River, McBaine, Missouri	Water (turbid)	0.09	4.9	0.20	—
Fish food and components	Commercial fish food	—	2,000	700	—
		—	7,000	60	DDT-30, dieldrin-60
	Casein	20	190	—	—
	Corn starch	20	170	80	—
	Gelatin	20	140	—	—
	Bone meal	30	400	—	—
	Wheat middlings	30	200	20	—
	Carboxymethyl cellulose	—	—	—	Chlordane-720

Taken from Meyer et al., (1972) Nature 238, 411.

DNBP, di-n-butyl phthalate: DEHP, di-2-ethylhexyl phthalate.

*Residues approximated by 'Aroclor' 1254 (80%), 1248, and traces of 1232.

[†]Residues presented for this group are the means of values for forty fish. Di-2-ethylhexyl phthalate residues ranged from 1,000 to 7,500 ng/g.

Table VIII.—"No effect" level of some insecticides, PCB, and phthalate esters.

Compound	mg/kg body wt/day (rat)
Dieldrin*	0.025
Endrin*	0.05
Chlordane*	1.0
PCB	0.5
Phthalic acid esters	65-1000

*FAO/WHO evaluation of some pesticide residues in food/1970.

References

1. Cagianut, B: Keratitis and Toxic Nephritis After Ingestion of Dibutyl Phthalate, *Schweiz Med Wochenschr* **84**:1243, 1954.
2. Lehman, AJ: Insect Repellants, *Ass Food & Drug Office US Quart Bulletin* **19**:87-99, 1955.
3. Smith, CC: Toxicity of Butyl Stearate, Dibutyl Sebacate, Dibutyl Phthalate and Methoxyethyl oleate, *Arch Ind Hyg Occup Med* **7**:310-318, 1953.
4. Bornmann, G *et al*: Behaviour of the Organism as Influenced by Various Plasticizers, *Z. Lebensm-Unters. Forsch* **103**:413, 1956.
5. Gaunt, I *et al*: Acute (Rat and Mouse) and Short-term (Rat) Toxicity of Dialkyl Phthalate, *Bibra Information Bulletin* **7**:118-119, 1968.
6. Erickson, NG: The Metabolism of Diphenyl Phthalate and Butyl-benzyl Phthalate in the Beagle Dog, *Diss Abstr* **26**:3014, 1965.
7. Hodge, HC *et al*: Chronic Oral Toxicity of Ethyl Phthalyl Ethyl Glycolate in Rats and Dogs, *Arch Ind Hyg Occup Med* **8**:289-295, 1953.
8. Shaffer, CB; Carpenter, CP; and Smyth, HF: Acute and Sub-acute Toxicity of Di-(2-ethylhexyl) Phthalate with Note Upon Its Metabolism, *J Ind Hyg Toxicol* **27**:130-135, 1945.
9. Carpenter, CP; Weil, CS; and Smyth, HF: Chronic Oral Toxicity of Di-(2-ethylhexyl) Phthalate for Rats, Guinea Pigs, and Dogs, *Arch Ind Hyg Toxicol* **8**:219-226, 1953.
10. Harris, RS *et al*: Chronic Oral Toxicity of 2-ethylhexyl Phthalate in Rats and Dogs, *AMA Arch Ind Health* **13**:259, 1956.
11. Smyth HF and Carpenter, CP: Further Experience with the Range Finding Test in the Industrial Toxicology Laboratory, *J Ind Hyg* **30**:63, 1948.
12. Dewey and Alma: Chemical Division of W. R. Grace & Co., Unpublished data submitted to FDA, 1968.

13. McLaughlin, J Jr *et al*: The Injection of Chemicals Into the Yolk Sac of Fertile Eggs Prior to Incubation as a Toxicity Test, *Toxicol Appl Pharmacol* **5**:760-771, 1963.

14. Bower, RK; Haberman, S; and Minton, PD: Teratogenic Effects in Chick Embryo Caused by Esters of Phthalic Acid, *J Pharmacol Exp Ther* **171**:314-324, 1970.

15. Singh, AR; Lawrence, WH; and Autian, J: Teratogenicity of Phthalate Esters in Rats, *J Pharm Sci* **61**:51-55, 1972.

16. Dillingham, EO and Autian, J: Teratofenicity, Mutagenicity and Cellular Toxicity of Phthalate Esters. Presented at Phthalic Acid Esters Meeting, Pinehurst, North Carolina, Sept. 1972.

17. Chambon, P, *et al*: Etude du Metabolisme des Phthalates de Dibutyle et de Diethyle chez le Rat, *C R Acad Sci*, (Paris) **273**:2165-2168, 1971.

18. Schulz, CO and Rubin, RJ: Distribution, Metabolism, and Excretion of Di-(2-ethylhexyl) Phthalate in the Rat, presented at Phthalic Acid Esters Meeting, Pinehurst, North Carolina, Sept, 1972.

19. Jaeger, RJ and Rubin, RJ: Plasticizers from Plastic Devices: Extraction, Metabolism and Accumulation by Biological Systems, *Science* **170**:460-462 1970.

20. Nazir, DJ *et al*: Isolation and Identification and Specific Localization of Di-(2-ethylhexyl) Phthalate in Bovine Heart Muscle Mitochondria, *Biochemistry* **10**:4228-4332, 1971.

21. Meyer, FL: Stalling, DL; and Johnson, JL: Phthalate Esters as Environmental Contaminants, *Nature* **238**:411-413, 1972.

Etiology and Prevention of Cancer

JOHN H. WEISBURGER, Ph.D.

To grasp a proper perspective of the current status of mor·
tality due to chronic diseases, the vital statistics of the United
States, of 1968, show that out of 100% of all deaths, heart
disease accounted for 38% and cancer for about 17% (Figure 1).
Some cancers of many types can be demonstrated as being
probably environmentally caused. Factors bearing on their etiology, therefore, warrant further discussion, as basis of rational
preventive measures.

Data produced by Silverberg and Holleb[1] of the American
Cancer Society, on cancer incidence over the last 40 years reveal
that with some types of cancer, for example, lung cancer, the
incidence is increasing at a frightful and dramatic rate (Figure
2). In contrast, other types of cancer such as gastric cancer,
have been occurring at a decreased rate. Some types of cancer
are found at a very low rate nationally, yet the incidence is high
in select groups in our population. In the United States, cancer
of the esophagus, for instance, is noted primarily among black
people living in underprivileged areas, with a mortality rate of
20 per 100,000. This kind of data that shows areas of high
incidence as compared to those areas of low incidence, are
useful in focusing on causative factors of cancer.

The concept that many types of cancer are environmentally
caused developed from the studies of migrants, due chiefly to
Segi, Hirayama, Wynder, Haenzel, and Doll.[2] This data shows
that in respect to stomach cancer, Japan has the highest rate,
whereas the United States Caucasian population has one of the
lowest rates, and other countries are intermediary (Figure 3).
One could conclude that Japanese are genetically different from
Americans and, thus, they are more prone to this type of

Rank	Cause of Death	Number of Deaths	Death Rate Per 100,000 Population	Percent of Total Deaths
All Causes		**1,930,082**	**965.8**	**100.0**
1 Diseases of Heart		744,658	372.6	38.6
2 Cancer		318,547	159.4	16.5
3 Stroke (Cerebrovascular Diseases)		211,390	105.8	11.0
4 Accidents		114,864	57.5	6.0
	Motor-Vehicles Accidents	54,862	27.5	2.8
	All Other Accidents	60,002	30.0	3.2
5 Influenza and Pneumonia		73,492	36.8	3.8
6 Certain Diseases of Early Infancy		43,840	21.9	2.3
7 Diabetes Mellitus		38,352	19.2	2.0

Source: Vital Statistics of the United States, 1968

Figure 1.—Various forms of cancer constitute the second most important cause of deaths in the United States.[1]

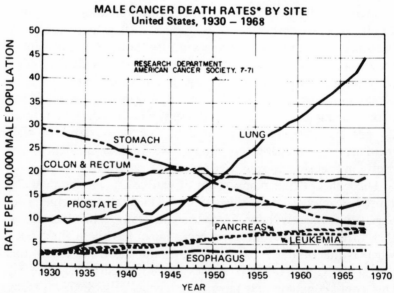

Figure 2.—Death rates due to cancer at various sites as a function of time. Note the impressive increase rates in lung cancer, and the decrease in stomach cancer[1].

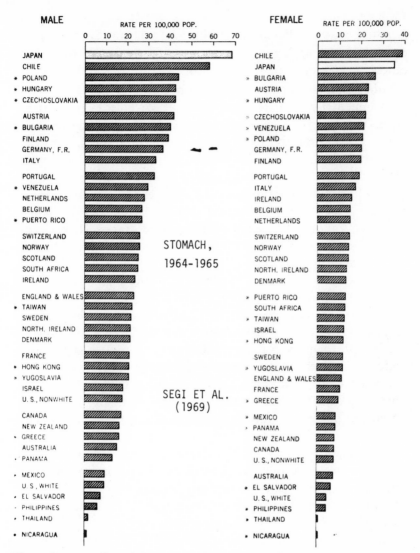

Figure 3.—Age-adjusted death rates from cancer of the stomach in various countries. Source: M. Segi and M. Kurihara[19].

cancer. However, epidemiologic studies on the incidence of gastric cancer in Japanese migrants to America demonstrate that such migrants assume the same lower risk in later generations as the American population. With respect to intestinal cancer, we see the reverse situation: Cancer of the colon, in particular, is among the highest in the United States population and lowest in Japan (Figure 4). People migrating from Japan lose their propensity for stomach cancer and acquire a propensity for colon cancer. The key change is the environment.

Other human data suggest or prove that some cancers are environmentally mediated and caused. [3] We must examine these causes, which may involve not necessarily synthetic substances, but more importantly, naturally-occurring substances. Figure 5 is a tabulation of chemicals proven to be carcinogenic in man. Bladder cancer has been induced by certain amines such as 2-naphthylamine, benzidine, and similar chemicals. Also, some alkylating agents such as the drug chlornaphazine and the industrial chemical dimethyl-sulfate have induced cancer. These occupational or iatrogenic cancers affect only a limited number of our population. Currently, little quantitative information on dose-response is available, although it seems that doses in the exposed groups may have been large.

Cigarette smoking can be categorized as a problem under polycyclic aromatic hydrocarbons and tars. There is some quantitative information in the area of cigarette smoking. Data show quite conclusively that a person smoking 30 cigarettes a day is at a much higher risk than a person smoking 10 cigarettes a day. There is a dose-response in man in relation to cigarette smoking which can be demonstrated experimentally in animal systems as well.[4]

All of these chemicals and mixtures that are carcinogenic to man have demonstrated carcinogenicity in one or more animal systems. Carcinogenicity in animals implies that the reverse is also true. If a product is reliably carcinogenic in animals, there are certain risks imposed upon some men some of the time.[5]

Man is quite heterogeneous. This question is often asked of me, "What do your animal systems mean to man?" and I reply, "Which man, you or me?" There are differences in response. A person smoking 30 cigarettes a day and who is 75 years old may show little effect while others who smoke the same amount may die of pulmonary cancer at the age of 38. Differences among us make it difficult to extrapolate directly the results of a given animal system. Nonetheless, if a chemical is reliably

Figure 4.—Age-adjusted death rates from cancer of the intestine in various countries. Source: M. Segi and M. Kurihara[19].

carcinogenic in animal systems, we must conclude that a portion of the world population is at risk, were it exposed. We need test systems to assess relative sensitivity of humans, involving a variety of parameters such as biochemical or immunologic competence.

POLYNUCLEAR AROMATIC HYDROCARBONS—Soots, Pitch, Coal Tar and Products; Creosote, Shale, Mineral, Petroleum and Cutting Oils; Cigarette, Cigar and Pipe Smoke

AROMATIC AMINES—2-Naphthylamine, Benzidine and Derivatives, 4-Biphenylamine, 4-Nitrobiphenyl, Auramine and Magenta

ALKYLATING AGENTS—Chlornaphthazine [Bis(β-Chloroethyl)-2-Naphthylamine], Mustard Gas [Bis(βChloroethyl) Sulfide], Melphalan (l-[p-Bis(β-Chloroethylamino)-Phenyl] Alanine), Busulfan (1, 4-Butanediol Dimethanesulfonate); Bis(Chloromethyl) Ether; Dimethyl Sulfate.

NICKEL CARBONYL

ISOPROPYL OIL MANUFACTURE (process discontinued)

BETEL NUT, NASS, TOBACCO chewing

CHROMATES, INORGANIC ARSENICALS, ASBESTOS

RADIATION—Ionizing, Ultraviolet (Solar), X-rays, Nuclear Fission Products, Uranium, Radon, Radium, Thorotrast

MIXTURES OF AGENTS

BENZENE?

MYCOTOXINS, SENECIO ALKALOIDS, PLANT CARCINOGENS?

HORMONAL IMBALANCE?

VIRUSES?

Figure 5.—Actual or suspected carcinogens in man[4].

Thus, classically, we use tumor-induction in animals as a means of revealing any possible carcinogenic risks to man.[6] These studies, particularly those concerning weak carcinogens, are cumbersome, slow, and expensive. It costs at least $70,000 to properly evaluate the carcinogenic potential of one chemical, and for a weak carcinogen it requires the full lifetime of an animal. Currently, in cooperation with several other institutions, the National Cancer Institute and we at the American Health Foundation, are developing new possible test systems, based on recent, fundamental developments in molecular biology and in carcinogenesis.[7,8] Current views imply that cancer is the result of genetic change or a key alteration affecting DNA. Thus, we can, with proper safeguards and controls, utilize mutagenesis as a preliminary assay system (Figures 6 and 7).

---

a. DIRECT-ACTING ALKYLATING AGENTS

b. PROCARCINOGENS, ACTIVE AFTER BIOCHEMICAL CHANGE.

Figure 6.—Relationship between carcinogenicity and mutagenicity.

PROCARCINOGENS ARE USUALLY NOT

MUTAGENIC, OR CARCINOGENIC *IN VITRO*,

UNLESS THE TEST SYSTEM HAS THE

BIOCHEMICAL COMPETENCE TO ACTIVATE

AGENT.

Figure 7.—Use of mutagenicity tests to detect chemical carcinogens.

This can be accomplished in microorganisms in as little as 15 days by using methods of quick screening. Transformation of animal and even human cell cultures is also being explored.[9,10] It would be advantageous to use systems such as those we are about to develop as a prescreen for pinpointing positives, for subsequent testing by long-term animal systems. Also, unreliable or doubtful results from chronic animal studies can be supported, validated or denied by such accessory, soundly obtained data on mutagenicity or other *in vitro* tests.

Carcinogenic risk to man is not merely risk of exposure to a single chemical. We are exposed to a myriad of agents and they sometimes have antagonistic effects, but also they can have additive or synergistic effects. Thus, when we state that a chemical is safe on the basis of a single test on a single animal species, we have to consider the additional problem of mixtures of chemicsls. Future toxicology must address itself to this problem of select and realistic chemical mixtures in the environment which may be carcinogenic risks to man.

Types of cancer that are induced by environmental factors are numerous, but this presentation will consider only three. Smoked and salted foods, nitrites or nitrates, and mycotoxins (Figure 8) are being questioned as etiologic factors of gastric cancer in man. [11],[12] Developments of the last six years yielded reliable ways of inducing gastric cancer in animals. The agents inducing cancer are all nitrosamide derivatives, such as N-methylnitrosourea, N-methyl-N'-nitro-N-nitrosoguanidine and N'-acetyl-N-methylnitrosourea. Our foods and food additives of today are more wholesome than the food additives utilized 100 years ago. In my view, better foods and improved preservation are responsible for the decline in gastric cancer. Microorganisms have been found to reduce the nitrates contained in our food to nitrites, which can form nitrosamines and nitrosamides. In the past, without refrigeration, cooked food standing at room temperatures could well have developed a microflora, which, it can

EXPERIMENTAL GASTRIC CANCER

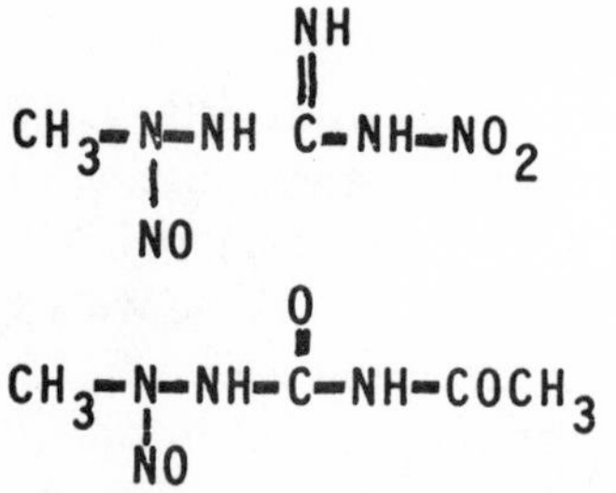

$$CH_3-N-NH\ \overset{\overset{\displaystyle NH}{\|}}{C}-NH-NO_2 \qquad \text{Methyl-nitro-nitroso-guanidine}$$
$$\underset{NO}{|}$$

$$CH_3-N-NH-\overset{\overset{\displaystyle O}{\|}}{C}-NH-COCH_3 \qquad \text{Methyl-acetyl nitrosourea}$$
$$\underset{NO}{|}$$

HUMAN GASTRIC CANCER

Smoked and salted foods?

Nitrite or nitrate?

Mycotoxins?

Figure 8.—Chemicals or situations leading to gastric cancer in animals and man. In view of the striking carcinogenic effect of alkylnitrosoureas and analogs for the stomach, in animals, this type of chemical may be implicated in the etiology of this cancer in man[20].

be speculated, effects a reduction of nitrate to nitrite. This would react with an unknown substrate to produce nitrosamides which cause gastric cancer. This problem no longer exists because refrigeration for our cooked and fresh foods is now available. Antioxidants and other preservatives are also used to improve the quality of our food. It is probably also safe to say that carcinogenic mycotoxins [13] occur in foods less today than they did 50 or 100 years ago.

It is necessary to secure data on causes of other key types of cancer as well as to apply what we know about the ongoing decrease of the incidence of liver and stomach cancer. This will assist us in solving the problem of the etiology of such other types of cancer.

For example, let us consider cancer of the esophagus (Figure 9). Data show that the high risk population in the United States consists of the poor, black people. The combination of consuming certain alcoholic beverages and excessive smoking is one cause of this type of cancer. There are studies underway testing

EXPERIMENTAL ESOPHAGUS CANCER

$$CH_3 - \underset{\underset{NO}{|}}{N} - \quad \begin{matrix} Alkyl \\[4pt] (Aryl) \end{matrix} \quad \begin{matrix} Methylalkylnitrosamines \\[4pt] Methylarylnitrosamines \end{matrix}$$

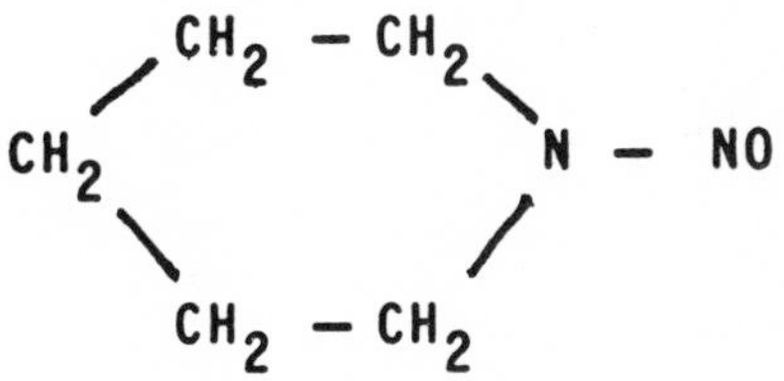

$$CH_2 \underset{CH_2 - CH_2}{\overset{CH_2 - CH_2}{\diagdown\diagup}} N - NO \quad Cyclic\ nitrosamines$$

HUMAN ESOPHAGUS CANCER

Alcoholic beverages and smoking?
Herbal medicines?
Vitamin A deficiency as auxiliary factor?

Figure 9.—Chemicals or situations leading to esophageal cancer in animal and man.

herbal medicines consumed in some islands in the Caribbean where the incidence of cancer of the esophagus is also very high.

It has been shown in experimental systems that vitamin A deficiency may potentiate the effect of certain chemical carcinogens in the epithelial tissues, such as the lung, stomach, and intestinal tract. [14-16] Recently it was stated by official sources that the general public does not need vitamin supplements. Yet, Canadian studies note that in certain areas of Canada there are people who have borderline tissue levels of vitamin A. We need to evaluate our diets as to whether they include enough vitamin A, especially in underprivileged populations. Do they consume proper diets? Do they receive adequate amounts of vitamin A and other co-factors of micronutrients which may provide protective mechanisms?

Cancer of the colon is high in the United States as well as in other Anglo-Saxon countries. Figures 10 and 11 illustrate some documented ways whereby cancer of the colon can be induced in experimental systems. We do not understand the causes of this type of cancer in man. We do know, however, that in countries where diets are consumed that provide substantial numbers of calories through animal fat and animal protein, the risk of cancer of the colon is higher than in areas such as Japan where the consumption of animal fats is much lower, and the protein is in the form of varied seafood[2,11,12,17] (Figures 12 and 13). If we can scientifically and reliably document the relationship of high animal fat and high animal protein to cancer of the colon, then it will be useful to educate the public and recommend a revision of dietary habits. The tradition, even centuries old, of eating certain foods may have to be changed if there is substantial evidence that the high consumption of such foods leads to diseases such as some types of cancer which have also existed for centuries because of the stability of counter-indicated dietary habits. Cancer of the colon and rectum has exhibited a similar incidence over the last 30 years (Figure 2). In other words, the same factors that cause it now were present years ago. The latent period for these cancers is of the order of 30 or more years. The average age of a person presenting with cancer of the colon is about 55 to 65. It would take years for this disease to become apparent and it can be concluded that conditions causing colon cancer have been invariant.

COLON CANCER BY CHEMICALS

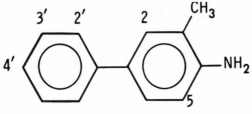

3-METHYL-4-AMINOBIPHENYL

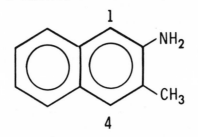

3-METHYL-2-AMINONAPHTHALENE

Figure 10.—Chemicals inducing colon cancer in rats[12]

COLON CANCER BY CHEMICALS

$CH_3 - N = N - CH_2O - \beta - glucoside$
$\downarrow$
O

CYCASIN

$CH_3 - N = N - CH_2OH$
$\downarrow$
O

METHYLAZOXYMETHANOL

$CH_3 - N = N - CH_3$
$\downarrow$
O

AZOXYMETHANE

$CH_3 - N - CO - NH_2$
$|$
NO

N – NITROSOMETHYLUREA

$CH_3 - NH - NH - CH_3$

1,2-DIMETHYLHYDRAZINE

Figure 11.—Chemicals inducing colon cancer in animals[12]

In contrast, lung cancer has increased enormously over the last 40 years. Heavy smoking of commercial cigarettes became popular among men after World War I.[4] An upward trend in lung cancer among women became evident in 1965. Women did not begin smoking heavily until after World War II. If a 30-year latent period must be taken into account, it seems evident that a connection exists between extensive smoking by men and women, and lung cancer. Thus, we know some of the causative factors of lung cancer, and we can take some measures to prevent it. On the basis of such data, the cigarette industry has reduced the amount of tar present per cigarette in half by modifying the type and form of tobacco, and by taking measures such as adding filters. It is up to industry to continue

COLON CANCER — CRITICAL DATA

HIGH RISK - Diets rich in animal fats and meats
Diets with low residue - Digestible carbohydrates; mineral elements? Genetic factor?

LOW RISK - Diets with low fats, Varied proteins,
with high residues and fibers

Figure 12.—Environmental conditions, mostly dietary, presenting a high and low risk of colon cancer.[2,11,12,17]

COLON CANCER - CAUSATIVE FACTORS

Exogenous: 1—Direct passage through gut
2—Absorption, liver metabolism,
Secretion in bile, liberation of active
Metabolite by microbial action

Endogenous: 1—Food constituent metabolized by
gut microorganisms
2—Toxin elaborated by gut
microorganism

Figure 13.—Possible mechanisms and causative factors leading to colorectal cancer.[12]

reducing the amount of tar per cigarette even more, and to the public to accept such modified smoking products. We must develop a "less harmful cigarette", a term coined by Dr. Wynder of the American Health Foundation. [2,18]

Pancreatic cancer is increasing. Current data on etiologic factors involve nutritional elements as well. This area needs to be studied in detail, in order to curtail the incidence of this and other types of cancer. This is our aim at the American Health Foundation, nationally and worldwide. We hope to develop facts, knowledge, and practical systems which will decrease the incidence and mortality rate of all types of cancer on the basis of rational research approaches. Furthermore, it seems that some of the etiologic factors relating to breast, prostate, colon and rectal cancers may also bear on cardiovascular disease. Thus, it is our hope that our extensive research program on cancer etiology will also lead to greater knowledge of the basis of cardiovascular disease, and its prevention.

References

1. Silverberg, E and Holleb, AI: Cancer Statistics, 1973. *CA, A Journal for Clinicians,* **23**:22 27, 1973.
2. Wynder, EL and Mabuchi, K: Etiological and Preventive Aspects of Human Cancer, *Preventive Med* 1:300-334, 1972.
3. Wynder, EL and Hoffmann, D: Less Harmful Ways of Smoking, *J Natl Cancer Inst* **48**:1748-1891, 1972.
4. Weisburger, JH: Chemical Carcinogenesis, In Holland J and Frei, E (eds.), *Cancer Medicine.* Philadelphia, Lea and Febiger, 1973.
5. Weisburger, JH and Rall, DP: Do Animal Models Predict Carcinogenic Hazards for Man? In M.D. Anderson Symposium, Baltimore, Williams and Wilkins, 437-452, 1972.
6. Weisburger, JH and Weisburger, EK: Tests for Chemical Carcinogens, In Busch, H, (ed.), *Methods in Cancer Research.* New York Academic Press, 1:307-398, 1967.
7. Miller, EC and Miller, JA: The Mutagenicity of Chemical Carcinogens: Correlations, Problems and Interpretations, In Hollander, A, (ed.), *Chemical Mutagens* New York, Plenum Press, 1:83-120, 1971.
8. Farber, E: Chemical Carcinogenesis, In Anfinsen, CB, Potter, M, Schechter, AN, (eds.), *Current Research In Oncology.* New York, Academic Press, pp 95-125, 1973.
9. Huberman, E et al: Transformation of Hamster Embryo Cells by Epoxides and Other Derivatives of Polycyclic Hydrocarbons, *Cancer Res* **32**:1391-1396, 1972.

10. Huberman, E, Donovan, PJ and Di Paolo, JA: Cytogenetics and Cytology of Cultured Mammalian Cells by N-Acetoxy-N-2-Fluorenylacetalnide, *J Natl Cancer Inst* **48**:837-840, 1972.
11. Berg, JW: Epidemiology of Gastrointestinal Cancer, In Proceedings of the Seventh National Cancer Conference, Philadelphia, J. B. Lippincott, in press.
12. Weisburger, JH: Chemical Carcinogenesis of Gastrointestinal Cancer, In Proceedings of the Seventh National Cancer Conference, Philadelphia, J. B. Lippincott, in press.
13. Wogan, GN: Metabolism and Biochemical Effects of Aflatoxins, In Goldblatt, LA (ed.), *Aflatoxin-Scientific Background, Control and Implications.* New York, Academic Press, pp 151-186, 1969.
14. Saffiotti, U et al: Studies on Experimental Lung Cancer: Inhibition by Vitamin A of the Induction of Tracheobronchial Squamous Metaplasia and Squamous Cell Tumors, *Cancer* **20**:857-864, 1967.
15. Newberne, PM and Rogers, AE: Colon Carcinomas with Aflatoxin and Marginal Vitamin A, *J Natl Cancer Inst* **50**:#2, 439-448, Feb, 1973.
16. Cone, VM and Nettesheim, P: Effects of Vitamin A on 3-Methylcholanthrene-Induced Squamous Metaplasias and Early Tumors in the Respiratory Tract of Rats, *J Natl Cancer Inst* **50**:1599-1106, 1973.
17. Wynder, EL and Reddy, B: Studies of Large-Bowel Cancer: Human Leads to Experimental Application, *J Natl Cancer Inst* **50**:1099-1106, 1973.
18. Wynder, EL and Hoffmann, D (eds.): Toward A Less Harmful Cigarette, National Cancer Institute Monograph 28. U S Government Printing Office, Washington, 1968.
19. Segi, M. and Kurihara, M: Cancer Mortality for Selected Sites in 24 Countries. Number 5 (1964-65), Tohoku University School of Medicine, Sendai, Japan, 1969.
20. Raineri and Weisburger: *Proc. Am. Assn. Cancer Res.,* **15**:1974 (in press).

Definition of Risk;
Priority for Safety

SAMUEL S. EPSTEIN, M.D.

In discussions on socially acceptable risks, references have been made by other speakers to scientific objectivity, social acceptability, and social responsibility. I believe that the problems that confront us now are not largely scientific, but rather public interest issues.

It is abundantly clear that there are major defects in the federal decision making process, in general, and in the regulatory process, in particular. The system of checks and balances, inherent in the democratic process, is largely absent from regulatory practice. Apart from limited *post-hoc* recourse, the citizen, or the consumer, and those who represent his interests scientifically and legally, are virtually excluded from involvement in vital decisions affecting them. The concept of matching benefits against risks has been applied to maximize short-term benefits to industry, even though this may entail minimal benefits and maximal risks to the consumer. Such an approach is often detrimental and counterproductive to the long-term interest of industry, which may suffer major economic dislocation when hazardous products, to which major commitments have been improperly developed, are belatedly banned from commerce.

Such problems are, in a large measure, attributable to crippling constraints that have developed in the total regulatory process. Responsibility for such constraints must be shared with the FDA, by the legislature, the scientific community, and by consumers and citizens who have not yet developed adequate mechanisms for protecting their own vital interests and rights.

Specters with which we have been confronted by previous

speakers are starvation of mankind and gross malnutrition, which have largely been prevented by the use of chemical additives. Now, nobody, generally, has any argument against the use of chemicals that serve broadly useful societal functions. Arguments arise when chemicals are used that do not serve broad and societally useful functions and when the hazards of such chemicals are improperly assessed.

To understand the whole problem of benefit and risk, one must make practical distinctions between technological innovations and new chemical products which have not yet been built into commerce, for which it is possible to develop more restrictive regulatory approaches, and chemical products which are already built into commerce, and for which, major economic dislocations can ensue if restrictions are developed.

To evaluate the risk benefit relationship, you need a data base, and the data base relates to three basic components:

- The efficacy of the material. Does the product serve a useful purpose?
- What is the chemical identity of the product?
- Is the product safe not only for human beings, but also ecologically safe?

Having said that you need data on these three components—efficacy, identity, and safety—the question is "What is the quality of the data on which you base these judgments?" I propose to indicate that certain data submitted to regulatory agencies suffer from a variety of constraints, ranging from the fraudulent and manipulated to sub-conscious bias.

Let us first of all examine what we mean by efficacy. Efficacy is defined in two distinct ways. Efficacy can mean, in the narrow Federal Trade Commission (FTC) sense of the term, that a product will achieve its stated objective. In other words, if you have a green or yellow Florida or Alabama orange and you make it red with a synthetic dye, then that dye will achieve the stated objective of making the orange red. That is the narrow FTC sense of the term.

The broader concept of efficacy relates to the question of whether there are societal benefits, attendant to the use of the product. Are there societal benefits in the massive use of cosmetic food additives to make food look more attractive and fresh than it really is? There is a flourishing market in this country of cosmetic food additives. For instance, as far as nitrites are concerned—excluding the preservative function of nitrites—their major use is to make meat look redder and fresher than it really is.

So, I make distinctions between the narrow FTC sense of efficacy, in which products achieve their stated objective, to the broader concept of efficacy insofar as the products serve a broadly useful societal purpose, such as preservation of food, making it available to large human populations. It is the latter type of broad societal efficacy which is clearly important, and to which we should properly address ourselves when we discuss the risk benefit calculus.

What benefits are there to society from cosmetic food additives in general, and what benefits are there to society from adding cyclamates and caffeine in soda pop which young children massively consume? What use is there in adding monosodium glutamate to baby foods, when there is no evidence that babies preferentially discriminate in favor of flavored foods? So, when we talk about benefit, let us really be clear what we mean by benefit. Do we mean benefit to a narrow economic segment of the community that produces cosmetic food additives, or do we mean broad societal benefit?

When we talk about identity, and this is the second important question, what exactly are the chemicals we are adding to our food? There are no requirements for complete ingredient labelling and disclosure of identity. So, we don't know exactly what food additives are in our food. There are 600 or more compounds on the Generally Recognized As Safe (GRAS) list, but the food industry has also apparently reserved for itself the right to treat other food additives as though they are on the GRAS list, although formal petitions have never been filed for these. The consumer does not have options in this matter, as he does not know what industry has put into his food.

In my view, the requirements for complete disclosure of identity are critical. When we are talking about a chemical product, we are not only talking about the chemical itself, but we are also talking about its contaminants, pyrolytic, degradation, and metabolic products. For instance, with cyclamates, the major problem is not with the cyclamate itself, but with cyclohexylamine, its contaminant and metabolic product. With the class of phenoxy herbicides, the major public health problem was not basically with the phenoxy herbicides themselves, but also with their dioxin contaminants and pyrolytic products.

Thirdly, what do we mean by safety? We mean, primarily, safety to man and safety to the environment. Why are we concerned about problems of safety? Largely, because there is growing realization that much human disease is environmentally induced. There is a growing consensus, amongst leading professional cancer researchers, that 60% to 80% of human cancer is environmental in origin. So, when we are talking about safety, we are talking about major public health issues, such as cancer and birth defects, not esoteric problems of concern to an extreme few.

Evaluation of toxicity is developed in one of two ways, either by testing in animals, on an anticipatory basis, or by epidemiology, which means examining human populations to evaluate what happens on a *post hoc* basis. We make sharp distinctions between toxicity *per se,* which is a reversible phenomenon, and is basically a function of dose, and carcinogenicity, mutagenicity, and teratogenicity, which are, unique, specific and irreversible phenomena.

Evaluation of carcinogenicity involves a set of special problems, quite apart from the long latent period, and quite apart from the difficulty in sometimes demonstrating causal relationships on an epidemiological basis. When you test chemicals for carcinogencity, mutagenicity, and teratogenicity, clearly you should select a route that reflects human exposure. It is also clear that you should use more than one animal species.

In testing, one must accept the fact that toxicology is a very insensitive test system. Let us assume that you introduce into a commerce an additive, which produces cancer or birth defects in one in every 10,000 humans. Let us also assume that the sensitivity of the rat or mouse to this additive is the same as that of man. You would then need 10,000 rats or 10,000 mice to get one cancer or one birth defect; for statistical significance, you may need 30,000 rats or 30,000 mice. In practice only 30 to 50 animals are used in a test group. So therefore, if you test animals with levels at which humans are exposed, your chances of detecting carcinogenic or teratogenic effects are virtually nil. In an attempt to reduce the gross insensitivity of the test system, you should use a series of dosages which extend to the maximum tolerated. The maximum tolerated dose means just that dosage you can give during the lifetime of the animal, without inducing weight loss of any overt evidence of toxicity whatsoever.

Assumptions of equal sensitivity or similar sensitivity of rodents and human beings are, of course, questionable. In some instances, humans are more sensitive and in some instances they are less sensitive to the adverse effects of a particular chemical. For instance, man is very sensitive to aromatic amines, which produce cancer of the bladder in man, but not in mice or rats. Women are 700 more times sensitive to the teratogenic effects of thalidomide than are hamsters. You can not predict in advance whether humans are more or less sensitive to any particular chemical; thus, you have no option but to test at higher levels than those to which humans are exposed if you are seriously interested in trying to decide whether the agents you are introducing into foods will produce cancer, birth defects or adverse genetic effects.

The idea that you can make any chemical carcinogenic by testing it at high dosages is just not true. Reports from The International Union Against Cancer, The National Cancer Institute, and The Surgeon General's Ad Hoc Committee on Low Levels of Environmental Carcinogens have never suggested that testing of non-carcinogenic chemicals at high dosages will non-specifically induce cancer. In the Bionetic study, sponsored by The National Cancer Institute, 150 chemicals and pesticides, selected on grounds of possible carcinogenicity, were tested for carcinogenicity, with commencing exposure in infancy, using maximally tolerated doses. Less than 10% of these chemicals proved to be carcinogenic!

It is clear that industry is entitled to know exactly what tests are expected of them. In this respect, I believe that the situation would be greatly facilitated if protocols were promulgated in the Federal Register, together with guidelines for evaluation of resulting data.

As far as epidemiology is concerned, the argument that we

have used chemical agents for a long time and that they appear to be safe on the basis of apparently safe human experience is not reasonable. In between the time of human exposure to chemicals and the resulting cancer, there may be a latent period of 10 to 30 years; in addition, it is difficult to isolate the effects of any one chemical in the environment from the masses of other chemicals to which human beings are concurrently exposed, and for which there are no sharp differentials in human exposure. Even with cigarettes, for example, in studies of humans who previously smoked five packs, four packs, three packs, two packs, or no packs per day and with control groups, (*eg.* using populations in which there were sharp differentials in expsoure), it took several decades to establish the causal direct relationship between cigarette smoking and lung cancer. In the case of chemicals that are widely disseminated in the environment, which are in food in many instances, and without the consumer necessarily knowing they are in his food, there are no simple ways of demonstrating epidemiological relationships. Hence, the idea that the human experience is a guide to safety is not acceptable.

Let me return now to the quality of the data base. At the present moment, data are generated by industry, either by commercial scientists or by commercial testing houses. These data are submitted in secrecy to the regulatory agencies and decisions are made behind closed doors. No mechanisms have been developed for involvement of the citizen or consumer or of his scientific and legal representatives in the regulatory decision-making process. There is ample evidence of close and intimate associations between regulatory agencies and industry. The top management of the FDA has been largely recruited from industry. Again, senior FDA officials often enter the industry they have previously regulated at retirement. Restrictive employment mobility clauses, are commonplace in certain industries, and these may prevent an employee leaving a certain industry to take related jobs in a competitive industry for some period of time afterwards. We do not have such restricted employment mobility clauses for senior officials in the FDA, or other regulatory agencies, who came from industry or who may subsequently go to industry.

Closely allied interests have developed between industry and commercial testing houses. A look at the cyclamate literature indicates that studies sponsored by its manufacturer generally show that cyclamates are acceptable as sweetening agents from a safety viewpoint. Contrastingly, studies sponsored by the Sugar Research Foundation have tended to show that cyclamates are harmful.

As far as the question of poor quality data or of manipulation of data is concerned, let me give you one or two examples. In 1967, 50% of all petitions submitted to the FDA in support of food additives were rejected by Commissioner Ley because of incomplete, inadequate, and nonspecific data; such decisions are of course costly to industry. Fraudulent manipulation of data has been clearly and legally established with drugs such as MER-29, for which officials of Richardson-Merril Co. were criminally convicted; Dornwall, in which Wallace and Tiernan Co. were found guilty of submitting false data; Flexin, for which McNeil Laboratories pleaded *nolo contenedre* to charges of willfully concealing information; and Panalba, withdrawn from the market on discovery in March, 1969, by an FDA inspector of secret laboratory files indicating its non-efficacy.

Let us proceed to the Food Protection Committee of the National Academy of Sciences. This is a group to which the FDA in the past 12 years has consistently turned for advice. Let us examine the nature of this committee, their objectivity, their social responsibility, and their composition, especially as we have heard much from previous speakers on objectivity and responsibility. The Food Protection Committee of the National Academy of Sciences has been strongly supported by grants from the food, chemical, and packaging industries. In April 1969, a nine-man task force of this committee, of whom five were industrial employees, one a commercial testing house director and the other three academic scientists, with long and intimate association with industrial interests, released a report entitled, "Guidelines for Estimating Toxicologically Insignificant Levels of Chemicals in Food". The point about this is that nearly all of these committee members had major economic commitments to the food industry. It is also important to state that none of the authors of this report is recognized as knowl-

edgeable, let alone informed, in the field of chemical carcinogenesis. I challenge any member of this task force to state his
qualifications in the field of chemical carcinogenesis. This lack
of familiarity of the fundamental problems of carcinogenesis,
coupled with inherent economic constraints, expressed themselves in views such as, "if a chemical has been used in commerce for five years without evidence of overt-toxicity, that it is
consistent with sound toxicological judgment to conclude that
small amounts in the human diet are toxicologically insignificant."

Dean Harvey Brooks, Chairman of the National Academy of
Science's Committee on Science and Public Policy, has been
explicit on this. He recently stated, "It is true that some of our
bodies, the Highway Research Board, the Food and Nutrition
Board, the Building Research Advisory Board, and the Space
Science Board, for instance, may be constituted too completely
with those who have an economic or institutional interest in the
outcome of their work."

Notes

Notes

Notes

Notes